Winning the Profit Game

PRAISE FOR *WINNING THE PROFIT GAME*

"I enjoyed this book very much, and found it applicable to many of the critical market issues in telecommunications and new media. The book demonstrates the management differences between the industry players who thrive, and those who 'just survive.' Very useful for what's new, and what is a reminder."

> —Tracy Korman, Executive Vice President, Customer Relationship Management, BroadView Networks, Inc.

"Smarter pricing can improve bottom-line results for any business; yet pricing remains an underutilized tool. *Winning the Profit Game* provides clear, organized, and practical approaches to improve your business' pricing in any situation. It is a pricing 'how to' manual that belongs front and center on every manager's bookshelf."

> —Andrew A. Stern, Chairman & CEO, USinternetworking

"Pricing strategy and branding are critical but often overlooked elements of improving business performance. *Winning the Profit Game* provides important insights into pricing opportunities and challenges facing companies in various industries. Any general manager could apply the tools in this book to get more pricing (and profit) leverage from branding and customer interactions."

> —Mark Gallion, Division President, Emerson

"If you want to improve your company's profitability, if you want to learn how price, brand, and product can be linked to achieve this, then this book is a must read. A real gem. It's one of the most insightful pieces I've read in a long time. In the introduction to this book the authors suggest picking the chapters most relevant to your business situation, but I think top management should read the whole book."

> —Robert A. Ferchat, Chairman and CEO of Bell Canada Mobility, retired, former president of Nortel Networks, Canada, and author of *Tangled Up in the Past*

"*Winning the Profit Game* delivers on its promise to improve corporate profit performance. The book is a sophisticated exposition of pricing strategies, and is unique in that it integrates pricing with its inseparable partner—branding. Brand and price are, in my experience, the most powerful tools available to management today to significantly raise prices and grow the bottom line. The book is not academic—it steers clear of technical minutia, in favor of describing concrete management initiatives."

> —Charles E. Lehr, General Manager Marketing (Chief Marketing Officer), International Division, ExxonMobil Corporation, retired.

"*Winning the Profit Game* delivers valuable insights and tools for business leaders—from entrepreneurs in Silicon Valley to pricing professionals in Detroit and the leaders of Fortune 100 Corporations. The book's innovative approaches to integrated pricing include turning created value into money (monetization), key to the entrepreneur trying to survive until the next funding round, or to the P&L manager who needs to deliver the next quarter's or year's profits. Business leaders in Silicon Valley and other dynamic and challenging markets should read this book prior to making critical product, price and brand decisions."

> —Jeffrey Depew, Silicon Valley serial entrepreneur and former President of General Electric Electrical Distribution and Control, Asia/Pacific

Winning the Profit Game

Smarter Pricing, Smarter Branding

**Robert G. Docters
Michael R. Reopel
Jeanne-Mey Sun
Stephen M. Tanny**

McGraw-Hill

New York Chicago San Francisco Lisbon London
Madrid Mexico City Milan New Delhi San Juan
Seoul Singapore Sydney Toronto

This publication is designed to provide accurate and authoritative information in regard to the subject matter covered. It is sold with the understanding that neither the author nor the publisher is engaged in rendering legal, accounting, or other professional service. If legal advice or other expert assistance is required, the services of a competent professional person should be sought.

> —*From a Declaration of Principles jointly*
> *adopted by a Committee of the American Bar*
> *Association and a Committee of Publishers*

McGraw-Hill books are available at special quantity discounts to use as premiums and sales promotions, or for use in corporate training programs. For more information, please write to the Director of Special Sales, McGraw-Hill, 2 Penn Plaza, New York, NY 10121. Or contact your local bookstore.

 This book is printed on recycled, acid-free paper containing a minimum of 50% recycled de-inked fiber.

Contents

Acknowledgments

When four authors from three different organizations write a book, a team of colleagues provides support of many kinds—editorial, factual, intellectual, and emotional. The authors of *Winning the Profit Game* want to express their joint and individual gratitude to all those who helped make this book possible.

Rob would like to acknowledge the valuable contributions of Daniel E. Aks, Marty Hyman, Paul L. Katz, Andrei Jezierski, Pam Docters, Patrick Thiede, Stephen C. Lipton, Graham King, Neil Posner, Gayle Maurin, Linda S. Sullivan, Sen. John Struthers, Phebe Prescott Greenwood, Mery Parra, John Grim, Dr. K. Raymond Wolfe, Julio Zamora, his coauthors, his consulting clients, and Eric Mitchell of the Professional Pricing Society. In particular, he would like to thank G.J.G. (Bob) Docters, Nancy S. Lothrop, Ann M. Docters, Bert Schefers, and Dan Aks for their tireless chapter reviews and thoughtful suggestions and additions.

Jeanne-Mey and Mike would like to thank their A.T. Kearney colleagues for their support. Marc Hochman and Donna Hagerman of A.T. Kearney's eBreviate division and Ricardo Ruiz-Huidobro of A.T. Kearney's Alexandria office provided insights on the "Turning

Online Auctions to Your Advantage" chapter. Karen Kaluzsa of A.T. Kearney's Chicago office provided her usual knowledgeable research assistance.

Steve would like to thank Khadija Siddiqi for research assistance, and Professor Frank Mathewson, Dr. Avery Shenfeld, and Brian Wanless for helpful discussions, suggestions, and encouragement during the writing of this book.

All of the authors would like to recognize and thank Kay Polit of A.T. Kearney's Costa Mesa office, Jim Shand and Eric Stettler of the Plano office, Alex Tserelov of the Alexandria office, and Jim Manocchi of the Cambridge office for their significant intellectual contributions to this work. In addition, the authors would like to thank Patricia Sibo and Nancy Bishop of the Marketing and Communications department for their project management, editing, and wise counsel, and Kevin Peschke for adding his design touch. Lorraine Keleher and Jeanne Hudock provided administrative assistance to the team. We would like to especially thank Randy Burgess of *usable-thought.com*, for his extensive editing and coordination of the manuscript.

Finally and wholeheartedly, we want to thank Mary Glenn, our senior editor at McGraw-Hill, for her support. She not only believed in our topic; she believed in our ability to make it fascinating.

Chapter One | Introduction: How to Read This Book

This book is about smarter ways of improving the bottom line. It's aimed at business leaders and managers such as you who help to shape that bottom line, and who often have specific revenue responsibilities.

The past decade has seen the reengineering of business processes, wholesale staff reductions, new purchasing strategies, a focus on quality, customer relationship management (CRM), automation, and the development of a slew of new channels and technologies for reaching customers. All of these have played an important role in improving results, but today they're part of nearly every top company's repertoire—long past the impact, excitement, and competitive advantage they initially offered. Smart managers and smart companies are already asking, what's next? How do we stay ahead?

This book takes a simple position: To keep improving the bottom line, business must now shift its sights and focus on growing the *top* line. There are two fundamental tools for doing so: price and brand.

What can possibly be new about price and brand? The answer is—a lot. To begin with, the level of competence in using these tools varies drastically among competitors. This is especially true of price skills:

Pricing today by major companies ranges from the brilliant to the stupid. This means that anyone who *does* learn to price well can achieve a huge competitive edge. (See Chapter 1 for proof.) This is in contrast to tools such as promotions or channel management—most companies do promotions pretty well, and no company today has a monopoly on sales-channel smarts.

Sophisticated yet commonsense approaches are now available that make pricing a logical, high-return activity that is integral to the development of new products and services. Brand is part of this activity—it isn't the fuzzy, mysterious thing that branding gurus persist in making it out to be. Rather, it is absolutely linked to price, so much so that a superior price strategy cannot exist without a detailed brand strategy.

This linkage is really the spur behind this book. Our goal is to show you how to optimize price, brand, costs, and product development for any business, whether manufacturing or services. More than that, we'll show you both why and how to integrate your pricing and brand strategies. The end result is that you'll be able to grow the top line in *any* environment, no matter how tough. As our title has it, you'll win the profit game.

Why did we mention costs in the preceding paragraph? Isn't this a book about growing the top line? The truth is that there are neglected links between price and costs as well, and all of these factors must and can be understood together. So what has hindered such understanding to date?

One reason many managers don't focus enough on price and brand is that their efforts in these areas don't seem to bear a linear relationship to revenue growth. In other words, you can double your efforts on price and brand, but this never seems to yield double the revenues. Something as simple as a price increase will work fine one time, fail the next time—with no logic to explain the difference in outcome. Even if an increase succeeds, you're forced to wonder whether it was as big as it could have been, or whether you've left money on the table. How can you know? In every way, results from pricing and branding seem uncertain and arbitrary.

What's really going on here is not that pricing is uncertain, but most managers aren't equipped with the tools required to be confident of their pricing. That's where this book will help, as we trace through previously neglected steps in manipulating product and profit, price and cost, brand and price, value and revenue.

For example, do you assume—as many managers do—that an immediate and natural connection exists between creating value and obtaining revenues? If so, Chapter 11 will show you that this is anything but the case. Without a deliberate strategy for turning value into money—a process known as monetization—you have only limited control of your revenues, perhaps no more than accidental control. Do *you* have a clear monetization strategy for your company?

Or take branding, another area where results often seem disconnected from effort. Let's say your business devotes significant resources to brand—can you quantify exactly *how* this effort improves your top line, your cost position, your bottom line? If not, most likely these resources are being wasted. Contrary to what brand gurus might tell you, brand awareness by itself can be worth very little—and in fact, without a clear value proposition, can be downright *harmful*. For example, Isuzu, the maker of economical midpriced cars, outspent its competitors on advertising on a per-car basis, thereby creating big brand awareness. The only problem was, this leap in awareness didn't help sales: A study shows that few visitors to an Isuzu showroom left having bought an Isuzu, as compared to the preponderance of visitors to Mercedes showrooms who left with a Mercedes. Imagine the needless expense to Isuzu, both in branding and in the sales channel. The Isuzu branding effort resulted in higher selling costs, while Mercedes branding has resulted in lower selling costs—and higher revenues. (See Chapter 3 for how to connect branding dollars to desired customer behavior.)

This isn't an academic book. Our goal is to lay out the principles simply, then provide you with an abundance of real-world frameworks for how to price. We believe that these frameworks, combined with success stories from a wide range of industries, will help you where it counts: improving your company's results.

PLAN OF THE BOOK

Time is key to our readers. If you have the time to read this book cover to cover, great—but if you have only 20 minutes to prepare for a key decision, this book can still serve as a quick injection of understanding and experience. Thus we have written many of our chapters as how-to guides, readable in a few minutes on their own. Need advice on raising price? Turn to Chapter 14. On managing sales channels? Take a look at Chapter 21. Pricing new products or services? Chapter 9 presents some powerful new approaches. On automating your pricing capabilities? Turn to Chapter 22. About how to handle a "lowest cost" auction? Take a look at Chapter 17. Whatever your immediate need, flip through the table of contents, then turn directly to the relevant section or chapter.

If you *do* have more time, we intend to provide you with a complete yet concise background in the tools and methodologies you need. We suggest you begin with Part One, but feel free to skip to the section that best suits your immediate objectives.

Part One: Take a New Look at Price and Brand

This first section provides the conceptual underpinnings of revenue. We explain the dynamics of price, including the forces that push prices higher or lower; look at the link between brand and price and how to use it to advantage; explore segmentation as a way to create additional value; and examine the somewhat surprising relationship of cost to price. Lastly, by way of gathering these various threads together, we show how businesses can build revenue in both boom times and recession.

Part Two: How to Set Price and Create Revenue

This section discusses the various ways to frame a revenue strategy and set initial price levels, especially when you have a clean slate, and makes clear that pricing is actually an important language for speaking to customers. Other topics include how to create new value through bundling, tiering, or solutions, as well as how to fully monetize existing value—that is, extract cash from customers.

Part Three: How to Manage Ongoing Price and Revenues

It's just as crucial to know how to improve price performance in an ongoing business, one with established goods and services. Key questions include how to penetrate markets, raise or lower prices, react to auctions, improve profit in the aftermarket, and manage discounting. We end with a chapter detailing some "quick hits" to meet budgets: These can help an organization achieve rapid gains in revenue and ultimately move toward better revenue skills.

Part Four: Building Revenue Capabilities

It's not enough for you as an individual manager to understand the topics in this book; ultimately, your entire organization must evolve to support the integration of pricing, branding, and related activities. In addition, powerful systems are becoming available that can take pricing experiments beyond what you might have thought possible. Accordingly, this section focuses on best practices in processes, organization, systems, and skills.

THE WAY FORWARD

Once you've read this book, we believe you'll be convinced of the rewards of spending time on revenue and pricing. You will have the tools to be as confident of price optimization as you are today of cost reduction efforts—but what then? Can you afford to divert your efforts from other activities and increase your company's efforts and resources in these areas? Put another way, can you afford *not* to? If these activities have been neglected in the past, now might be the time to break out of the vicious cycle of low priority leading to minimal results, leading to still lower priority and still worse results.

But isn't pricing someone else's responsibility—say, the marketing department's? Perhaps today it is, but this can't continue. The ability to rapidly adjust price levels and structures flows across many departments and requires high-level understanding.[1] A broad range of management must become involved—in marketing, finance, operations, IT, and sales. Linking the top and the bottom lines offers remarkable returns to your company. We invite you to read on and see for yourself.

---

[1] This is particularly true if the marketing department is obsessed with promotion and sales support. Einstein once said: "Problems cannot be solved at the same level of understanding as that which created them."

Winning the Profit Game

Part One

Take a New Look at Price and Brand

Chapter One | Winning the Profit Game

Rock 'n roll finds power in the driving beat of drums and the riff of multiple guitars. The Swing era's big bands relied on thundering brass sections whose synchronized refrains would rattle the dance hall roof. Classical music produced masterpieces built around virtuoso string sections capable of producing sounds ranging from glissando to pizzicato. Every era has its own music and its own signature instruments.

If we make the analogy with business, what skill is emerging even now as the lead instrument of the 2000s? What will be the key to success in an environment that's tougher, more competitive than ever before, and evolving as you read this? This book argues that it's pricing—not pricing alone, but pricing integrated with brand, cost management, and product development. And here is the crux of our musical metaphor: Previously these disciplines all played solo lines, going pretty much their own way—but to succeed today they must play in unison, with price carrying the melody.

But can pricing really be that important? Apparently so. Let's demonstrate by breaking our assertion down into smaller components: price and brand, price and cost, price and product development. In each case, the principle is the same. In each case, we'll illustrate it with examples of success.

Price and brand must be inseparable if you wish to maximize profitability. A business issue faced by the U.S. Postal Service illustrates the point: Today the USPS offers multiple types of postage, including first class and bulk rates. While the two have distinct levels of service, the major difference between them is far more subtle: Postal recipients, like you and me, tend to open letters with first class stamps but throw away those with bulk mail stamps—so much so that bulk mail letters are three times as likely to get trashed unopened. It appears that first class postage has a "brand," and that you and I are very sensitive to that brand.

Now consider that junk mailers, an important USPS customer group, live and die by how many people open their letters. Thus, many bulk mailers actually use the costly first class stamp, even though the 16.9-cent bulk mail stamp would get the letter there. Wanting the best of both worlds, they have been lobbying the USPS to get the two stamps to look alike—thereby letting them cut costs while effectively stealing the benefits of the brand. Only by analyzing its customers' economics (and the behavior of its customers' customers), and by likewise calculating how much the price difference is worth to its own revenues, has the USPS known to resist these requests. This has preserved the first class brand, and with it, that high-profit revenue stream.

Here's another illustration, with a setting familiar to all business travelers who were around before cell phones: AT&T knew that payphone users feared being gouged by pirate payphones with huge hidden charges, and that the AT&T brand represented a guarantee against this sort of extreme pricing. The result? At many airports, there was often a line for an AT&T payphone, even as independent payphones sat idle. The phones were functionally identical, and often the independent's rates were lower, not higher. But because customers did not actually know the tariffs, they preferred to wait for the AT&T phones. Because AT&T was aware of this behavior, it was able to charge a premium for its brand—maximizing profit.

Price and cost are inseparable. Many managers believe that costs drive price, and some of the time this is true. However, equally often *price drives cost.* How price can actually be used to *reduce* costs is a key tool every manager ought to know. For example, a leading commercial printer, tired of the operational nightmare of rush orders, restructured his pricing so that overtime pay and other added costs for such orders were reflected in his price. Soon the number of rush orders went down without any apparent loss of customers—the new pricing simply forced customers to plan better, to the printer's benefit.

Even more impressive, smart manufacturing companies such as Dell Computer do "forward pricing" of products. They ask what price the market requires for best volumes, then use these target prices and volumes to force subcontractors to adjust their prices (and therefore Dell's costs) to meet the market price. Subcontractors do this because they too want higher volumes. This strategy is made viable only through tight linkages among marketing, manufacturing, and procurement—but it can be done.

Price and product are integral. Smart companies have already begun to integrate price and product development, knowing that how you price determines both your customer and your competition. A choice often overlooked is whether to offer a product or a service to the market. For example, GE makes aircraft engines, but came up with the novel idea of offering aircraft engines as a service, rather than only as a product. The result is "power by the hour" contracts with airplane operators, whereby the unit of sale is an hour of engine use by commercial airlines. Similarly, IBM now offers "computing on demand" as an alternative to the purchase of processors. In both cases, customers enjoy reduced risk and fewer operational burdens, even as the vendors enjoy better profits. Another example comes from the cellular telephone industry: Cellular service companies have for years given away phones, choosing instead to make their money from networks. This practice has successfully insulated them from cutthroat international competition for equipment.

Similar examples of price defining an offering can be found in the field of the arts. Whereas many movie theaters offer only one price at

all times, the large independent theaters offer off-price matinees and spe-
cial-price showings—a pricing technique known as tiering. The result has
been a material uplift in revenues. The Houston Society for the Performing Arts, meanwhile, has made use of simple simulation tools to experiment with different combinations of shows, seating, and discounts for its
season ticket holders—a sophisticated version of bundling. Such bundles
have boosted revenues by 17 percent, with minimal risk to attendance.

WINNING THE PROFIT GAME WITH PRICING

The price initiatives described above have been able to lift prices anywhere
from 5 to 25 percent and more on a sustained basis for the companies

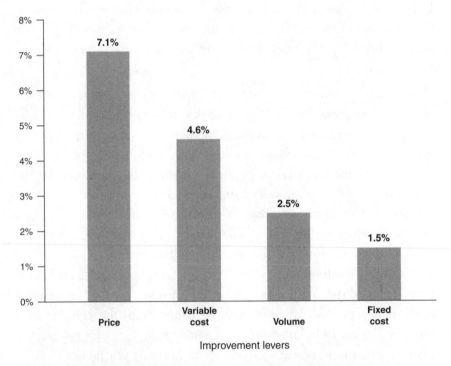

Comparison of profit levers[1]

[1]Based on S&P 500 Average Economics, 2001 data, shows impact of 1 percent improvement to price,
variable cost, volume, and fixed cost on operating profit. Typical improvement programs include pricing
optimization, sourcing, growth strategies, and asset effectiveness.

Sources: Compustat; A.T. Kearney analysis

Figure 1.1a.   Pricing is the most powerful profit lever.

involved. This range of improvement is material in any business and should occupy a high priority for any management. Price improvement is actually *a better use of management time than cost-reduction projects*, because even though cost can sometimes be reduced by higher percentages, price improvements have greater leverage on the bottom line. Take a look at Figure 1.1a. It shows that for the S&P 500, a 1-percent improvement in price results in a 7.1-percent improvement in operating profit. This dwarfs the return on a 1-percent increase in volume. And it's more than double the return on a 1-percent cost reduction, which nets only a 2.5-percent improvement. These figures show that price is the most powerful management tool—and that it can be applied to every industry, as shown in Figure 1.1b.

Here are more examples of smart managers using pricing to improve revenues: Demand management in airlines supported by Sabre, the pricing and ticketing system developed by American Airlines, reprices seats every six minutes and manages dozens of distinct

(Impact of 1-percent price improvement on operating profit[1])

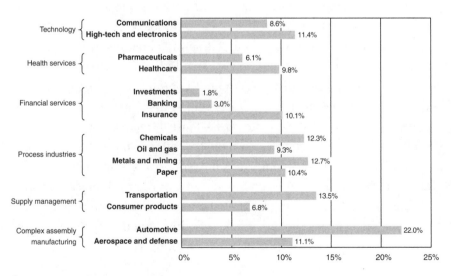

[1]Based on S&P 500 companies with available breakdown of 2001 financial data. Improvement initiative holds constant all other variables except variable of interest.

Sources: Compustat and A.T. Kearney analysis

Figure 1.1b. **Pricing optimization affects operating profit in many industries.**

price categories. This sophisticated capability adds 15 percent to revenues. HP's North American enterprise systems division says that smarter pricing adds 4 percent to its top line and has helped increase market share. Even a commodity business such as Alcoa Aluminum attributes a 5-percent revenue uplift to its extensive pricing program.

Brand, too, can be linked to higher prices and thus to improved revenues. As we've shown, a strong brand lets you charge a premium for otherwise identical products, depending on your industry, this effect can boost your price by 20-plus percent and more than double your profits. For example, Heinz and Del Monte offer identical tomato pastes, yet the premium brand Heinz commands a 61 percent higher price. The same is true for the identical table salts made by Morton and Arrow—the premium brand here commands an 18 percent higher price.

Intelligent pricing can also grow margins through analyzing connections between unit price and customers. For example, most steel producers base their prices on the *types* of steel they have identified as most profitable—in other words, by product. But one strategic manufacturer decided to take a different tack. He realized that because his blast furnace represented his principal capital asset, which could run only 24 hours a day during good times, its use should be prioritized not by type of steel, but by profitability per ton and *profitability per minute*. Based on this insight, the manufacturer developed a segmentation and price scheme that allowed it to focus on its most attractive customers. The result has been high profits in an industry with few profitable players.

Ironically, every day companies have dozens of smart people looking to improve sales volumes, reduce costs, or reduce the cost of capital. But usually it's only the CEO or the head of P&L who tries to connect the dots between the top and bottom lines—and even this tends to occur only in scarce moments of reflection amid various crises.

INSTITUTIONAL OBSTACLES

Many companies unconsciously create formidable obstacles to the coordination of price, brand, cost, and product development. For a start, they spread these four functions in separate organizational pyramids—most often marketing, finance, line management, technology, and operations—which don't meet face-to-face until they reach the CEO reporting level. If that is not bad enough, the cultures of each of these four functions are quite alien to each other. Often you can tell at a glance if you're dealing with back-office pricers, the flamboyant, creative branding staff, the hard-nosed cost-cutters with rolled-up shirtsleeves, or the idiosyncratic product developers confined to incubators or laboratories.

Finally, and perhaps most important, these four functions have very little in common regarding their missions and operational measures for success. Branding often measures success primarily by awareness, pricing by incidence of discounting, marketing by short-term revenues, and product developers by patents or the reliability of products. Only the CEO and P&L heads are on the hook for the bottom line.

This was not always the case. Once upon a time, there was less of a divide in business functions: Henry Ford personally managed product design, brand, costs, and price. The same with Steve Jobs and Steve Wozniak at Apple, who jointly designed, built, and positioned the Apple computer line. The same with Bob Crandall, who was the decisive element at American Airlines in airplane choice, price, brand, and more. But this book does not call for more centralized or autocratic corporate control. To the contrary, we've seen the four elements come together in a wide range of reporting relationships. We explore the potential for change at an organizational, process, and capability level in Chapter 20.

A BROADER DEFINITION OF PRICE

Price uplifts don't just happen because the CEO orders a price increase. Companies obtain higher prices because they can integrate price, brand, cost, and product management, and because they understand the impact of all this on markets. This ability to both execute and understand is what we mean by price capabilities. These capabilities go beyond organization, culture, and process—they are the ultimate test of a company's business strategy.

The first step in building your company's price capabilities is to understand what motivates your customers' spending habits. These are called price drivers, and they form the basis for a sound price strategy. Take the familiar example of selling a house. Anyone who has ever sold or bought can recite a long list of potential price drivers—house size, lot size, location, condition, neatness, presentation, architecture, among others—but as we discover in Chapter 2, only two of these drivers actually matter.

Similarly, when your company sells goods and services, only a few characteristics are likely to influence pricing. Here's an example from the data communications market: The primary driver of one device (called a multiplexer) was how much this device could save you in monthly charges from the telephone company. If the multiplexer saved three lines, it was worth $700, and if it saved six lines, it was worth $1400. All other drivers were secondary. The same kind of analysis applies to greeting cards, toothbrushes, information services, automobiles, and many others. It's an immensely powerful analytic tool—but only if you use it correctly.

Finally, pricing must be a senior management agenda item. Strategic price capabilities are often not amenable to execution by middle management. In Chapter 14, we discuss how the president of Pfizer struck a deal with the state of Florida when the company found its pricing hindered by Medicaid and other state-administered health care programs. This was a CEO-level pricing initiative with potentially big payouts.

PRICING MISTAKES

With bad pricing, huge amounts of money are left on the table. However, unlike ill-fated mergers, or poor purchasing practices, the harm of bad pricing is often invisible. Leaving money on the table doesn't result in telltale fingerprints on accounting records—other than lackluster performance.

When a company's desire to affect price and markets exceeds its pricing capabilities, profitability is often harmed rather than helped.

For example, as advertising spending fell during the early 2000s, one media CEO blamed the sales and marketing function. He ordered the sales and marketing team to stand firm on price—and saw revenues slip even further until he was fired by the shareholders. Similarly, a few years ago a leading cigarette manufacturer offered a significant price break to its wholesalers, but failed to structure the new price so as to force the wholesalers to pass along the savings to end users, which was to have been the whole point. As a result, the wholesalers got a one-time windfall and the manufacturer failed to win new market share.

Excuses for unresponsive pricing include the difficulty of physically relabeling prices on shelves, too many products, too much data, or any number of reasons—but all these problems can be fixed. Notwithstanding this, one well-known retail chain has in fact used such excuses to go as long as 18 months without a reprice of convenience items, a luxury few companies can afford. A more encouraging example is Toys "R" Us. In the face of head-on competition with Wal-Mart, it decided to abandon price tags altogether. It now has kiosks where customers can go to scan any piece of merchandise to see its price. Repricing can now be instantaneous, and the system provides invaluable information about customer decisions after seeing the price displayed at the kiosk. This gives a direct read on the gap between the customer's perceived value and the set price, a very powerful capability.

Information technology capabilities are equally crucial in some markets. When young upstart MCI challenged AT&T for market share through the innovative "Friends and Family" program, MCI succeeded in cheaply winning over a million customers through customer referrals and highly effective direct marketing.[1] AT&T, saddled with legacy systems at the time, was unable to respond and saw its share erode over many painful years.

---

[1] The Friends and Family Program created what MCI called "calling circles." An MCI subscriber would be offered a discount to callers in her "circle" who also subscribed to MCI. MCI would then contact the circle members named by the subscriber and, in general, enjoyed great success in converting and keeping them. In pricing terms, we can say that MCI used conditional discounts for lead generation and improved retention.

If a company's pricing actions exceed its IT capabilities, the result can be explosively counterproductive—an exception to our earlier generalization about pricing blunders going unnoticed. For example, a leading long-distance telephone company unintentionally sent almost one million checks, designed to induce long-distance users to change vendors, to its own customers—needlessly costing the company more than $30 million.

Even this gaffe pales in comparison to the debacle at Greyhound. Looking to increase revenues and reduce costs, the bus line attempted to install a reservation and pricing system modeled on a similar system successfully used by airlines. However, bus routes are more complex than those of airlines, placing the necessary IT well beyond the company's capabilities. It pushed forward regardless, however, going so far as to sell off many of its buses in anticipation of expected efficiencies and touting revenue gains to investors. The result was a complete systems crash upon launch, riots at bus stops as passengers fought to board infrequent buses, and a crash in stock value.[2] A worthwhile lesson to the rest of us, although an expensive one for the formerly high-flying bus line.

A REWARD FOR EFFORT

Going forward in this book, you're about to read how price, brand, and cost have been made to work together, and how leading-edge pricing can be a powerful solo instrument when the situation calls for it. But what will this knowledge require of you? Of your organization?

Consider that smart companies in every industry have begun treating the intangibles of price and brand as products in their own right. After a highly successful product relaunch, white-goods manufacturer Whirlpool said that it now thinks of launching a new price as requiring the same process as launching a new dishwasher or dryer.[3] There is the same value in market research, innovative thinking, and careful exe-

---

[2] "Real Dog: How Greyhound Lines Re-Engineered Itself Into A Deep Hole," *The Wall Street Journal*, October 20, 1994.

[3] "The Price is Wrong," *The Economist*, May 23, 2002.

cution. Brand too can be considered a product, with the right message and value proposition to the customer being keys to success in the market. The rewards of this new mindset are great—jumps in the top line of 5 to 25 percent, even bigger jumps in profit. Yet the effort required is not trivial.

Not willing to make that effort are those companies that believe they can shrink their way to superior results, or that allow themselves the luxury of mediocre returns. Companies on this side of the divide will continue to plod along with separate and isolated functional management in brand, pricing, operations, sales, customer service, finance, and IT. But for how long? The 2000s represent a tougher economic climate than the 1990s, and sooner or later a broad range of their competitors will learn to integrate price with brand and the other disciplines. Those that lag will face severe pressures as their competitors hone pricing skills, use them to build profit margins, then invest these same margins in improving pricing capabilities still further.

Which side of the pricing equation do you want to be on?

Chapter Two | The Secret Life of Price

On television there is a game show where contestants are shown various consumer goods, ranging from snack foods to boats, and are then asked to guess the price.[1] When we watch that show, it's fascinating to see the contestants struggling to come up with an estimate, and we feel a genuine sense of closure when the real price is revealed.[2]

Good entertainment—but upon reflection, a flawed view of the world. At best, it's an idealized view of a very small part of the world, namely consumer goods. But it's still missing too much of the intriguing variety of pricing. On the show there appears to be only one price for the product, no discount opportunities, no warranties or related charges, and the products are sold only through an attractive model's hand gestures. Finally, no one questions the prices, or even wonders why the prices are what they are.

---

[1] *The Price is Right*, with Bob Barker on CBS, is apparently the longest-running top-rated show.

[2] This is probably why we write books on pricing.

In the real world, there are many variations in price for a particular good or service. By way of example, some retail prices found around Canada are shown in Figure 2.1. This chart illustrates that, in addition to there being no single price for each of these goods, in some cases the range of differences, or spread, is wide. In other cases, the spread is narrow.

A simple chart—but it gives rise to questions that are anything but simple. Why are some goods priced high while others are priced low? Why do prices vary so much, sometimes even for the same item in the same city? Why do prices for some items vary more than for others? What are the forces at work? This chapter takes us on a journey beneath the surface of prices, into a varied and sometimes complex world—yet a world with answers that are highly rational and useful once we understand them. In some ways, this chapter is key to the rest of the book: It describes what price really is.

Industry	Product or service	Vendor A	Vendor B	Extent of price variation*
Grocery	Peanut butter	Ajax: $3.29	Toronto: $3.69	12%
Telco	Telephone basic phone line per month	Toronto: $22.05	Missisauga: $25.60	16%
Utility	Cable basic channel per month	Oshawa: $16.48	Toronto: $20.20	23%
Fast Food	Pizza large, two toppings	Barrie: $12.99	Missisauga: $16.99	31%
Tourism	Car rental compact car for one week	Vancouver: $189.00	Toronto: $299.89	59%
Telco	Cellular phone 100 minutes per month	Halifax: $20.00 per month (no activation fee)	Toronto: $25.00 ($25.00 activation fee)	25%
Telco	Internet service provider per month	Windsor: $24.98	Toronto: $29.98	20%
Legal	Divorce	Calgary: $399.00	Toronto: $499.00	25%
Tourism	Westin Hotel (A rating) 1 night, deluxe room	Vancouver: $159.00	Toronto: $249.00	57%
Religious Services	Wedding (same denomination)	North Bay: $100 or donation	Toronto: $250 ñ $500	150%+

*Figures have been rounded to nearest percent

Figure 2.1. Price differences in Canada.

THE THREE ELEMENTS OF PRICE

There are many influences on price, and therefore in different markets, different influences will dominate. However, we believe that the three strongest influences—those that have the greatest applicability across industries—are the *value* of a good or service, the degree of *competitive intensity*, and the importance of *brand*. In some cases, all three of these influences will matter. Yet in every pricing situation, it's worth asking if there is one that matters more than the other two. Let's discuss each in turn.[3]

The Clarity of Value

Both television and popular conceptions of price convey the idea that price is directly related to the value of the service being offered. As it happens, value is the cornerstone of price in the real world, too. To learn more, let's look at the technique of value-based pricing—one of the best pricing methods, when feasible.

An example comes from a well-known chemical company. This company had developed a new hot-melt adhesive for use in sealing and packaging consumer goods—that is, gluing up boxes for everything from computers to breakfast cereal. The new adhesive had a number of advantages over competing products: stronger, lower-density, and more stable at high temperatures. But how to price it? What was the *value* of all these advantages?

To find out the answer to this question, the company interviewed potential customers, spent time on the packaging lines of current customers, and jointly worked up financials with purchasing officers who would have to sign off on the purchase. After this effort the chemical company was able to identify three distinct benefits: First, the product

---

[3] Daniel E. Aks, COO of a leading magazine conglomerate, points out that value, competition, and brand are really another way of describing supply and demand—but they are more useful to line managers than trying to measure supply and demand. We do, however, discuss ways of using supply and demand to determine price levels in Chapters 8 and 15.

stuck better, so less was needed and fewer boxes would burst or fail. This in turn meant less breakage and fewer claims for returned merchandise. Second, the adhesive reduced factory maintenance because it was less prone to plug up customer's nozzles and hoses. And third, the higher thermal stability meant a better appearance for the final product—less discoloration.

The company then quantified—wherever possible—the value that the adhesive would create for customers by reducing the customer's cost of ownership in the packaging process. The reduced costs in the packaging process, and reduced clogging of hoses, were highly quantifiable, and worth about $480,000 a year to a company doing a million boxes per month. Other benefits could not be so easily quantified, such as the value of better appearance.

The company worked with customers to communicate and validate the value created for them. This involved working with different stakeholders inside customer organizations, running trials, and building the credibility of the claims of savings and advantage. Another way of looking at this process is that although the company came with a fair degree of credibility, it nonetheless had to create a brand for the new adhesive—a reminder that although one of the big three factors might dominate a situation, as value does here, the others are usually present as well.

The company decided it would price the product to capture the value of all the quantifiable cost savings, giving away to customers only the fuzzier, harder-to-quantify benefits, such as improved appearance. This proved a sound strategy because the typical customer required hard numbers on cost savings before paying a higher price—but was pleased to see additional benefits such as a neater appearance, for which the customer was *not* being charged.

The value-based approach resulted in a market price that was 40 percent higher than a cost-based approach would have produced. Also worth noting is that this price carried a 30-percent premium over the next highest price in the market. And because the company had taken the time to communicate the value of the new adhesive, and had chosen a price closely tied to demonstrable benefits, the new adhesive rap-idly gained a big share of the market.[4]

Note that value changes, depending on the buyer's point of view. Farmers value tractors more than accountants do; baby boomers value the Beatles more than their parents do. This is the notion behind seg-mentation, the practice discussed in Chapter 4 of charging different prices to different groups of customers for the same product.

The Discipline of Competition

It's no surprise that the level of competition drives prices, but how you measure the effect isn't nearly so obvious. It depends on the nature of the market. The simple number of competitors can be useful for determining price in some markets—yet in the case of airlines, it's not the total num-ber of airlines that determines average ticket price, but rather the number of airlines serving a particular route. An airline with no competition can command a premium price—but add a second carrier, and prices drop an average of 22 percent. Add a third competitor, and prices dip a further 20 percent. Additional competitors depress prices by another 10 percent.

What happens if there are always dozens of ruthless competitors competing for every sale? In that case, differences in price can become so subtle as to be hidden, as they are in some commodity markets—for example, steel.[5] One roll of cold-rolled steel costs the same as any other conforming roll from another source. Automobile manufacturers, an important customer base for cold-rolled steel, at first glance appear to ignore quality differences among vendors—meaning they refuse to pay more to any given source.

---

[4] To value price, you must be able to meaningfully differentiate your product or ser-vice from competing offers. If value propositions are identical, the price ends up being set by the least sophisticated or most aggressive competitor. Such competitors typi-cally don't focus on customer value, and therefore might underprice, destroying the market in the process. For more, see Benson P. Shapiro, "Precision Pricing for Profit in the New World Order," *Harvard Business Review*, December 1998.

[5] Although many managers call their market a commodity market, a real commod-ity exists only when buyers refuse to pay any more to one up-to-spec vendor than to another.

And yet markets such as this do still draw distinctions. In this case, Dofasco, a leading integrated steel producer, makes its steel to stricter tolerances, and in run-experiments with Toyota, has shown that its steel runs through stamping machines 20 percent faster than other steels. At first glance Dofasco's quality would appear to go unrewarded with no price premium, but that is not true. Each automobile manufacturer has plans for which steel providers to drop in the event of a downturn. For its superior quality, Dofasco will be among the last providers to be dropped while others will be forced to shut down factories. This is crucial to long-term cash flows and operating costs. Thus, in this particular commodity market, the price rewards for value cannot be seen in the short run—only in the longer run.[6]

Brand

Brand is the third major element of price. Whether it is a product such as laundry soap, or services such as legal representation, sellers who enjoy prestige, familiarity, and cachet will command a higher price than those without brand references. A classic example of brand and price: Matches from a drugstore will light the candles on your birthday cake and cost nothing. A $1.49 plastic BIC lighter will do the same; so will a sleek $70 Colibri piezoelectric lighter. Each offers the same degree of utility—but each has a very different brand value.

You'll note we just used "value" again. Strictly speaking, brand is a form of value—there is distinct value to buyers in purchasing a product or service with a strong brand. Buyers benefit in several ways, including: *Brand awareness* makes it easier to identify candidates for purchase. For example, if you're shopping for a car, you don't need to

---

[6] Other ways that price results can be made invisible, or at least obscure, include barter—the exchange of goods and services for goods and services. This is common in many endeavors ranging from not-for-profit organizations to large defense contracts. See "A Well Kept Military Secret. Foreigners Exact Trade-Offs from U.S. Contractors," *The New York Times*, February 10, 2003, Sec. 3:1; also "Buying Your Way Into College. So, Just How Much do You Need to Donate To Get Your Kid In?" *The Wall Street Journal*, March 12, 2003: D1. This article suggests that a $1 million donation can get anyone into Harvard—along with the regular tuition payment.

spend a lot of time compiling lists of manufacturers—a brand that fits
your requirements will spring to mind.

Perceived brand quality allows buyers to abbreviate their product
testing and decision making, confident that the seller has thought
through the product requirements, and the product will perform as
advertised. In corporate purchasing, brand allows buyers to feel comfortable that their senior managers won't second-guess the decision.

Brand loyalty comes about when buyers feel reassured that the
product is the best it can be. Even better, users of luxury brands often
feel better for driving their Mercedes, or wearing an Armani suit, or a
Tiffany ring. For individuals, brand is a reflection of their personality.

The appeal to sellers is that brand offers an effective way to
acquire, satisfy, and retain customers, beyond the vagaries of product
specifications or the lowest price. As we discuss in the next chapter,
this works best when there is a complexity or an unknown aspect to the
product. The more customers know every aspect of a product and its
alternatives, the more they believe that all such products are functionally identical, and the greater their skepticism about taking differences
on faith, the less important brand will be to price.

PRICES IN REAL LIFE

The more we look at specific prices in specific markets, the more we see
how prices vary. In fact, we have only to glance back at our contradictory list of prices in Canada to realize that we will rarely see uniform
prices, even for the same branded item.

We know that in most markets, products and services differ in quality, as well as in shipping costs, after-sales service, and in other ways—
and, naturally, these varied factors affect price. And we can guess that
different companies choose price for different objectives: for example,
to gain an immediate maximization of profit or share gain. These factors too must have an impact.[7]

---

[7] For instance, during the late 1990s, many markets were affected by new Internet-
based participants striving for market share and capital market approval, while
incumbents sought profitability and defense of markets.

Another reason for different prices is the difference between the list price and the actual price the customer pays and the seller realizes—the realized price or "pocket price." As a result, *any product or service has more than one price*. Between the list price and the final pocket price lie many potential changes, some foreseen, others not. Figure 2.2 shows the realized price of a household good and illustrates how discounts and adjustments in the pocket price can alter list price. In this case, the realized price was half that of the list price.

The multiple components of realized price have the effect of making actual market prices highly variable. For example, one buyer might receive a deep discount; the other does not. One buyer might purchase under a long-term contract; another does not. To add to the confusion, some costs and benefits not tangibly related to the specific transaction also have an impact on price. Customer loyalty programs such as promotional gifts are a factor in some industries. Additional adjustments such as vendor financing and volume rebates can sometimes make it hard for anyone to understand the price of a particular transaction.

Finally, there is the chaos of the real world. The management of Mercedes-Benz USA has a clear notion of the prices at which its cars should sell. With good German clarity, the company has even designated its cars numerically to reflect chassis size and engine strength, so that bigger numbers mean more valuable cars. Every car has been considered, every car has its number and precise list price—and yet the actual prices realized by Mercedes-Benz dealers deviate considerably from this grand scheme. Recent sales at one dealer revealed some typical reasons for this: a bargain sale to an angry influential customer who had returned his car as a "lemon," the sale of a previous year's model at a price no one could account for, a fleet sale of several cars, and a car that arrived without the options ordered by the customer. Thus, even when an overall price structure is known, it can be difficult to see it clearly reflected in actual prices.

And in some cases the pattern is deliberately obscured. Customers typically like simple, unambiguous pricing, often called *transparent* pricing. It allows easy comparison. Yet transparency is often not to the

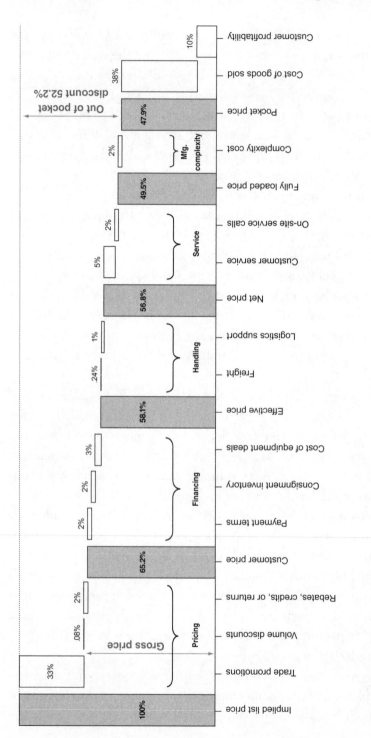

Figure 2.2. Net realized price or "pocket price."

Note: Percentages in pricing, financing, handling and service are rounded up
Source: Client data and A.T. Kearney analysis

seller's advantage, and thus *opaque* pricing is common, particularly in industrial markets.

Ironically, complex pricing is often opaque to the sellers as well. When developing a record of final or pocket prices for a particular good or service, we often find that almost no one associated with the seller actually knows these prices—and many people who *thought* they knew turn out to be mistaken. For example, we once surveyed a sales force and asked what prices had been obtained the prior month for specific sales. Later, we compared the survey results to cash results posted on the general ledger. The correlation between actual prices and the remembered prices showed a correlation of only 65 percent—not a close match. Interestingly, there is often little or no correlation between discounts and volumes: A low-volume customer might receive more favorable discounts than higher-volume, more strategic customers.

PRICE DRIVERS

We now arrive at the action-oriented part of this chapter. Despite all the confusion that price variations can present us with, nonetheless price patterns can be found. These patterns are a reflection of how a particular market defines value, the competition in that market, brand, and dozens of other factors. Understand the patterns in your market, and you can maximize the value your company realizes from the market. Know the patterns, and the better you can take advantage of price patterns and changes.

The good news is that price has distinct patterns. Even better news is that these patterns are often simple. You don't need to know higher mathematics to leverage price patterns in most cases. Often a simple relationship, or a simple mathematical tool, will allow your company to understand how to optimize its prices. We call such a pattern a "price driver." Knowledge of price drivers is like having radar in a fog—if value can't be given shape, and if prices obscure rather than reveal, you can easily run aground. But once you can quantify value by means of price drivers, you can see where you actually are and how to get the ship home safely.

Let's take a familiar example of pricing and discuss the price drivers: residential housing prices. When buying a home, most of us look at different houses for sale within a neighborhood, get advice from a realtor, then put in an offer to purchase a house. This works fairly well if there are similar houses on the market within a narrow area, and the realtor has good judgment. But we can do better.

For example, we looked at houses sold during 2003 within one small New England town. We compared sales prices with a number of features that sellers and realtors commonly believe important to selling price: size of house, lot size, how well the house is maintained, how many bathrooms, whether or not there is a garage, landscaping, dry basement, or "charm." Using a statistical technique that looks for connections between these features and the selling price, we were able to separate those features that mattered from those that didn't—in other words, to identify the true drivers.

As it turns out, there were only two: the size of the house measured by the number of square feet of floor space, and the size of the lot in acres. The statistical analysis said these two factors accounted for 97 percent of the house price.[8] Specifically, if you multiplied the square feet by $325 per square foot, and the acreage by $125,000 per acre, you could predict the selling price almost exactly. Obviously, this was not news to real estate developers who had been building bigger and bigger (and less and less charming) houses in this area for years—bigger meant a higher selling price. Knowing price drivers allows businesses such as developers to single-mindedly maximize their profit margins.

The analysis also suggested that this market did allow for a modest premium for lots of more than half an acre—but not much, and certainly less than the cost of additional land. Hence, large houses on

---

[8] A statistical measure of how well-observed prices can be explained by price drivers can be obtained through a process called regression analysis. If the fit is perfect, the "R-squared" is 1.00 (or 100 percent). The R2 tells you how much of the variation in prices is explained by the price driver or drivers being tested. Also, brand can play a role in real estate pricing but apparently within this town, brand was consistent. Inside New York City, the name of a building can affect the price. See "The High Stakes Game of the Name," *The New York Times*, July 27, 2003: 1, real estate section.

small lots. Oddly, the numbers suggested that there was no systematic value associated with neatness or care and maintenance. In some cases, we suspect this was because older homes were being torn down and rebuilt. In such cases, whether a home was poorly maintained or well maintained didn't matter to the developer. If these price patterns differ from what buyers say they want, we can only observe that sales prices show what buyers are actually willing to pay.

What factors drive prices in other markets? The answer depends on the market, of course. However, across a broad range of markets there are typical drivers that should be examined when asking why prices behave as they do. The usual suspects are number of competitors, geography, cost-to-serve, and customer benefits created by the product or service. Two examples follow.

Geography

Geography affects not only sellers' costs, but also demand, competitive mix, and other price components. Prices posted on Marriott Corporation's Web site for its hotel rooms show that prices are highest in the center of Manhattan and at the two major New York airports, and fall as you move away from these centers (see Figure 2.3). Other geographic drivers we have observed include the distance to a manufacturer's factory and the distance from a major transportation hub, such as a rail link.

Benefits

This criterion suggests that if a machine is three times as productive as another machine, it will be worth three times as much. Although not always true, it's often a good guide.[9] For example, printing presses are priced primarily on their speed per minute. Agricultural goods, such as hybrid seeds, are priced based on their productivity per acre. Such benefits are carefully measured, and companies devote tremendous resources to demonstrating to customers the exact increases in produc-

[9] In some cases, companies decide to forego the higher price in favor of increasing market share by offering a superior value proposition, so sometimes value will relate to total revenues rather than simply to price.

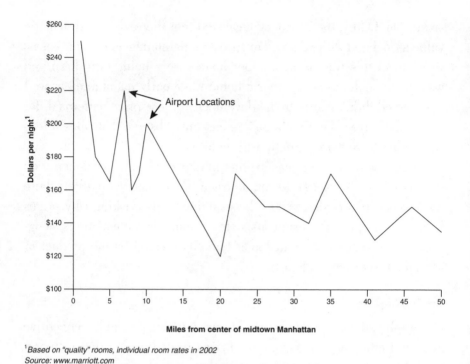

[1] Based on "quality" rooms, individual room rates in 2002
Source: www.marriott.com

Figure 2.3. Hotel room prices and geography.

tivity. For example, Pioneer, one of the developers of hybrid seeds, funds test acres in agricultural communities to prove results to farmers.

Other examples where value or productivity drives price include the size of buses and their drivers' salaries, computer code output and dollars per hour for software developers, and financial portfolio managers' performances and bonuses.[10] You can find still more examples in later chapters.

PRICES OVER TIME

Don't forget that prices also vary over time, which gives us another important driver. Airplane ticket prices vary as you get closer to the time

[10] See, for example, Moses Abramovitz, National Income Lectures, Stanford University, 1979.

of scheduled takeoff. Gasoline prices along highways vary in the course of a week.[11] Magazine renewal prices drop as your subscription nears an end. Timing can be everything, as when Cisco routers moved from selling near list prices in 2000 to selling for pennies on the dollar on eBay—this after the tech bubble burst in 2001 and bankrupt dot.coms sold their equipment to pay off employees and creditors.

Relationships change over time, including those between buyer and seller. Even in industries where the customer is normally king, there are moments when the balance of power shifts. Many sellers of goods or services lacking meaningful differentiation have found ways of temporarily obtaining higher prices—for example, the surcharge for rush orders. It's a hard life selling an undifferentiated product, but smart pricing and pricing that takes advantage of changes over time can lift returns dramatically.

To see why price matters over time, consider the development and manufacture of an industrial good. The typical pattern is that in the beginning, prices are relatively low. Later, after the product has been well established in the market, opportunities will come about to increase price significantly—but to seize these opportunities, you need to be alert and actively managing price. Otherwise, you might miss the most lucrative parts in the cycle, such as the aftermarket. We discuss the aftermarket specifically in Chapter 18, but suffice it here to quote Henry Ford: "I would give my cars away for free if I could be guaranteed spare parts sales."

Smart magazine publishers also understand price life cycles. One example is the efforts they undertake to retain subscribers, all of which are reflected by price changes and channel choices—typical for superior pricers that tend to vary other elements of a marketing program along with price. The issue here is the dreaded nonrenewal. To avoid it,

---

[11] Regarding gasoline prices, the pattern observed is low prices on Monday, rising to higher prices on Friday. This reflects the fact that much of highway traffic is commuters. These workers can visit local low-priced stations over the weekend and start the week with full tanks of gasoline. By Friday, they often need a fill-up and have little choice but to use the service stations located on the highways.

publishers use increasingly high-cost methods, while offering increasingly attractive prices. To wit:

- Some months before a subscription ends, inexpensive little cards ("blow-in cards") are inserted into the magazine, offering very ordinary renewal rates.
- If no response is forthcoming, a letter is sent with a better price offer.
- If there is still no response, shortly before the subscription lapses, a telemarketer will call—sometimes with the same price, sometimes lower, but always at a higher cost to the publisher.
- After the subscription lapses comes the grace continuation (free issues) and a letter.
- Finally, when all hope is gone, the name and contact information might be sold to Publishers Clearinghouse or a similar organization, which offers the publisher its lowest margins.

In a host of industries, companies have used price patterns over time to squeeze the last dollar out of a product. In the film industry today, often it's the revenues after the initial theater run that push a movie into the black. Similarly, retailer Best Buy for many years derived more of its profit margins from selling extended service warranties than from selling the actual merchandise. The tougher the core market, the more ingenuity is needed in the pricing of related services.

Even if times are good in your industry, knowing a typical industry price evolution can help you prepare for a future that might be different than today. Many industries go through similar stages in their pricing evolution. In each case, as prices evolve, their administration becomes more complex. One example is the telecom industry, which has moved from uniform transparent pricing to highly varied, promotional pricing, as shown in Figure 2.4.

Managers must look ahead to possible pricing changes, or else billing and back office systems won't be able to accommodate more complex pricing; accounting systems won't produce the required cost analysis; channels won't be able to sell new price plans; and marketing won't be adept at developing creative and effective new structures.

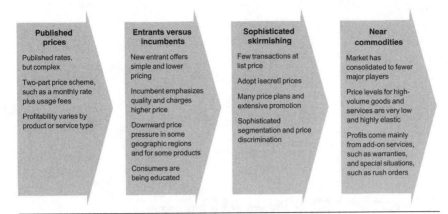

Figure 2.4. Typical price evolution.

Without foresight, increased pricing pressure will truly be bad news—your company will not be able to adapt in time.

SEEING THROUGH CHAOS: THE POWER OF DRIVERS

Even at their most complex, prices are secretly rational. The world is filled with buyers, sellers, and intermediaries, all pursuing radically different objectives with different time frames, values, budgets, skills, knowledge, and execution capabilities. This can make it hard to discern the true price drivers in your market. Yet by keeping close track of realized prices and applying the appropriate analytic tools, you can understand the drivers and penetrate the price fog to develop a strong price strategy.

Whatever form it takes, a good price strategy must recognize the limitations to setting a price. Don't be surprised when you set a price and the product or service sells at anything *but* the target price. Develop a price strategy that's compatible with the chaos of real prices. The ability of your company to thrive in an increasingly competitive environment might well depend on recognizing emerging price patterns—and price drivers are the starting point.

Chapter Three | Branding for Profit

Many managers have come to regard brand as a fuzzy topic, requiring broad measures. This is wrong. Brand in fact has specific purposes, and businesses should invest in it only with specific aims in mind. A sure sign of fuzzy thinking (and poor strategy as a result) is the mistaken belief that customer awareness is the same as brand strength. Other signs of fuzzy thinking are internal memos with "brand" listed as a company strength without further elaboration. Specificity is required to move brand from "feel good" to hard financial results.

Here's a statement shocking to those still mired in fuzziness: Brand is at its most valuable *as a tool for pricing*. For a given market segment, if you understand brand, the value of your offers, and the competitive dynamics, you can optimize your price. The question thus becomes, how do we understand brand in price terms?

Brand is a form of information. Brand is most valuable where customers have the least specific information, the least ability to obtain information, the least clarity on evaluation criteria, and the least time or inclination to obtain product information. Brand equity produces the highest returns when products or services are complex, difficult to compare, difficult to evaluate in regard to success, and expensive to evaluate relative to price. The brand message is most powerful when it's clear, crisp, and communicates a relevant vision or value to the customer. This is why companies such as Coca-Cola, McDonald's, and IBM are so focused on providing a consistent product or service. Product variation would damage the nonverbal proposition of what you expect in a McDonald's hamburger, the contents of a Coca-Cola bottle, or an IBM computer.

We believe that brand and the utility of brand vary sharply by product, market, and channel. Therefore, unless you offer only one kind of product to a homogenous market, your brand strategies must be highly varied, along with your level of effort and expenditure.

Brand is best understood by examining how your customers make decisions regarding your product or service. For example, as described in Chapter 1, direct mail advertisers must decide to buy either first class or bulk mail stamps for their letters. Their decision-making process illustrates the need to understand customer decision criteria: Many mailers pay for first-class mail although, functionally, bulk mail (standard A mail) gets the letter there within an acceptable length of time. Why pay more? The reason is that in some markets, mail recipients are three times more likely to open a first-class envelope than a bulk mail envelope. Over time, mail recipients have learned that envelopes with first-class stamps tend to contain more important messages—a bill, a legal notice, or business correspondence. Bulk mail tends to be a waste of their time, so they don't open it. Because bulk mailers' business relies on how many people open their envelopes, many pay for first-class stamps.

Another example is automotive spare parts. A Mercedes diesel camshaft purchased from a Mercedes-Benz dealer runs $500. The same camshaft, in the same box with the same manufacturer's logo stamped on it, can be had for $150 from an independent parts supplier. Other parts also show threefold price differences.

Still another example is sunglasses. Surveys show that many people buying sunglasses pay for a better brand because they believe those glasses offer superior UV protection. In fact, an independent study recently showed that there are no discernable differences in UV protection in sunglasses that cost more than $5.

In each case, consumers made the choices they did because of lack of information. If mail recipients could somehow know what was in an envelope, they wouldn't rely on the type of stamp when deciding whether to trash a letter or open it. Likewise, if car owners knew they were buying exactly the same part, they would opt for the lower-priced component. Finally, if sunglass purchasers knew that all sunglasses offer UV protection, many would spend less.

Channel influences the importance of brand. On the Internet, the ability of brands to provide information is even more crucial. Faced with an inability to touch, smell, and inspect food and grocery items, for example, patrons of online groceries tend to be more brand-oriented and less price-sensitive than shoppers in conventional grocery stores. Brand is used as a proxy for quality.

BRAND AND PRODUCT

Brand equity varies by type of product, as do its dynamics. Why? Because available information, as well as the inclination to obtain such information, also varies by product. Here are three examples of this:

Example 1: 3M's branding decisions for its lines of clear adhesive tapes are based on how much attention consumers give adhesive tape (very little, it appears). According to the 3M product manager, the "Scotch" and "Highland" brands are kept separate because they offer distinctly different levels of quality. For example, Scotch, the premium brand, can be removed from paper without tearing the surface of the paper. Lower-priced Highland will tear the paper and appears less transparent. Because 3M knows that few if any consumers will take the time to read the specifications of their adhesive tape, the only way to maintain clarity as to quality is to separately brand the two tapes. Each has a different market focus: Scotch appeals to customers who are price-insensitive, while Highland competes with discount brands of adhesive tape.

Example 2: Car manufacturers, unlike 3M, have the luxury of knowing that most purchasers view a car as a major purchase decision and will therefore invest a fair chunk of time in investigating purchase options. Thus car manufacturers can support multiple levels of quality under the general umbrella of the total company brand. BMW wants potential purchasers to believe that it produces "The Ultimate Driving Experience" for different price levels. Although its low-end 3 Series might underperform its other cars, BMW believes consumers will have the sophistication to understand that *for its class*, the 3 Series offers superior handling compared to competitors.

Example 3: In big-ticket industrial purchases, customers are willing to spend a *lot* of time evaluating product quality. In preparing for a major outsourcing decision ($600 million per year for five years), one leading utility spent $350,000 on consultants and an equal amount on internal employees' time to thoroughly evaluate two of its options: IBM versus EDS. IBM's reputation and credibility among top management was acknowledged to be superior, but the utility chose EDS after concluding that it offered the better long-term performance. Brand failed to win the day.

Brand and Price

Often, brand and price serve a similar purpose—to inform purchasers about their potential purchase.[1] For example, telling consumers that a car is priced at $60,000 will deliver much the same message as telling him the car is built by Mercedes, Lexus, Jaguar, or BMW. While the nuances differ, in both cases the message is essentially the same: "It's a luxury car." In general, brand and price are often close reflections of each other.

A much-asked question is whether or not brand can create a price premium. The answer is yes: Some of the smartest companies in the world cultivate brand because it does in fact result in higher prices and thus higher profit margins. In some cases, these premiums appear to exist without much basis. For example, the U.S. Supreme Court found

[1] "Price Strategy: Time to Choose Your Weapons," *The Journal of Business Strategy*, September–October 1997:11–15.

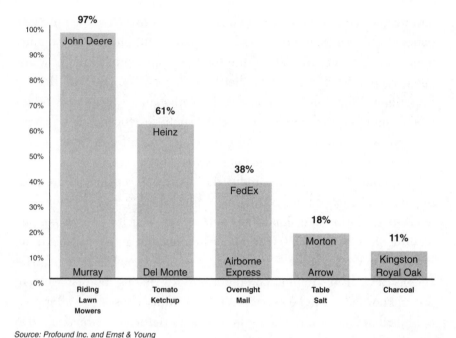

Source: Profound Inc. and Ernst & Young

Figure 3.1. Difference in price between leading and contender brands.

in one famous antitrust suit that chlorine laundry bleaches are identical in function and performance. Consumers apparently don't agree, however—Clorox routinely commands a gross margin of 58 percent, versus less than half that for competitors.[2]

If we associate brand with market share, whether as driver or result, there emerges a clear link between brand and price. Figure 3.1 shows this for various products. In the case of perfumes, cosmetics, fashion accessories, toys, and similar products, the combination of design and brand often matters far more than the cost of materials, manufacturing, and distribution. For example, manufacturing costs for perfume and fashion clothing are often less than 15 percent of the retail purchase price.[3] High profit margins are possible because fashion designers such

[2] Clorox annual report, 1998.
[3] French Fragrances, Inc., 1998 10K.

as Ralph Lauren have "built [their companies] into aspirational lifestyle brands reflecting the good life."[4] Brand in this context offers the consumer guidance on how to achieve such lifestyle aspirations: Fashion products claim to be the keys "for successful living" (Benetton) or the stuff of "new dreams and legends" (Hermes). Designers operate in a rapidly changing and impressionistic segment in which product evaluation is uncertain, hence, consumers will pay a premium for a brand that assures them of a product's merits.

While some areas of human endeavor will always remain a mystery (such as how to dress fashionably), others evolve over time. In the 1960s, oil companies were heavy advertisers, and many consumers believed there were significant differences among major brands of petroleum. Since then, most of us have become aware that the differences are minimal.[5] We've become correspondingly more price-sensitive, and as a result there is no longer an oil company on the *Ad Age* list of top 200 advertisers.

The Internet remains an area of relative uncertainty for both consumers and businesses, and so, not surprisingly, brand remains key in this market. By signaling trust, an online brand can leverage a price premium, even for nearly identical products and services. For example, one study found that *Amazon.com*, which enjoys strong customer trust, has been able to sustain prices 7 to 12 percent higher than online competitors such as *Books.com*.[6] The study further found that despite beating Amazon's prices 99 percent of the time, *Books.com's* share of online book traffic remained miniscule at 2.2 percent.[7]

Offline, too, many industries grant a premium to brand strength. The automobile sector offers an example: Toyota and GM cooperated to

---

[4] Richard Baum, Goldman Sachs Retailing Conference, Tokyo, Japan, October 12, 1998.

[5] In fact, petroleum brands might have shared distribution agreements—meaning it might be a Mobil product coming out of a Chevron pump.

[6] Michael D. Smith, Joseph Bailey, and Erik Brynjolfsson, "Understanding Digital Markets: Review and Assessment," July 1999.

[7] "The Power of Smart Pricing," *Business Week*, April 10, 2000. *Books.com* is now part of *barnesandnoble.com*.

build and sell a car known variously as the Geo Prism or Toyota Corolla. The Corolla and Geo were identical coming off the same assembly line, and shared all but a handful of mainly cosmetic parts. Yet the Toyota sells for more than $2800 than the Geo. There can be only one reason: brand.

Where product quality is obvious, however, the power of brand is limited. For example, one Canadian brick manufacturer decided to brand its products and invested in advertising and other tools to do so. While consumers eventually learned to recognize this brand, it had no impact on brick prices or market share, so the experiment was dropped. In a commodity business, brand usually isn't worth the effort. Hence, in his book on brand equity, David Aaker values brand equity in the stone, glass, and clay industry as zero.[8]

BRAND AND COSTS

Brand influences costs. A strong brand will not only allow a price premium, but will in addition make potential customers more inclined to pay attention to advertisements. A strong brand provides a platform for further communication with customers.

A meaningful, distinct, and consistent brand can have an enormous impact on the selling process. A powerful example comes from the automobile industry, which has a range of well-known brands. On the one hand, we have the striking statistic that almost 80 percent of the visitors to Mercedes automobile showrooms end up buying a Mercedes. On the other hand, we find that only a few visitors to Isuzu showrooms end up buying an Isuzu. Clearly, despite a clever and memorable advertising campaign involving "Joe Isuzu," brand awareness did not translate into purchases for this importer of reliable, moderately priced cars.

The effect on selling costs is dramatic. Instead of spending their days on productive prospects, Isuzu dealerships must filter through many wasted prospects. Probably this is just the beginning of the financial burden: lower compensation for salespeople, a higher rate of dealer

---

[8] David Aaker, "Managing Brand Equity," 1991 (Free Press).

dissatisfaction, sinking morale, and less care taken with prospects. All conspire to create a vicious cycle. Better branding could fix this cycle.

BRAND AND MARKET SHARE

For some consumer-packaged goods, there is solid statistical evidence that brand awareness, as measured by advertising, is related to market share. The definitive study of beer brewers' market battles showed that when Anheuser-Busch and Miller outspent local rivals by a factor of two, their share of market expanded over the next several years to match their share of advertising "voice." The correlation between advertising and market share (albeit lagged) is 50 percent—a pretty strong result in a dynamic marketplace.[9]

Some important caveats exist to this powerful prescription. The study warns that the advertising share advantage must be constant over time and must be considered locality by locality. Further, this rule might not apply to niche markets. This is another way of saying that advertising must have an impact on the consumer decision-making process—general advertising to niche markets is not effective. For example, advertising aimed at New Yorkers doesn't affect consumer decisions in Los Angeles.

Brand also plays a role in industrial purchases when drawing up the Request for Proposal "short list." While purchasers will eventually know the merits of competing offers in detail, when drawing up the RFP list, they're forced by their initial ignorance to rely on brand to decide who might bid. Brand might also play a role when the buyer's decision-maker is worried that the soundness of his or her decision can't be effectively communicated to senior management. Hence the 1960s slogan, "No data processing manager was ever fired for choosing IBM."

Bundling of consumer products and services tends to intensify the importance of brand. Customers view bundles as natural combinations and generally believe there is a bargain in the bundle.[10] Given the

[9] James C. Schroer, "Ad Spending: Growing Market Share," *Harvard Business Review*, Jan./Feb. 1990.

[10] Focus groups in five major U.S. cities queried on various potential service bundles, May 1997.

many permutations of bundled offers, consumers can't generally make direct comparisons to competing offers—and even if they could, they probably wouldn't take the time required to do it right. Given this disinclination on the part of consumers to investigate the actual economics, brand plays a key role. A good brand might convince the consumer that a bundle is likely to represent a bargain and a well-integrated set of service components, while a poor brand will lead consumers to avoid a decision. This is why bundling is a tool that generally favors market incumbents.[11]

LIMITS TO BRAND IMPACT

A lot of money is being spent on corporate brand advertising by telecommunications competitors. Yet the overall efficacy of such broad-based advertising is unclear. Increasingly, consumers have come to believe that there are no significant differences among telephone companies. Indeed, competitors AT&T, MCI, Sprint, Verizon, SBC, BellSouth, and others offer fairly similar levels of service, have similar prices, similar sales channels, and fairly similar histories. There are, however, major differences in advertising levels. AT&T spends more than $1 billion annually, while SBC Ameritech spends less than $100 million annually. Has this made a difference in brand?

Probably not. Each company is ranked according to reputation by *Fortune* magazine each year (see Figure 3.2). If reputation is a proxy for brand, it appears that advertising levels have had no impact on brand. Regression analysis of reputation and advertising dollars (either as a share of revenue or in absolute terms, lagged or instantaneous) shows no relationship—that is, no explanatory power. (In technical jargon, R-squared is low or nil.)

Unlike the beer market, it appears that the telecommunications market cannot be won by brute force. Just as IBM has found that the

---

[11] Market leaders often can wait up to a year before following minor players in bundling initiatives, without significant share loss. However, minor players (those with less than 40-percent share) must follow share leaders in less than six months, or else get shut out of a new bundle niche. "The New Wholesalers," *Telephony*, January 21, 1998.

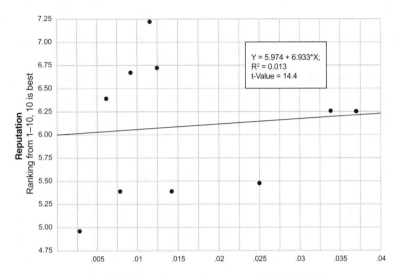

Total advertising spent as a proportion of revenues

Sources: Fortune *Survey of Corporate Reputations,* Advertising Age, *and authorsí analysis*

Figure 3.2. Comparison of advertising spending and corporate "reputation" for U.S. Telcos.

power of its formidable brand has eroded over time (the disappearance of the famous "IBM Premium") because of an increasingly open computing world, telecommunications giants might be discovering that ad spending is also no longer the key to brand.

DAMAGE TO BRAND

The personal computer industry has recently seen a major shift in market power based on brand. Evidence of this comes from a recent poll of potential buyers of personal computers, which shows that more than 67 percent of new PC purchasers would have bought a different brand to save $100, and 82 percent would have done so for a savings of $200.[12]

This wasn't always the case. At one point, Compaq, IBM, and others were powerful brands in the personal computing world. What ended this comfortable state of affairs was the "Intel Inside" campaign, which

[12] Sanford Bernstein Research, survey of PC buyers.

most PC manufacturers eagerly but perhaps mistakenly joined. This campaign initially underscored the observation (then true) that some software ran better with an Intel processor. Unfortunately for the PC manufacturers, the campaign had the side effect of telling PC purchasers that the most important thing about a PC isn't the manufacturer—it's the chip (for example, the Pentium III). Thus, as a result of the "Intel Inside" campaign, many consumers now place far less value on the brand of PC they buy.

Meanwhile, the one brand that never had anything to do with Intel—namely, Apple—is today the most secure against price-based switching by existing users. This is shown in the survey depicted in Figure 3.3, where we see a mere 2 percent of users citing price as the main reason for buying an Apple.

Apple is secure primarily because its product is distinct, but this is reinforced by a branding campaign to reinforce the distinctiveness of Apple's "Think Different" brand. Dell also scores well in price insensitivity, perhaps because of its emphasis on tailoring PC features to

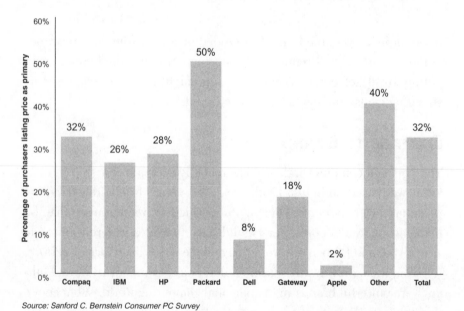

Source: Sanford C. Bernstein Consumer PC Survey

Figure 3.3. Importance of price as the primary selection criterion by brand.

users' needs. These differences in brand equity exist despite some observers' beliefs that for most PCs, performance is quite similar.[13]

The lesson from the PC industry is that brand power resides in those markets with the greatest uncertainty. PC consumers have concluded that the differences among PCs mean little or nothing. Asked to explain the differences among chips made by Intel, Cyrix, and AMD, most consumers have no idea. They *do* know that credible entities, in the form of PC manufacturers, have been telling them there are important differences in these chips. From that knowledge gap springs the power of Intel's brand.

Another source of brand erosion is when brand, price, message, and performance diverge. In the late 1980s, various studies commissioned by Mercedes-Benz USA indicated that the Japanese car lines Lexus and Infiniti were both producing cars comparable in quality to the Mercedes line. Worse yet, they were being priced at 20 to 30 percent less than Mercedes. When Mercedes management refused to reduce price, the inevitable result was share loss to the Japanese. All of this was exacerbated by a lack of clarity on brand. While Mercedes claims to dominate the field in all aspects of quality, in fact they are viewed as leading in only two aspects: safety and prestige (see Figure 3.4).

Mercedes' advertising claims ("Sacrifice Nothing," "The Complete Automotive Experience," "Passion") are at odds with its actual advantages. Mercedes ads, unlike Volvo, do not mention safety. Mercedes ads also do not use the word "prestige," or a synonym. (The ads do emphasize quality, but that is common to many brands—including some distinctly down-market brands.) While its advertising might not correspond closely to Mercedes' comparative advantages, fortunately its price goes a long way to reinforcing the prestige advantage.

In contrast, BMW's perceived advantage regarding "driveability" is highly consistent with its claims to be The Ultimate Driving Experience. Perhaps as a result, BMW has come from behind to pass Mercedes in U.S. car volume. BMW now dominates the performance lux-

---

[13] "Comparison of PC Performance," *PC Week*, March 22, 1999.

Quality attributes	BMW 535	Lexus 400	Lincoln Continental	Mercedes 300
Trouble-free	6.3	8.6	6.9	7.3
Comfortable	7.0	8.2	8.0	7.5
Safe	6.6	7.2	7.2	8.7
Driveable	8.6	8.0	6.8	7.4
Good service	6.7	8.2	6.4	7.4
Pleasing aesthetics	6.8	7.7	6.2	6.5
Large, roomy	5.8	7.0	8.9	7.2
Good fuel economy	5.8	6.0	4.6	5.2
Prestigous	8.3	8.1	6.8	8.8
U.S.-made	1.0	1.2	8.2	1.7

Source: Bradley Gale speech at IIR Pricing Conference.

Figure 3.4. How luxury car brands were rated on different buying factors, on a scale of 1 to 10.

ury car segment, and has taken pains (to the tune of $150 million per year spent on U.S. advertising) to drive that point home.

Although brand is closely related to advertising, success in branding might have nothing to do with advertising. Brand is a function of experience also. For example, a *New York Times Magazine* article talked about how Prince Charles of England had engaged a public relations firm to improve his "brand" (also known as image).[14] As a result of that firm's efforts and the Prince's increased contact with the public, his approval ratings rose from a low of 41 percent to more than 60 percent.

Other groups and institutions have developed positive or negative brands without the benefit of advertising. For example, a recent poll found high regard for pharmacists and low regard for politicians. It's unlikely that most of us know much about either profession in detail, but we might have been disappointed by bad results from the smoke-

[14] *The New York Times Magazine*, November 22, 1998.

filled rooms of legislatures and pleased at our good experiences with pharmacists—all of this with little advertising.

RULES REGARDING BRAND

Based on a number of markets, there are at least three widely applicable rules regarding branding and profit. Each rule requires a detailed understanding of how purchase decisions are made by customers.

Rule 1: Brand is a Function of Audience, Product, Price, and Message, Not Your Company

Brand parameters are set by the nature of the product, not the company. Both 3M and BMW are large, prestigious companies. However, the brand dynamics for the two companies are very different. 3M's Scotch Tape brand cannot support two levels of product quality, while BMW has several levels of automobile size and quality. It's not that BMW is a better company than 3M, it's just that the branding dynamics differ due to product and customer interest levels. As advertising veteran Roger Kenrick observes: "Companies don't own brands—customers do."

The question to ask is: Where does your company's product fall— toward the Scotch Tape or the BMW side of the spectrum? An interesting example of such a quandary exists in the telecommunications industry, which is seeing the rollout of a new product: Internet telephony.

Today, telephone companies are launching voice-over-Internet products. Unlike traditional ("PSTN") telephony, which is highly reliable, easy to use, and high quality, Internet telephony has (so far) been unreliable, difficult for the average user to master, and highly variable in quality. For example, telephone central offices are engineered to fail less than 30 minutes every 40 years. On the other hand, some personal computers crash on a daily basis, and Internet-based voice calls are often cut off during conversation. Voice quality on most Internet calls is mediocre, at best. However, Internet calls are either inexpensive or free, depending on how you measure it.

Can telephone companies such as Verizon, Bell Canada, British Telecom, and others afford to offer Internet telephony under their corporate names? If telephony were like adhesive tape, the answer would clearly be no: Keep inexpensive, low-quality Internet calls as a separate brand, far away from high-quality, high-cost PSTN telephony. Consumers might not care about the differences in specifications and guarantees between PSTN and Internet telephony—but they will nonetheless think poorly of a service provider when the latter fails to perform to PSTN standards. However, if telephone companies think consumers view telephony like automobiles (that is, interesting and worth investigating) then they might well offer both services under one umbrella brand.

Rule 2: Target the Decisions, If You Can

Brand is a form of information to help decision makers. For well-established companies, generalized, content-free brand advertising has only limited utility. Potential purchasers already know of the existence and size of most major suppliers. (This might be different for smaller competitors, or new entrants.) If the existence of the company is already well known, a brand message needs to address the specific questions facing decision makers.

Targeting specific decisions allows companies to build brand. Examples of a solid understanding of customer values include the decision by credit card companies to offer competitive foreign exchange rates to customers—they recognize this as a high-visibility issue for international travelers, one where any appearance of profiteering on exchange rates will undercut the basic message of support while traveling. Thus credit card companies keep exchange commissions low because this reduces customer defections. Similarly, focus groups in the early 1990s made it clear that the key feature they appreciated in Cisco routers was the number of protocols supported. This guided both product design and branding. Cisco's lead in protocols made it "The Easiest Decision I've Ever Made" among IT managers.

Customers might "own" a brand, but they aren't always its best caretaker—in fact, sometimes you might have to ignore their expressed desires. The question is when to do so. To answer correctly, you must understand the customer decision-making process.

For example, professional services firms face constant attempts by their clients to appropriate the value of the firm's name. Audit firms have their reputation at stake when they sign company SEC filings. Where there is financial mismanagement, such as at Enron, the company being audited will use its auditor's approval as a shield. Yet, when the mismanagement becomes known, the audit firm suffers brand and financial loss. Similarly, many management consulting firms find themselves approached by clients who want to use the consultant's prestige to obtain their board of directors' approval of risky new business ventures and controversial decisions. If the new venture goes sour or the decision proves flawed, then the consultant's reputation suffers.

Customers want the benefit of premium brands, but don't want to pay for them. Chevrolet owners would probably enjoy having a Cadillac marquee on their cars, and Nissan owners might prefer an Infiniti marquee. The temptation to give customers what they want is tempered by the potential erosion of the premium brand. Both General Motors and Nissan have in fact used such branding tactics to temporarily boost sales and realized prices—yet possibly at the longer-term expense of brand.

Who should make brand decisions? We discuss the organizational aspects of brand and price more fully in Chapter 20. However, the crucial requirement is for direct involvement by the same managers who make price and product decisions. Often, brand is given solely to staff managers who have functional expertise in advertising. This is a mistake. Unless managers are intimately knowledgeable about the customer decision-making process, they can't leverage that process in deciding how to brand. Brand managers not familiar with the market can only act as police to ensure that logos are not misused—useful, but not likely to turn brand into a significant competitive advantage.

Rule 3: Be Selective in Spending on Brand

The lesson from the beer wars is that more spending on brand is better. But in many industries and markets, this isn't true. For industrial marketers, brand must be targeted. Most industrial organizations are far more complex and heterogeneous than beverage or packaged goods companies. GE has more than 300 profit centers, each with hundreds or thousands of products. Sony has dozens of distinct businesses, each offering hundreds (sometimes thousands) of different products ranging from motion pictures to personal computers. A typical Telco has a dozen profit centers and more than 30,000 discrete products and services, covering scores of distinct markets (local service, voice, data, residential and business, yellow pages, network management, and public telephones). These permutations mean that one message will never fit all requirements.

Broad spending might create awareness, but this doesn't necessarily mean increased opportunities, revenues, or profits. This has been the lesson from Joe Isuzu, the telecom industry, and the commodity industries. Before spending on broad-gauge media, decide if your market truly looks like beer and cars.

SUMMARY

Brand is an important element of both corporate success and superior pricing. Although there *are* a few industries where there's no point in seeking a price premium through brand, in most others, brand improves price, costs, the sales process, and market share.

Many managers view brand as the overall impression that a company wants to create, or else equate brand only with customer awareness. But in fact, brand is most powerful when tailored to decisions made by customers. If targeted at decisions and products for which the customer has the least familiarity and the least ability or inclination to research, brand can affect price dramatically—a 100-percent price premium is not uncommon. Brand is a superior tool for swaying customers and potential customers who will not fully investigate all aspects of their purchase decision.

Remember that execution matters. The wrong brand message can destroy loyalty and the ability to command a premium. Superior brand is meaningful, distinct, and true—and an important part of a company's profitability tool chest.

Chapter Four | Segmentation: Beauty Is in the Eye of the Beholder

 ooking for love in all the wrong places?[1] This chapter describes how to find the love, revenues, and customers you want.

Beauty is in the eye of the beholder, and so is value both for individuals and for companies. In Chapter 2 we described the marketing of a new adhesive, one whose attributes made it very valuable to packagers in need of a strong, reliable, attractive glue for their packaging process. This adhesive was a success within its target segment. For some packagers, however, these qualities weren't worth the premium price charged, and so they continued to use less-expensive adhesives.

Segmentation can be described as the process of identifying groups of buyers with common buying desires, characteristics, and similar price sensitivity. The objective of identifying such groups is to tailor product, marketing effort, brand, and price to suit those groups'

---

[1] Johnny Lee, "Lookin' For Love," 1980. This hit song laments, "Lookin' for love in all the wrong places, looking for love in too many faces, lookin' for a trace of what I'm dreamin' of." To this, Mr. Lee adds: "Don't know where it started or where it might end." Segmentation is a good beginning, in our opinion.

requirements. The benefit of segmentation is to maximize your profits from each segment—leaving no money on the table. Additionally, you can attract new customers by appealing to new segments.

A single price or brand approach is unlikely to work across multiple segments, as in some respects each segment is its own market—even if they've been lumped together by the government in its SIC classification. A single price will be too high for some potential buyers, and less than what other buyers would pay if requested. This is why price sensitivity is the basis for profitable segmentation.[2]

In this chapter we'll discuss the relative merits of:

- *Behavior-based segmentation*, which categorizes customers based on their actions (either directly or through inference from their demographic characteristics)
- *Needs-based segmentation*, which categorizes customers based on their self-reported priorities or requirements
- *Evolutionary segmentation*. This is a new and powerful framework for segmentation. In contrast to other approaches, it categorizes customers by how individuals, companies, and industry segments change over time.

Each of these three bases for segmentation has advantages and disadvantages. However, with the right segmentation, there will be clear, manageable, and executable differences among segments.

BEHAVIORAL SEGMENTATION

A commonly used form of segmentation, behavioral segmentation, focuses on objective and observable characteristics—for example, whether or not a potential customer for luggage has traveled in the past 12 months. Behavioral approaches also include demographic features,

---

[2] See R. Frank, F. Massey and Y. Wind, *Economic Principles of Market Segmentation*. Some companies perform segmentation based on product characteristics. Although product-based segmentation is simple to develop, it rarely yields good pricing-related insights. See Philip Kotler, *Marketing Management*, 6th Ed. (Prentice Hall, 1988).

such as if a potential customer for acne medicine is teenaged or middle-aged, or if a potential customer for audit services is a privately or publicly held firm.

The advantages of behavioral segmentation are twofold: This information is often available from existing sources and it is objective, thereby avoiding the danger of self-reporting. As an example, current automobile ownership combined with personal income has generally turned out to be a better predictor of future car expenditures than self-reported intentions and transportation needs. (People want Mercedes, but they buy Chevys.)

The disadvantage of behavioral data is that sometimes there is no observable characteristic that answers the questions you wish to ask: How much are you willing to spend on my *future* product? On an *improved* product? How will your view change over time?

Still, insightful analysis of behavioral characteristics can say a lot about the value created through a product and how to capture that value. For example, ethnic affiliation and subscriptions to ethnic-language publications can be an almost-perfect predictor of international calling patterns and the willingness to pay for certain calling plans. Similarly, the combination of test scores and household income is an effective predictor of which students are likely to attend certain colleges. On another front, corporate ownership of computer equipment, when combined with corporate size measured in revenues, is a strong predictor of the need for training on that equipment.

NEEDS-BASED SEGMENTATION

Needs-based segmentation provides insight into the internal conditions, whether of a firm or a consumer, that motivate the use and purchase of a particular product or service. Thus, this kind of segmentation is very useful for identifying the best brand strategy and the optimal price level for a customer group.

Understanding needs lets you assess customers' willingness to pay, given the perceived benefits of the product or service and available competitive alternatives. Additionally, this approach helps identify segments in which you can deliver unique value at competitive advantage. Examples of corporate needs that can form the basis for this kind of segmentation include:

- Top-line growth at the expense of profit margins
- Profit growth and cost-cutting at the expense of revenue growth
- Improved product quality
- Defense of markets
- Prestige, self-esteem
- Minimization of risks

Insight into a customer's need to minimize risks, for example, can have a direct impact on price. The same computer can be sold to the same corporation for a different price, depending on whether it will be used for major manufacturing work flows, on the one hand, or for monthly administrative processing, on the other. Because most companies are more concerned with the fault-tolerance of manufacturing processors than with administrative systems, they'll pay more for the computer intended for manufacturing.

Such improved insights can also be applied to brand. Perhaps one computer must be reliable and resist harsh environments (such as the production floor), while another must be easy to integrate with financial systems. These are very different propositions and are one reason that HP and Compaq are so strong on factory floors while IBM is so strong in the back office. Similarly, the positioning of a woman's handbag could not be more different than that of a shopping bag—one bag speaks to status, the other to utility.

The disadvantages of needs-based segmentation include the frailties of customer self-reporting and the burden of surveying and assessing potential customers.[3] This burden can in fact be decisive, as the

---

[3] However, perhaps in the future that will be less of a problem. See "This Man Can Read Your Mind," *Fortune*, January 20, 2003, and "The Future of Mind Control," *The Economist*, September 2002. Both articles suggest that through brain scans and digital imaging, machines are increasingly able to assess the mental activities of subjects. Gerald Zaltman of the Harvard Business School suggests that such readings are more accurate than self-reporting under some circumstances.

costs of surveying might exceed any potential profit margin on the product or service. Few needs-based surveys can be performed for less than $50 per respondent, and usually they cost far more, especially if person-to-person interviews are required. This is no problem when surveying potential customers for a $15 million locomotive, but it's prohibitive when identifying potential customers for a $30 bunch of flowers.

An actionable needs-based segmentation can be developed through the following process:

1. Identify and prioritize customers' buying factors
2. Define segments based on these buying factors
3. Create segment value maps to show relevant pricing opportunities for each customer segment

1. Identify and Prioritize Customers' Buying Factors

Start by developing a comprehensive understanding of which product or service features are most important to your customers in their buying decisions, and why. For this, you need well-designed customer interviews to highlight the relative importance of buying factors that differ across customer segments. For example, in the coated-steel industry, we found that some customers preferred full-service distributors and some preferred low-cost distributors. A key factor underpinning this difference was that full-service distributors offer short lead times for orders, and low-cost distributors do not. A distinct difference in needs.

2. Define Segments Based on Buying Factors

The key step that distinguishes the insightful from the humdrum is taking the information you've gleaned about the relative importance of purchasing factors and using it to define convincing segments. For instance, inside one sector of the chemicals industry, we found that customers exhibited four distinct needs and related needs-based behaviors. Smaller-volume, family-owned customers indicated that although price was important to them, they placed more value on the security of their relationships with their suppliers. For them, dealing with their suppliers was akin to a tradition, henceforth this segment became known as "traditionalists." Other segments, as shown in Figure 4.1, were nicknamed total sourcers, specialists, and price buyers or bottom feeders.

Compared with cold, unfeeling usage statistics, these descriptions are richer and more usable. They allow more intuitive, better-developed pricing structures and price levels that are better able to capture value.

3. Create Segment Value Maps to Show Relative Pricing Opportunities for Each Customer Segment

One you've captured characteristics and data for each segment, you can create "value maps" to drive home pricing-related insights. A value map compares a product's market *price* to its *value* for customers (measured with respect to customer needs or benefits). For example, a value map developed for the specialists and prisoners segment in our chemicals industry example would show that customers in this segment face inor-

Segment	Characteristics
Price buyers and bottom feeders	Price is the primary driver for these customers as product quality comes in a distant second on the importance scale. These customers generally purchase small quantities from both domestic and overseas suppliers with almost no switching costs associated with competing products. Standard service levels are adequate and limited, or no additional technical services are required.
Total sourcers	Price is important but not as important as the total cost of the product. Service attributes such as delivery reliability, technical support, and problem resolution are essential to doing business with these customers. Large-volume specialty chemical purchases help this segment wield a lot of buying power. Additionally, total sourcers tend to have sophisticated purchasing organizations replete with advanced purchasing tools, training, metrics, and indexes, among other things.
Specialists and prisoners	Strong product uniformity and quality is important to the specialists. These customers buy ìbest of breedî products and services to ensure uniformity in their specialized applications. Very high switching costs drive a reluctance or inability to switch. Technical support is also key for these customers as they have challenges with meeting customer specifications and product-formulation requirements.
Traditionalists	The relationship rules with these customers, given their concern with the security of supply and delivery reliability. Most traditionalists have a long-standing history with their supplier and place significant trust in that supplier. Suppliers act as a source of information and as trusted advisors, so these customers will avoid switching if possible.

Source: A.T. Kearney analysis

Figure 4.1. Segments in a specialty chemicals market.

dinately high switching costs due to product formulation requirements, specific product attributes, or customer specifications that make it difficult to switch suppliers or products. A value map would illustrate how suppliers could exploit this fact. For example, suppliers that provide the least value to the customer can charge higher prices because they could not economically be replaced.

EVOLUTIONARY SEGMENTATION

Market segments evolve over time—they can grow, decline, or disappear. They change for a number of reasons: new demographic trends, technological advances, increasing competition, regulatory impositions, and economic cycles. This leads to shifts in their needs, purchasing patterns, and loyalties.[4]

Unlike the other two forms of segmentation, evolutionary segmentation focuses on the changes in a market. Knowing how an industry will evolve can be immensely valuable. Even knowing something about when and how such changes occur is crucial. The most important market opportunity is the moment when a company or person is changing a business model or life stage. For instance, new computers are purchased when a company migrates from one IT architecture to another; life insurance is purchased shortly after a family has its first child. Once those moments pass, breakthrough opportunities are relatively scarce and competitors might already be in place—and price competition might be intense because all the competitors have figured out the opportunity.[5]

Therefore, this form of segmentation focuses on stages, or events, in the life of an individual or company. It recognizes that although a company might have the same name and address, it will change beyond recognition every few years. The logical sequence is to ask at what

---

[4] Robert S. Duboff, "Marketing to Maximize Profitability," *Journal of Business Strategy*, November–December 1992, pp. 10–13. Duboff observes that in today's environment, it's difficult to keep customers loyal.

[5] R. Docters, J. Grim, and J. McGady, "Segments In Time," *Journal of Business & Strategy*, January 1997.

stage or juncture in its evolution does a company need your services most? Least? Armed with this knowledge, you can make sure you're on that company's doorstep just ahead of that moment in its development.

Evolutionary segmentation is possible because there tend to be well-defined patterns within an industry, covering 95 percent of the population.[6] While not perfect, this is good enough for dramatic results. Knowing that a particular individual or company will be needing your service in the next six months allows you to tailor your brand message and price to that moment. Thus the key moment to sell the value of a human-resources software package is not when everything is "business as usual," but when a firm has decided to reduce its human resources staff count or is merging with another firm.

There is always a logic shaping the evolution of the industry in question, but to find it, market planners must get their hands dirty with many industry interviews. These interviews will be the foundation to identifying patterns. For example, interviewees might say, "We used to do X, but now we do Y." The changes described will typically span organization, process, technology, mission, budgets, and buying processes. If you hear several interviewees say the same thing, there's a good chance you've found a pattern. Your goal is to become familiar with how finances, operations, strategy, and organization all interconnect. This will tell you what triggers the migration from one segment to another.

The final step is to develop a road map of how companies have progressed over time, what the triggers for change are, and how you can predict a change looking in from the outside.

In the case of data communications customers during the 1980s and 1990s, for example, the migration steps were complex but predictable. In the beginning almost all companies used mainframes from

---

[6] That is, 95 percent of companies are following in one another's footsteps. The remaining 5 percent represent potential "next generation" segments. Leading-edge companies form these new segments, to which other companies will eventually migrate. Fortunately, even in markets thought to be changing rapidly, it takes many years before the trailing 95 percent make it to the newest segments.

IBM or similar vendors. From a communications point of view these architectures were often very economical, but not very flexible. Thus many companies saw operational departments (manufacturing, customer service, and others) set up their own non-IBM computing platforms, with independent data networks to meet departmental needs. Thus the first step in the evolution was a shift in equipment, vendors, and organizational responsibility. It also turned out that departmental buyers were less concerned with price than flexibility and performance, and so with the first evolutionary step price levels (measured in dollars per MIPs) climbed significantly—good news for the vendors.[7]

After a while, the free-spending ways of computing departments were noticed. In some cases these data networks were consolidated under a corporate telecommunications department, or "utility." This department was keenly interested in costs, and so it curtailed spending. In other cases, the operational departments refused to go back to a central, unresponsive utility, and so they consolidated networks and computing platforms themselves. This way they saved money, but kept control.

In most cases, after many twists and turns, the typical company ended up with a client-server or mixed mainframe plus client-server environment, run by the IT department (the new name for the MIS department). Some companies skipped the intervening steps, stayed with their mainframes for a long time, then hopped directly to the client-server stage. A few have already left this stage behind and are experimenting with new architectures, organizations, and buying patterns to fit their needs. These shifts are shown in Figure 4.2.

The point to all this isn't to address the question of what constitutes the best architecture for data communications. Rather, it should be clear that to obtain the best price, computer equipment vendors needed to know not just what was happening now, but what would happen next. Otherwise, they could miss opportunities to price high, or cultivate the wrong approaches and contacts when the whole buying pattern in a particular company was about to change. With evolutionary segmentation,

---

[7] MIPs is defined as Millions of Instructions Per Second, a standard measure of a computer's processing power.

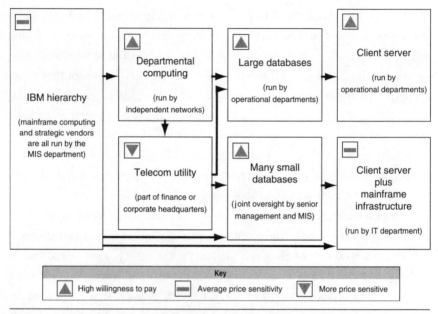

Figure 4.2. Stages in the evolution of data communications.

on the other hand, a vendor could know in advance—not guess, but *know*—if a potential customer was on the brink of a crisis in IT functionality propelling the move to "departmental computing," or if it was about to react to exploding IT costs by handing over control to the finance department (utility). In the former case, the winning message would show how the vendor's products could help overcome functional limitations. In the latter, it would stress value and cost control.

In some ways, evolutionary segmentation is analogous to the life-cycle marketing used by insurance companies and others to identify prospects.[8] For example, insurers track graduations, marriages, and births because these events often signal the need for life or health insurance. Evolutionary segmentation also tracks such events, but with one difference: We find that companies never repeat earlier stages—the world has changed too much.

[8] For example, see Lawrence Lepisto, "A Life Span Perspective of Consumer Behavior," *Advances in Consumer Research*, ed. E. Hirschman and M. Holbrook, XII (1985): 47ff.

Unlike static segmentation, which offers little structure in quantifying future market proportions, evolutionary segmentation allows accounting-like accuracy over time.[9] This is because inputs (number of companies at earlier stages of evolution) plus growth must equal outputs (number of companies at later stages of evolution). In other words, evolutionary segmentation tracks where specific customers come from and where they go, and thus gives a better indication of what the segment's growth shares will be like.

This approach isn't limited to highly technical industries. It has been used successfully to analyze banking customers, users of disposable plastic products, law firms, and dozens of other industries. Every company changes its purchasing habits from time to time, and such changes will happen in distinct stages. As companies pass through the various stages, they require different messages and exhibit different price sensitivities—sometimes higher, sometimes lower. In each case, the rewards of tailoring the message and the price have been significant: market success rather than failure, along with reduced sales costs.

If you don't believe that anticipating changes is important, consider that every step taken on the evolutionary journey changes what matters inside a potential customer's organization: decision makers, buying criteria, and budgets. If you can anticipate these changes, you can get to a new decision maker before competitors do. Being first, you can begin shaping the decision maker's time frames and criteria.[10] When the laggards finally arrive at the new decision-maker's door, they might find that it has already been closed.

SUMMARY

You have a choice of which approach to segmentation best addresses your company's needs. Effective pricing and branding depend on having a solid understanding of the market and its segments. Behavioral needs,

---

[9] Barbara G. Cohen, "A New Approach to Strategic Forecasting," *Journal of Business Strategy*, September–October 1988, pp. 38–42. Forecasting is often haphazard.

[10] See Jim Holden, *Power Base Selling* (John Wiley & Sons, 1990). This book describes the importance of identifying and influencing purchasing decision makers.

and evolutionary segmentation each have advantages and disadvantages, but when thoughtfully developed, each can be a powerful profit tool. You need to consider the trade-offs between the cost of implementing a segmentation scheme and the effectiveness of the segmentation. However, without solid segmentation, you'll underprice the least price-sensitive customers, fail to win share among the more price sensitive, and probably miss the branding opportunity.

Chapter Five | The Truth about Costs

A popular view of pricing maintains that costs are the basis for prices. A more sophisticated yet still conventional view says that costs set a long-term floor for price, but not much else. Our view is that costs often do influence prices—however, and far more important, in many markets *price strategy is the basis for shaping costs*.

Correspondingly, the first part of this chapter discusses situations in which price levels are determined largely by costs. With that as a basis, we move on to the second and more intriguing part of the chapter, in which we describe how managers—provided they understand their costs and are skilled at setting price structure and levels—can use pricing to actively reduce costs and build a significant competitive cost advantage.

Costs Influencing Price

Costs shape prices under many circumstances, but two important scenarios for cost-influenced pricing are worth describing in detail: first, when a low-cost competitor uses that cost advantage to lower prices and gain market share and, second, when a competitor has a significant but temporary product or service advantage and uses the opportunity to reap profits or recoup R&D costs.

Using a Cost Advantage to Lower Prices

Companies that enjoy a significant cost advantage have a greater range of options on how to set price compared with their higher-cost competitors. Typically there are several possible courses: Build market share by fully reflecting the cost advantage. For example, discount brokers enjoy a 30- to 50-percent cost advantage over full-service brokers and typically have reflected this cost advantage in their advertised list prices. This explains how Charles Schwab, for example, has increased its share of the total market from zero to more than 25 percent.

When competitors are less clear as to the extent and sustainability of their cost advantage, they adopt more subtle tactics. Many analysts believed that in the early 2000s, after years of cost-cutting, General Motors became the lowest-cost of the Big Three automobile manufacturers. GM used this advantage to gain market share at the expense of its U.S. competitors through incentives such as no-interest financing and other temporary tactics, rather than lower list prices as Schwab had done. "When I look at . . . how much we've been able to drive own our cost, it's allowed us to stay aggressive in the marketplace," said GM Chief Executive Rick Wagoner.[1]

Finally, some entities simply accept the prevailing market price and choose to reap superior profit margins. For example, some years ago a consortium of oil companies built an oil offloading facility near Freeport, Texas. The facility, called a Single Point Offshore Mooring, or SPOM, allowed tankers to sail up to a large buoy, pump their oil aboard, and sail on. The existing competition used traditional docks, which required tankers to come into port and pay for docking and tugboats. By comparison, the SPOM was far cheaper—however, its owners chose to price the service such that it offered only a modest savings to end-customers. In other words, the SPOM owners chose to capture increased profit margin, not volume.

---

[1] "GM's Deep-Discounting Strategy Helps Auto Maker Regain Ground," *The Wall Street Journal*, January 17, 2003: A1

A Market Window to Recoup Costs

From time to time, companies have the opportunity to price with little chance of competitor inroads or customer defections. A classic example is when a company enjoys an R&D breakthrough that competitors cannot match for many months. In many such cases, the desire to recoup up-front R&D costs drives price decisions.

In 2003, for example, Johnson & Johnson introduced a new form of stent (a medical implant for cardiac patients).[2] The new stents cost about the same as the old stents to manufacture but were coated with a useful drug that gradually seeps into the blood system, avoiding complications. Reportedly the new drug cost $800 million to develop. To recoup its R&D expenses in the period before competitors caught up, J&J charged $3200 for the new stent, far higher than the going rate of $1200 for an old-style stent.[3] Recouping costs in this fashion is a common initial price objective among companies with large R&D outlays in many industries, not just medicine.[4]

Another case where past costs can drive current pricing is when company ownership changes. As our example, we take two companies, one a publisher enjoying 60- to 70-percent gross margins, the other a professional services firm enjoying 80-percent-plus gross margins. These sorts of margins are generally considered to be admirable—yet in the circumstances we're about to describe, both these companies behaved with an unusual degree of cost-consciousness.

Why? Because in both cases, the firms had recently changed ownership. The publisher had been purchased at a premium, and the professional services firm had recently gone private. The new owners

[2] A stent is a little coil resembling a ballpoint pen spring; it is inserted in the arteries of heart patients during artery-clearing procedures. The new ones are coated in a medicine.

[3] "New Stents, a Boon for Patients, May Affect Rising Health Costs," *The Wall Street Journal*, December 24, 2002: A1.

[4] Interestingly, in some cases computer chip manufacturers haven't displayed quite the same behavior—however, they don't enjoy the price protection of FDA licensing delays. Also, chip markets are much more price-elastic than those for cardiac implants.

weren't content with pre-acquisition margins and profits—instead they set management compensation based on new cash flows and increased margins, since the sale and privatization prices had already incorporated the generous historical margins. Hence, behaviors resembled low-margin businesses.

This behavior, as it turned out, had another feature: It made both entities vulnerable to competition. Although they had substantial profit margins with which to combat competitor inroads, in fact, they both were reluctant to discount and respond with lower prices. As a result they held up a price umbrella, while losing market share to more flexible competitors.

SOME MARKETS PRECLUDE COST-DRIVEN PRICING

To the chagrin of many managers, prices need not rise to reflect increased costs. Many products have fallen in price even though their costs have risen and the product has remained the same quality, or perhaps even gotten better. In the early 1980s, a Burger King Whopper cost $1.40. Since then wages and real estate, the major components of restaurant prices, have doubled—yet the Whopper now sells for $0.99. Similarly, new car prices have fallen since 1996, both in nominal and real terms. A family earning the median income in 2003 needed about 20 weeks of pay for a new vehicle as compared to 29 weeks in 1996.[5] At the same time, cars have improved in reliability and mandated regulatory features.

As a generalization, it does appear that costs are more important to pricing strategy in an industry with thinner gross margins.[6] However, even in markets with razor-thin margins, such as commercial lending, there are exceptions to costs forming a floor on price. For example, while top-rated corporate borrowers generally obtain short-term financing within a dozen basis points above the benchmark LIBOR[7] source of

---

[5] "Lack of Pricing Power," *The New York Times*, Jan. 19, 2003.

[6] Andy Stern, ibid.

[7] London Inter-Bank Offered Rate, the international benchmark for cost of capital.

capital, there have been numerous examples where competitors have made below-LIBOR loans.[8]

In many industries, there is no simple relationship between price and cost. One needs to understand the economic and management motivations of industry players before hazarding forecasts of pricing based on costs.

PRICE INFLUENCES COSTS

Here is the fun part. Although many managers believe that costs drive price, often it's the other way around. The remainder of this chapter describes five important ways in which price can be used to drive costs:

- In support of a cost-based strategy
- To drive customer behavior
- To propel scale-based costs
- To improve product portfolio returns
- To improve account costs

Pricing to Support Cost-Based Strategy

Cost differences among sellers generally aren't across-the-board, but instead are associated with particular customer segments or geographic regions. In the case of cement producers, because freight is such a large component of the total delivered costs, each producer dominates the geography around its production facility.[9] Thus, areas of dominance are determined by geography and production costs.

Geographic dominance applies to other industries as well. For example, due to local loyalty, travel, and other burdens to attending school on opposite coasts, Harvard and Stanford Universities enjoy geographic dominance—Harvard has a higher acceptance rate in the East

---

[8] Such as by Japanese banks to U.S. borrowers during the late 1980s, and at times during the 1990s by HSBC and other Asian banks.

[9] At one point producers conspired to determine prices so that producers that sold under cartel prices arbitrarily became the lowest price spot in the country, but this was enjoined by an antitrust ruling. Now, actual freight prices predominate.

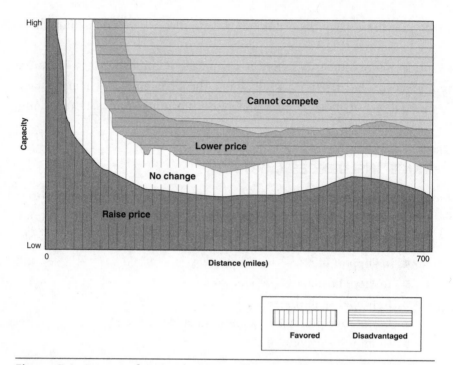

Figure 5.1. Range of cost advantage for a custom equipment maker.

and Southeast, Stanford has the highest acceptance rates in the West and Midwest. If educational institutions competed on price, we would expect that Stanford's tuition would be highest in California, lower in the transition states, and that the school would contemplate including airfare in its tuition, so as to challenge Harvard in the Northeast.[10]

An illustration of pricing linked to cost-based competitive advantage comes from a fabricator of custom manufacturing equipment. The two cost factors primary to this company's industry were the capacity of the manufacturing equipment and the distance from the fabrication center (the huge equipment components are expensive to transport). Charting these two factors against competitors and alternative technologies, Figure 5.1 shows the circumstances under which this equip-

---

[10] We recognize that differences in academic focus, culture, local attachments, and a desire by both schools for geographic diversity frame the situation, and that price is secondary—yet still not trivial.

ment maker enjoyed a cost advantage, as well as those under which it was disadvantaged. The company appeared to be better at constructing low-capacity equipment, and (not surprisingly) enjoyed lower transportation costs when operating near its base. The figure demonstrates that above the divide, the company would experience higher costs than the competition, while below the divide, its costs were lower than the competition's.

In some industries, these cost differences wouldn't be crucial—but in this market, they're key drivers: buyers are highly price-sensitive, competitors have comparable quality, and profit margins are thin. As a result, this fabricator chose to adopt a price strategy based on costs.

The fabricator raised prices where it was heavily advantaged, while leaving them unchanged near the divide line. To pick up some incremental business, the company lowered its prices to customers both adjacent to and above the divide line—customers unwilling to pay the fully saturated costs of the projects, but who would still pay more than variable costs. This gave management greater flexibility not only to compete, but also to improve capacity utilization. The strategy made clear what business wasn't worth pursuing because the company couldn't compete on cost—although occasionally in such cases it would put in a spoiler bid, sometimes as a price signal.

The results of this cost-based strategy were dramatic and positive. Over the next two years, the fabricator's margins increased sixfold, while revenues doubled.

Pricing to Drive Customer Behavior

Costs related to customer behavior can often be regulated through price. The rule is that for every major cost, there should be some reflection in the price charged to the customer, though not necessarily a separate charge. For example, take a direct-mail advertising house that charges by the size and number of mailings, plus postage. As shown in Figure 5.2, its current price structure reflects many of its costs, but not all.

A better price structure—better because it better reflects the company's costs—would reflect costs such as artwork and production. These inclusions could reduce the number of low-margin, multiversion

Cost element	Percent of total cost	How reflected in price
Printing	15%	Reflected in size and quantity
Selling	10%	Not fully reflected—somewhat reflected in degree of account support to larger customers
Artwork, production and assembly	15%	Somewhat reflected in size and printing, but multiversion jobs are not fully captured
Postage	50%	Fully captured

Figure 5.2. Price structure for a direct-mail advertising house.

jobs bought under separate contracts. A long-term contract discount might be useful in reducing sales costs.

Tying price to the costs associated with a product is a useful strategy for several reasons—for one thing, it imposes fewer burdens on management. If you charge for a cost element, then customer use of that element might well become self-regulating. On the other hand, if you *don't* charge, customers might abuse that element. For example, some customers of an all-you-can-eat restaurant might eat only shrimp—very expensive for the restaurant owner. With a separate per-plate charge for the shrimp table, this sort of wanton abuse would be reduced or eliminated.

Another broad principle is to avoid charging all customers for expensive features or service elements used only by a few. This prevents competitors from swooping in to capture your majority customers using a lower price that reflects the lower cost to serve.

In some cases, you might prefer *not* to fully reflect costs in your price structure. For example, instituting an explicit pass-through rate for shipping costs implies that you're targeting a particular geography.[11] A contrary strategy would be to absorb geographic-related costs into your overall list price, thereby making a formerly divided geographic market into a national market. For example, self-service brokers have been more aggressive about adopting Internet and 800 numbers than

[11] Unless your shipper is insensitive to distance, as is the case with the U.S. Postal Service and its rates for domestic letters.

full-service brokers. This is because they feel (quite correctly) that they have a cost advantage and should therefore seek to attract price-sensitive customers regardless of geography. For a while, the full-service brokers continued to favor walk-ins and local telephone numbers because this suited their form of geographic organization.

Pricing to Propel Cost Decreases Due to Scale

Price is a major determinant of sales volume. Thus price is an important tool where there are economies of scale in purchasing, provision, or production. If companies set prices that maximize volume, this often has the effect of improving their clout with suppliers that offer lower prices for larger orders. Such "forward pricing" can be an important strategic tool for companies willing to act on observed price sensitivities.

In manufacturing, one finds both the classic scale curve, and the equally well-known experience curve.[12] Both of these curves suggest that the more units produced, the lower the unit costs over time. The amount of this cost reduction depends in part on the complexity of the product or service and on the economics of component suppliers.

Forward pricing suggests estimating sales volumes at different price levels, and then modeling how unit costs fall along with volume. Equipped with this knowledge, you can select a combination of sales volume and unit costs likely to give you an advantage in the market. An important part of this exercise is to incorporate volume savings for suppliers and to convince them to sell parts and service components at the lower prices appropriate to these volume savings.

This approach can be risky, however, because volumes might not meet expectations. Balancing this risk is the opposite risk that com-

---

[12] A scale curve is the ability to spread fixed costs over a greater number of unit outputs. For instance, GM is able to spread the costs of stamping molds over more cars than Chrysler. The experience curve is the ability of companies to introduce better techniques over time, and so reduce either or both the fixed and variable costs of production over time. For example, GE Aerospace observed that it could lower the cost of satellites by at least 2 percent per year simply due to process improvements discovered over time.

petitors will do forward pricing themselves and use it to launch offers at prices you can't match. To some extent, these risks are a function of your company's pricing expertise: As long as you understand market price sensitivities with precision, the risks are manageable.

Your company's price capabilities also affect your ability to persuade suppliers to go along with your strategy. If they lack confidence that you know the market price dynamics, they'll be reluctant to assume the risks of forward pricing. If they *are* confident, however, then their own search for higher volume will lead them to take the risks with you. In effect, your company's risks are minimized as these risks get assumed by your suppliers.

Forward pricing isn't confined to manufacturing industries; service firms can also profit from this strategy. For example, energy companies can do quite well buying forward energy contracts—but they must know volumes and price trends. Telecom firms have a choice of how many circuits to "pull" through an underground conduit, as well as how many plug-in circuit boards to forward-provision in their switches—if they understand market price sensitivities, they can optimize such provisioning in advance of customer sign-ups.

Pricing to Improve Product Portfolio Returns

Pricing of product lines can also be used to improve overall returns for a product portfolio. This is a two-step process. The first step is to match cost data to products and services, thereby calculating profitability in all cases. This isn't easy, but it can and should be done regularly. The second step is to unearth revenue numbers for each product. This too can be tough. However, once you've done all this, you'll have an overview of product and service profitability, typically revealing a wide range. Usually there are some borderline and even negative-margin products.

What to do with this result? As with the physician faced with patients in varying degrees of health, the next step is triage—in other words, sorting products into three categories: robustly profitable, clearly unprofitable, and those in the middle ground, which probably aren't returning their cost of capital.[13] Each category has a different price prescription: hold prices, reposition to increase price, and reposition or dispose.

Typically, some but not all of the middle earners can be repositioned. Let's look at how to handle such malingerers:

Badly priced products. Sometimes companies sustain large-revenue products that generate little profit. Increased prices, albeit at lower volumes, might be a good strategy.

Cannibalized products—at greater unit volume, these would become profitable. Often the impediment to greater volume is a similar product in the line. One or the other might be repriced as part of an effort to differentiate.

Mediocre-margin products. Some of these can be closely linked with stronger products. For example, in cosmetics, less-appealing hair care supplements are packaged and priced with popular ones, boosting the formers' sales.

Poor performers are generally disposable, but occasionally there are arguments for retaining them. These include:

- Loss leaders required to penetrate accounts or support profitable products.
- Products that complete a necessary portfolio of products and services—for example, products the company requires for credibility in the market.
- New products and services. Many products and services aren't immediately profitable. In this case, life-cycle analysis will suggest whether or not there is a reasonable expectation for longer-term profitability.
- Older products that might serve a new use, or that will be profitable as certain segments begin to buy them more.

[13] See R. G. Docters, "Improving Profitability Through Product Triage," *Indiana University Business Horizons*, January–February 1996.

In many cases, strong price management is required to pull products out of the unprofitable category. For example, one client found that special orders (custom and rush) were highly unprofitable. This was surprising, because usually special orders are an excellent source of profit margins (a rush order, or a special requirement, tends to mean the customer has fewer alternatives). After a dramatic price increase, these orders were reclassified as robustly profitable.

Pricing to Improve Customer Account Costs

Costs can also be compared to revenues by customer account, yielding profitability per customer. This, in turn, can produce useful price prescriptions. For example, one chemical company looked at its profitability across different customer accounts and noticed that profit margins were lower where its share of the customer's business was low. Investigating further, the company found that most accounts consumed about the same amount of sales, marketing, and administrative effort, but this effort was spread across different unit volumes. This resulted in different costs per product sold and, therefore, in different profit margins.

The company responded by customizing its volume bonuses (discounts) by account, so that customers were encouraged to go primarily with the chemical company, or else not at all. In addition, it made changes in sales force compensation and organization. The result was to influence customer behavior as hoped, allowing the chemical company to consolidate its position at some major accounts, while reducing its commitment to marginal accounts. Another benefit was improved transportation costs, because a higher volume per account made for fewer less-than-truckload shipments.

SUMMARY

The impact of costs on pricing suggests a closer look at costs. Low costs might allow a competitor to reduce its prices relative to competitors, and gain share. Companies might also use a window of competitive advantage and low price elasticity to increase prices—thereby defraying up-front costs such as R&D. There are many other examples of cost having an impact on price; yet to say that prices are set by costs is simplistic and often wrong. To the contrary, cost can be a useful basis for price strategy in a number of industries with narrow profit margins, or against competitors with less flexibility in delivering profits. None of this is easy—competitors' costs, and alternative technology costs, must be mapped against your company's costs—but the results can be more than worth it.

THE INFORMATION THAT UNDERLIES A COST-BASED PRICE STRATEGY

Attributing costs to product, segments, or customer accounts isn't easy. The reasons for this lie both in the varied and complex nature of cost accounting, and in simple human nature.

The threshold accounting issue is whether to look at variable cash costs, variable costs, incremental costs (which can be the same as variable costs, but often are different), or total costs (that is, those including overhead). As Gorden Shillinglaw, the prominent professor of accounting at Columbia University, once said: "If you ask me how much something costs, I need to ask you, 'Why do you want to know?' "[14]

Which measure of cost is relevant depends on the market. In the twilight of the Internet boom, for example, variable cash costs were what mattered to incumbent companies competing with doomed Internet startups. The goal of startups was to conserve their scanty cash in order to survive what they hoped was a short lull in the IPO market; the goal of the incumbents examining these variable cash costs was to hasten the end of the upstarts.[15]

Traditional standard costs systems are good both at reporting variable cash costs and producing a number for total costs. However, they have a harder time with incremental costs—just the sort of incremental cost data that management really needs. Incremental costs require judgment and, more important, require a decision about the appropriate time frame for the analysis. These are questions that machines

---

[14] G. Shillinglaw, *Managerial Cost Accounting* (Irwin, 1982).

[15] In some cases, however, startups rose from the dead after Chapter 11 with improved balance sheets—a conundrum.

traditionally don't handle well. For example, many older costing systems include corporate overhead that is arbitrarily spread among products—yet managers know that eliminating many of these products wouldn't affect overhead cost in the short term by one penny.[16]

Attributing costs is a thorny issue. For example, how to gauge the impact of a product line on marketing costs? If a product manager is directly associated with the product line, then adding her salary to the product line cost is easy. But suppose the marketing organization is organized by geography, not products? It is tougher to make the link. The economic rule is clear: joint costs can't be allocated.[17] However, some costs that are joint in the short run aren't joint in the longer run—for example, floor space that can't be reduced just yet, but *can* be adjusted when the company moves into a new plant. Good judgment on the part of the costing team is required to deal with this sort of thing.

Here's an example of the different conclusions that can be derived from an analysis based on "total cost" on the one hand, versus one based on "marginal cost" on the other. An integrated oil company was considering investing substantial capital funds for expanding its European marketing operations. As a first approach, the company made the calculation shown in Figure 5.3, basing it on total costs, including depreciation of existing capital equipment, and on net revenues. This calculation would seem to make it clear that the lion's share of available capital funds should be assigned to Country A. As the country with the largest volume, its superior profit margin would produce the highest returns.

However, a second analysis was performed, based on marginal cash costs and revenues, and omitting depreciation of existing capital equipment and some allocated marketing costs. The results of this are

---

[16] A key question for teams determining costs at the product level is this: Over what time frame do you look to see if the possible related cost is incremental? The authors have done studies that show that within an industry over a long enough period of time, corporate headquarters are closely proportionate to the size of the company as measured by revenues. However, in a one-year horizon, this effect is unlikely to be observed.

[17] Shillinglaw, supra.

Country	Volume (barrels per day)	Total supply cost (per barrel)	Net marketing revenue (per barrel)	Profit margin
A	100,000	$50	$60	$10
B	80,000	$52	$55	$3
C	60,000	$50	$52	$2
D	50,000	$55	$57	$2

NOTE: Total supply costs include the cost of crude oil delivered to the country in question, as well as refining costs. Net marketing revenues represents the proceeds of selling product minus distribution and marketing costs.

Figure 5.3. Initial calculation of costs, revenues, and profit margins for crude oil delivery.

shown in Figure 5.4. When adjusted to true marginal cash costs and marginal revenues, the conclusion was different: Countries B and C turned out to be the most attractive candidates for further capital infusions.

The story doesn't end there. One challenge in setting marginal costs against marginal revenues is that sometimes the marginal cost might not mirror the actual physical logistics. In the above example, suppose that low-cost oil for country C ($45 per barrel) could easily be diverted to country D. Country D would then offer the highest cash contribution per barrel, at $22 per barrel ($67 − $45 = $22). If the oil company decided to shrink its operations to maximize profitability, in the process terminating sales in one country, this would be very

Country	Volume (barrels per day)	Marginal cost	Marginal revenue	Cash margin
A	100,000	$48	$65	$15
B	80,000	$46	$64	$18
C	60,000	$45	$66	$21
D	50,000	$50	$67	$17

Figure 5.4. Subsequent analysis for crude oil delivery.

important. If oil could be supplied to country D at $45 per barrel (rather than the current cost of $50 per barrel), profit maximization would suggest discontinuing operations in country C rather than country D, even though C currently enjoyed wider margins per barrel.

Finally, it's worth noting some of the human and political obstacles to effective costing for price purposes. One such obstacle is the fear by product line managers that the profit study will reveal their products to be unprofitable. To the manager, this would be bad news, because downward profitability can be viewed as a reflection on the manager, and because it might also lead to a curtailing of resources for that product line—and still worse, increased intervention by senior management. A manager driven by such fears might be inclined to endlessly criticize the cost part of a pricing study as inaccurate.

Still other managers might be philosophically opposed to acknowledging cost variations in manufacturing and account management. We suspect this is principally because line management's mission is to work around such differences, and so they take a "no excuses, get the job done" approach to costing as well as to operations. Unfortunately, this view filters out precisely the variations being sought. In other words, a line manager with this attitude sees variations as something he should be able to correct (even though no line manager ever has), rather than as a problem with a pricing solution.

Costing isn't easy when done right. Those unfamiliar with the economic principles will resist the sophistication required for accurate results, while others will insist on complete accuracy to the point at which the effort will collapse. Despite all this, if done correctly, cost data forms a useful basis for price strategy and offers material rewards, particularly in low-margin environments.

Chapter Six | Doing It All in Boom and Bust

Facing an oncoming storm, the captain of a ship orders the ship secured, extra lashings on the cargo, meals prepared in advance, and course adjusted to avoid the worst of the weather. The captain has a clear and proven strategy for bad weather. Do you have a similarly proven strategy for economic turbulence?

We close the first section of this book by looking at profit prescriptions during industry boom and bust. Unlike the captain of a ship in a storm, managers don't have the benefit of hundreds of years of tradition to know what is required during a bust. Too much has changed since the last big downturn. A boom too has its dangers, not the least because boom and bust are perpetually trading places—what a company does in one period must inevitably affect its fortunes in the next. We therefore offer pricing and branding prescriptions that are specific to each period, yet reflect this mutual relationship. And though much of what we say is common sense, mixed in are strategies and tactics that are anything *but* common.

Because downturns carry heavier penalties, let's consider them first.

STRATEGY FOR A DOWNTURN

Let's begin with some fundamentals. In a downturn, the trade-off between goods and cash changes, for no other reason than that people's expectations of growth have diminished. It takes $100 to buy an asset growing at 5 percent, but only $50 to buy the same asset growing at 3 percent.[1] Money has become more valuable—it buys more. So what does this mean? It means that your branding plan to improve your customer perception is now out of date, your price strategy is out of date, and your capital budget is out of date.

Instead of moving forward with the old plans, consider new ones. If money has become more valuable, your customers will demand more for their dollars and expect to spend less overall. This gives you several questions to ask yourself.

- As customers adjust their spending, could my products or services substitute for someone else's more expensive goods or services?
- If so, how do I steer customers to my offers?
- If on the other hand I'm *not* one of the lucky companies that can benefit from substitution, then how best to adjust my prices to the new reality?

Starting with the first point, what are good examples of substitutes? High-end substitutes include all terrain vehicles (ATVs), billiard tables, and other toys. These, although expensive, serve the affluent as substitutes for even more expensive vacations in distant places. Hence, sales of such toys have skyrocketed since the U.S. economy turned down in 2001.[2] Similarly, at the low end, meat man-

---

[1] For those who like equations, the growing perpetuity model (using a 7-percent discount rate and a dividend of $2) is Present Value = dividend/(discount rate-growth rate) or $100 = $2/(.07 − .05) and $50 = $2/(.07 − .03).

[2] "Brand Fever Bucks Recession," *Journal of Japanese Trade and Industry*, September–October 2001; "In Uncertain Times, Americans Resort to Expensive Toys," *The Wall Street Journal*, 2002

ufacturer Hormel discovered that through further processing, it could make its chicken and pork products quicker to fix—and therefore a good substitute for eating out.[3]

Substitution possibilities are by no means rare. While prices generally fall during recessions, they don't fall uniformly—the alert eye can spot marked differences in price trends among goods, and between goods and services.[4] In 2001, for example, residential developers could choose between sites in the New York City area, where residential property prices rose more than 11 percent, and the Pittsburgh area, where these same prices fell almost 15 percent. Other industry segments showed similar divergences: Within electronics manufacturing, prices dropped 12 percent for televisions, even as they rose 20 percent for personal electronic devices such as PDAs. Similarly, while print fashion advertising revenues in the United States fell sharply from 2001 to 2002, advertisements for parent and baby magazines rose sharply.

BRAND IN RECESSION

In a downturn, brand becomes a key tool to divert consumer spending in your direction. In its essence, brand is what consumers think they are getting from a product or service. For example, Starbucks is thriving not only because of its product's merits, but also because of an important shift in the company's brand identity. Whereas Starbucks during the early 1990s was a Mecca for coffee-drinking connoisseurs, today it serves as a "brief escape from the office" and gets more than a billion dollars of its revenues from spiffy coffee drinks such as cold Frappucinos.[5] Brand is at its most powerful when influencing customers about

---

[3] "How to Thrive When Prices Fall," *Fortune*, May 12, 2003: 131–134.

[4] For example, see D. W. Carlton and J. M. Perloff, *Modern Industrial Organization* (HarperCollins, 1994).

[5] "Starbucks May Indeed Be a Robust Staple," *The Wall Street Journal*, Sept. 27, 2002. The article notes that Starbucks founder Howard D. Schultz originally opposed offering sugary noncoffee drinks.

when and what to buy—whether it's Starbucks in the middle of a business day, beer at sporting events, or photography while on vacation or traveling.[6]

Brand is also key to industrial markets—big-ticket budgets get reduced in a recession just as surely as the family budget. In many markets, a budget cut takes the form of fewer purchases, rather than the same number of purchases of cheaper goods. For example, in good times a library might buy three books on a particular topic, with these books spanning a range of prices and coverage. Faced with a cutback, the library might decide to buy just one book on that topic. Surprisingly, this one tome is seldom a lower-priced or less-extensive title, as one might have expected. The library's rationale: If we have to have just one, let's make it the best one. If this becomes a trend, the publisher of the premium book can actually *raise* prices, because in the absence of competing titles, library budgets can absorb an increase for the one book. A real-world example of this phenomenon is shown in Figure 6.1, which charts revenues for a set of reference books during the early years of a recession.

Diverging from brand for a moment, another shift that can actually improve revenues during a downturn is to determine whether or not a subset of your market can sustain a price rise. This requires market insight and some courage, but drug companies, electric utilities, and telecom service providers have all played this game. When drug companies were faced with price regulation in Europe, they responded by increasing prices in the United States.[7] When energy companies such as Duke Power faced chaos in their unregulated markets, they shifted

---

[6] A good example of branding failure in a recession involves boutique hotels. The price of a room at many such hotels is now comparable to a normal hotel, but they failed to communicate this in time; as a result, they've become passé in an era of restraint. "Travelers Bypass Boutique Hotels," *The Wall Street Journal*, February 27, 2002: B1.

[7] "How Americans May Subsidize Euro-Health Care," *The Wall Street Journal*, Dec. 26, 2002.

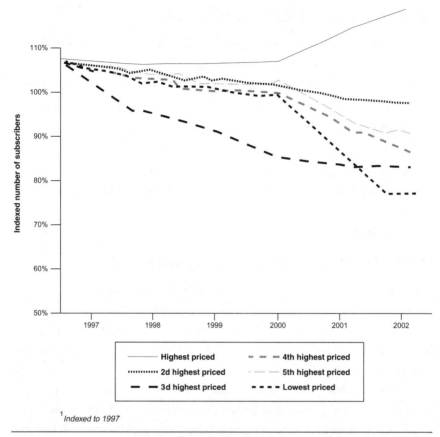

Figure 6.1. Subscription levels for six tiers of professional journals.[1]

---

costs and debt to their secure monopoly of electrical utilities.[8] Likewise, despite generally falling retail sales during the economic slowdown in Korea in 2001, some retailers featuring strong global luxury brands, such as Louis Vuitton, Celine, and Fendi, achieved double-digit sales growth.[9]

[8] "Beleaguered Energy Firms Try to Share Pain with Utility Units," *The Wall Street Journal*, December 20, 2002: A1.
[9] "Brand Fever Bucks Recession," *Journal of Japanese Trade and Industry*, September–October 2001.

IF YOU HAVE TO CUT, CUT SMART

Sadly, time constraints or the nature of your industry might not always allow you to offset the effects of a downturn, so that supporting current price levels becomes untenable. What then? You adjust your pricing, your offerings, or both as necessary. We recommend the following tactics and guidelines to accomplish this:

- Don't be a prisoner of your budgets
- Use tools other than list price to adjust price
- Innovative pricing and repackaging of goods and services
- Lock in your best customers
- Anticipate competitor moves, but avoid price wars

Don't Be a Prisoner of Your Budget Cycle

Some sellers hike their price in a downturn. They reason that as volume starts to slacken, unit price increases will make up the difference. And indeed, if switching costs are high and the switching cycle long, this logic has a certain short-run validity. For many managers, a further inducement is the yearly nature of their compensation plans—better to earn a good bonus now than invest in future earnings. At any rate, regardless of motivation, this tactic is quite common: A survey in 2001, involving 35 companies in a dozen industry categories, showed that five of these companies were still raising prices even as they instituted a hiring freeze.[10] It seems reasonable to assume the freezes meant *someone* at the company knew a downturn was coming.

Yet raising prices to meet now-unrealistic corporate financial goals is not only a bad idea for the long-term, but potentially damaging in the short-term as well. The New York commercial real estate rental market offers a good example of this kind of imprudent pricing. By mid-2001, it was clear that the decade-long boom for the U.S. economy was coming to a halt. If a steadily falling stock market was not enough, the tragic events of September 11 served to punctuate the end of an era and intro-

---

[10] Sectors included financial services, telecommunications, and publishing. Survey by Graham King, The Recruitment Company, New York.

duce severe economic strain, especially for metropolitan New York. Yet despite all of this, commercial real estate rental prices continued to increase on a per-square-foot basis through the end of 2001. Not surprisingly, vacancy rates, despite the destruction of the World Trade Center space, zoomed upward. In a dozen instances, prestige addresses that had raised prices by more than 5 percent were rewarded by an outflow of more than 20 percent of their tenants, leading to a wholly unnecessary plunge in revenues.[11]

To dissuade such inappropriate pricing maneuvers, top management should encourage an environment in which midcourse corrections to budgets and other goals can openly be entertained, in the event that the economy veers from the assumptions of the planning process. Structuring employee incentive schemes with performance targets that extend beyond one year will also help avoid such ultimately and counterproductive pricing behavior. The longer time frame makes it more likely that an improvement in the economy will come along to put the company back on track.

Use Tools Other Than List Price to Adjust Price

If your business requires high sales volumes to generate positive margins, then a downturn might require price reductions to sustain those volumes. We generally recommend against changes in list price to accomplish such reductions, for at least two reasons: First, once lowered, list prices might be difficult to raise when the opportunity presents itself again. Second, list prices reduce prices to *all* customers when there are probably some customers willing to continue paying the old prices.

Consider discounts and incentives instead. These can be implemented quickly and withdrawn at a later date more easily than changes to list price. Examples are *Amazon.com* reintroducing free delivery on book orders over a certain amount to stimulate sales following the dot.com meltdown; fitness clubs offering free memberships for anywhere from three to six months to new members; and wireless service

---

[11] Commercial rental data courtesy of PriMedia Corporation.

providers offering substantial incentives for new subscribers, including free phones and a period of free or heavily discounted service.

During 2001 to 2003, U.S. domestic automobile manufacturers relied on a similar approach, offering rebates to stimulate sales. In December 2002 these rebates averaged $3142, more than double their level two years earlier. The result was record unit sales for the industry. For cost leader General Motors, this resulted in significant profits, though other U.S. auto producers did not fare as well.

Similarly, in the personal computer industry, demand weakened as a result of tighter budgets and no real imperative to buy (in particular, no new killer application to drive sales). In this soft market environment, Dell led the move to substantial price reductions, in large measure through the persistent use of discounts and incentives. Despite the lower prices, Dell achieved record sales and profits in 2002, due both to gains in market share and effective cost cutting.

Meanwhile, weaker competitors in the computer and automobile industries suffered from the price cuts. In the final months of 2002, Chrysler's profit per car fell from €505 per car to about €125. Likewise, Dell's competitors felt the pain of discounts far more.

Weaker in this context needn't always mean smaller. AOL, the leader in online consumer services, was forced in 2001 to 2003 to reduce its advertising rates dramatically—in some cases to zero, meaning free. During this same period, however, *The Wall Street Journal* and *The New York Times* were able to sustain advertising rates for their own online sites without significant changes.[12] These two newspaper's Internet subsidiaries benefited from rock-solid franchises, so despite being smaller, they didn't suffer from significant attrition.

Innovative Pricing and Repackaging of Goods and Services

Downward price pressure takes the form of potential customers refusing to buy services or products. Some of the tools described in detail

---

[12] "Web Ads Hit Rock Bottom," *The Wall Street Journal*, September 10, 2002, and "If They Have To Pay, Will They Come?" *Business 2.0*, February 2003: 45.

later in this book—tiering of products and various forms of price discrimination—are even more vital in such an environment. The following offers a preview.

In 2001 some nine national theater companies filed for bankruptcy, representing more than one-third of the nation's screens. These chains had attempted to stay afloat by the rigid tactic of raising prices across the board. By contrast, chains such as AMC, as well as certain large independent cinemas, had begun exploring a range of innovative off-peak pricing plans, beginning with lower ticket prices for matinees. In pricing terms, these smarter theaters were tiering their product. Combined with content innovation, it proved a far more successful strategy—in this case, the difference between survival and failure.[13]

Repackaging your services might help to put them within the grasp of consumers now feeling less affluent. Some sports teams respond to falling demand by offering fans a broader range of ticket packages—for example, packages for 10, 20, or 40 games, rather than for the full season. This tactic can keep bleachers full enough to sustain significant price increases, even in the midst of a recession.[14]

Another innovation that can help sustain revenues during a downturn is converting your offer from a product to a service or vice versa. Why might this help? Consider that in 2002, a recession year, prices for goods in the core Consumer Price Index declined by around 1.5 percent, but prices for services *increased* by about 3.5 percent. Economists explained this divergence by noting that manufacturers were victims of intense competition from countries in Asia and elsewhere abroad, while service providers did not face such competition. As one article on the phenomenon put it, "If you need a plumber at 2 o'clock in the morning, you really can't call Bangkok and get one. You are going to call a local guy, and he is going to charge you $85 an hour."[15] Hence the costs of such handymen were up 5 percent.

---

[13] "Few Cinemas Dare to Innovate by Offering Creative Pricing," *The Pricing Advisor*, April 2001.

[14] "America's Pricing Paradox," *The Wall Street Journal*, May 16, 2003: B1.

[15] "America's Pricing Paradox," *The Wall Street Journal*, May 16, 2003: B1

At first blush it might seem as if the service providers were lucky and the product-makers weren't—but it's not quite that simple: Most companies have a choice of how to serve their customers, but typically only an alert few exercise that choice. One smart company moved from selling and installing light bulbs to large municipalities, to offering service contracts on streetlights to these same municipalities. The operational jump was a small one, but the associated benefit of avoiding competition was huge. Similarly, retailer Office Depot began moving toward contract printing rather than just selling photocopiers and supplies. And as described later in Chapter 9, other companies have made this same leap from goods to services by offering complete lease and servicing packages.

Lock in Your Best Customers

If you think you have better insight on the future prices of your company's goods and services than do your customers (and you probably do), and if in addition you believe prices will decline, then it's time to lock in your customers. Such lock-ins will make it difficult for desperate competitors to tempt your customers with lowball offers later on.

Contracts are a good way of achieving this goal. If you link prices to an objective index, customers will feel that the contract is fair and that both sides are participating in the risks. Note that this isn't necessarily the case—it depends on which index you choose. For example, LexisNexis, the big online information provider, cleverly linked its price increases to the prime interest rate, thus guaranteeing the increases even as overall prices in the information industry continued to steadily decline.

Another tactic to hold prices is volume discounts, or better yet, cumulative volume discounts. These make it suboptimal for customers to accept the occasional lowball offer. In addition, such complex discounts reduce the level of price transparency, making it harder for customers to calculate whether or not the occasional offer is indeed a bargain.

Anticipate Competitor Moves, but Avoid Price Wars

One peril associated with reducing prices to maintain volume during a recession is that you might trigger a price war. Such wars have proven to result in a loss of profits for everyone.[16] Research is contradictory as to whether price wars are more likely to break out in boom times or downturns—or merely when uncertainty increases, as during inflation.[17] But there is little doubt that soft markets and an ambitious and aggressive competitor are the makings of a combustible price environment. Automobiles, the long-distance telephone market, airlines, and the personal computer market are all good examples of the havoc that can be wreaked upon an industry and its profits as competitors chase volume and try to steal customers by slashing prices in a downturn.

How to avoid a price war? Your first step should be to signal early on to competitors where you'll fight on price and where you won't. This requires that you first make this decision for yourself. Bear in mind that not all customers or geographic areas are created equal. Some are strategic and valuable to your long-term growth, while others are of considerably less value. Remember, any customer that you lose on price, you can win back on price at a later date. Thus, if you gain in the long run by foregoing a price war, the value of doing so far outweighs the short-term loss of business.

Next you must communicate your position to your competitors. You don't have to wait for them to establish the boundaries—you'll often have a good idea of where they stand, simply by envisioning yourself in their positions and seeing where they're experiencing revenue loss and where they might seek to recover this loss. A speech on your part declaring segments X, Y, and Z as core to your business is often a very effective—and legal—signal. Properly publicized, it might keep your competitors from underestimating your reaction to an incursion. This sort of signaling is important in price-war-prone industries such as airlines, tires, cement, and high-tech.

In summary, a downturn is not a giant sucking sound, eliminating all of a company's pricing power. Through astute use of strategies such as these, many companies can continue to raise prices.

[16] "What are Price Wars Good For? Absolutely Nothing," *Fortune*, May 12, 1997: 156.
[17] Dennis Carlton and Jeffrey M. Perloff, *Modern Industrial Organization*, 2d Ed. (HarperCollins, 1994), 732.

PRICING DURING A BOOM

Thankfully, expansions are much longer and more pronounced than periods of slowdown or recession. However, the very different opportunities and stresses that come with a boom can have an equal impact on a company's fortunes in the long term.

In an upturn, customers generally are much less sensitive to higher prices. Growth projections rise, and so does the value of assets. This mirrors the decreases that occur during a downturn, so more money is generally required to buy an asset. Profits are rising, and business plans are more ambitious. As a result, corporate buyers in an upturn are less concerned about price and more concerned about security of supply. The cost of missing out on opportunities is greater than the potential gains of cost cutting. Likewise, consumers are less prone to scrutinize price tags because their disposable income is rising.

In a period of such buoyancy, the risks associated with a price increase tend to be greatly reduced. Therefore, it's an ideal time to initiate an increase. However, there are still guidelines to help maximize success and minimize the chances of a misstep. We recommend that you:

- Emphasize your ability to deliver
- Take price increases rapidly—don't wait for annual cycles
- Pass along cost increases quickly
- Don't be greedy: Resist the temptation of more market share
- Build in value and links to customer infrastructure
- Invest in price and brand

Emphasize Your Ability to Deliver

The network systems manufacturer Cisco Systems offers a good example of altering course to match changes in customer priorities. For much of the 1990s, Cisco doubled in size annually, meanwhile enjoying growth in share price at even higher rates. Seeking to maximize both market opportunities and Wall Street's focus on revenue growth rather than profit margins, the company focused on growth rather than costs. Specifically, it conducted repeated reviews of production bottlenecks, as well as new ways to speed product launches and upgrades. Appropriately, these reviews received CEO-level attention and support. Security of supply and more effective distribution were also major concerns.[18] Until about 2001, a Cisco supplier gained little by offering low price. Instead, suppliers gained favor by offering complete solutions, premium delivery schedules and terms, and absolute quality.

After the dot.com meltdown, however, Cisco found itself in a radically different environment, with customers highly focused on cost.[19] This led Cisco to focus on cost as well: Positions were eliminated, and supplier prices were examined with a fine-tooth comb. This was also fully appropriate but represented a fundamental shift in price sensitivity.

Take Price Increases Rapidly—
Don't Wait for Annual Cycles

As we have noted, a price increase is much more acceptable to customers during a boom. Even so, prices should never be raised without a corresponding explanation (see Chapters 7 and 14). The nice thing about an upturn is that a price increase can easily be explained as passing on an increase in costs. Customers accept this because it makes intuitive sense to them: After all, their own costs and incomes are also rising.

Despite these favorable conditions, many companies remain reluctant to raise prices in a boom. They fail to see that the overall market and stock market value propositions have changed—growth is now more important than earnings. No longer is low price as important, now that revenue growth and security of supply dominate. Those that hesitate risk losing leadership to the higher-growth competitors propelling the boom.

There are other problems in not raising prices when the rest of your industry is doing so. First, implicit in any decision to raise or not raise price is your choice of customers: *Not* raising price might by default

[18] "A Cloud of the Recovery: Businesses' New Frugal Ways," *The Wall Street Journal*, October 16, 2002. Also a 1997 request for proposal from Cisco to select consulting firms that emphasized the need to speed growth.

[19] "A Go-Go Giant of the Internet Age, Cisco is Learning to Go Slow," *The Wall Street Journal*, May 7, 2003: A1.

result in selecting cost-oriented laggards as your customer base. Second, failing to raise prices now might create a catch-up problem later on. If prices are rising 4 percent per semester, the company that misses a semester and then looks ahead to a price announcement covering an entire year might suddenly have to choose between a 12-percent rise or continuing to lag its input costs by 4 percent. Not a happy choice.

If in fact a key cost in your market *has* risen, such as for raw materials or other inputs, consider a surcharge as a way of raising price without risking complaints. Many industries have successfully used this approach. For example, transportation companies typically add fuel surcharges when oil prices rise, and publishers add a paper surcharge when the price of newsprint or other paper rises. The benefit here is that a surcharge implies a temporary price increase based on extraordinary cost conditions. Customers are more likely to accept the higher price, in expectation that the surcharge will be removed once these costs fall.

Don't Be Greedy: Resist the Temptation of More Market Share

Another reason some companies fail to raise prices is that they can't resist the temptation to win more market share. Many managers try to take advantage of a competitor's initial price increase to win a few customers—even though they fully intend to mirror the increase later on. But with repeated use this strategy is prone to backfire: It makes your competitors unwilling to take the lead to increase prices, and might even inspire them to try the same ploy against you if *you* attempt to raise prices. As a result, no one really wins.[20]

---

[20] A good example of such mutually destructive behavior is the airline industry, where established players frequently veto one another's price increases by failing to follow suit. This veto doesn't apply to low-cost entrants, which is why Southwest Airlines grew so rapidly. By 2002, Southwest enjoyed a market capitalization greater than that of all other major airlines combined (see Southwest Airlines Co.'s 2002 report to shareholders). It's clear to some industry observers that regulators should allow airlines to better coordinate service and fares to avoid more bankruptcies: "How About Letting Airlines Help Themselves," *The Wall Street Journal*, August 21, 2002: A13.

Therefore, if one or more of your competitors raises prices, be prepared to follow suit without hesitation. This will send a clear message that you too are interested in an industrywide price increase.

Invest in Price and Brand

Because customers during a boom are more sensitive to value than to price, brand assumes a crucial role: It becomes the vehicle for your value message. Offering a lower price won't promise better quality or security of delivery—indeed, it might well suggest the opposite, as described in Chapter 7. Therefore, when thinking about brand, think about investing in value.

As an example, now is the time to build in new features or services; because they add value, you're more likely to be rewarded. A boom is also a good time to consider restructuring prices to remove any costly freebies or value-added features you might have thrown in during a recession. Finally, implementing new price-related IT capabilities can pay a double dividend: the first, during the price fluctuations of an upturn and, the second during the downturn that follows, when these new capabilities might allow you to outmaneuver your competitors with innovative ways to avoid or minimize the impact of downward price pressures.

Some industry observers argue that recession is the better time to invest in growth. Clearly everyone would prefer to invest in brand and infrastructure when advertising and technology are cheaper and competitors are sidelined.[21] However, as some have discovered, it's tough to time such investments correctly. Brand messages aren't the same in an upturn as in a downturn, so your timing must be exact. In addition, if your product isn't recession-proof and the economy continues to fall rather than recover, shareholder value will be destroyed.

SAILING CLEAR

Exploiting times of high demand and salvaging value from periods of weakness are the foundation of profitable pricing. So it's not surprising

[21] "Signs of Life," *Business Week*, July 14, 2003: 32–34.

that all of your pricing decisions need to be designed and reviewed with an eye to existing and developing economic conditions. The fundamentals of pricing and branding never change, but applying these fundamentals calls for opposite tacks as expectations of growth rise and fall. A brand message appropriate for an upturn will probably be quite different than that required for a downturn. In an upturn, quality and security of delivery might be the keys to brand identity. In a downturn, the keys might be ensuring that customers see your offer as competitive in both value and price.

Strong leadership is essential in making sound pricing and brand decisions at every point in the cycle. The ability to rapidly raise or lower price early in a boom or a bust is a competitive advantage. Getting the brand mission right is crucial. Understanding the price to win allows you to design to cost and manage cost-to-serve. Such decisions aren't easy, nor are they the province of middle management. It is top management that must make the strategic bets required to handle a broad economic shift—it is top management that must adjust course and sail the ship clear of the storm.

Part Two

How to Set Price and Create Revenue

Chapter Seven | Price as a Language to Customers

Companies like to talk to their potential customers. From the sales force to the marketing department to the executive suites, everyone is eager to explain the value of a company's product or service. Rather foreign, however, is the idea of speaking to customers in prices and price structures. Hence a past chairman of GE insisted on seeing all TV commercials personally, but only rarely reviewed individual price points.

Actually, sometimes a price is worth a thousand words, a thousand commercials, or a thousand other marketing vehicles. Studies have shown that customers can often recall prices from years or even decades ago.[1] In fact, along with personal experience of a product or service, price can be the single most important message a company can send to a potential customer.

What is the language of price? Some of its elements are simple and known to us all. For example, when comparing prices between compet-

---

[1] Russell S. Winer, "A Reference Model of Brand Choice for Frequently Purchased Products," *Journal of Consumer Research*, September 13, 1986: pp. 250ff.

ing products, a higher price generally signals that there is something better about that product, whether it be the product itself, its terms, or the degree to which it serves a particular niche market.

Other elements of the language are more ambiguous, complex, and occasionally confusing. An example of a message with several possible interpretations: a new customer discount at a department store. Department stores often offer 15 percent off all credit card purchases the first day a customer uses the store's charge card. This can be read in several ways:

- "You don't know us yet, so we will make it worth your while to shop here for a day. And once you shop here, you'll know us and love us."
- "We really want new customers, and for one day we'll give you an incentive to shop here."
- "We know it's a nuisance for you to open a charge card account, so we'll make it worth your while."

By way of contrast, in many cases you will see special sales for existing customers only. Brooks Brothers every year mails out discount cards to its existing customers, along with an invitation to a sale that will only later be advertised to the general public. The message here is quite different: "We value our existing customers more than new ones, so here is tangible proof of that preference."

But let's suppose a firm does both—offers incentives to new customers, and promotions to existing customers? Such a store would run the danger of sending an unintended message: "My normal price levels are lower than the nominal sticker price on the goods. You should avoid randomly buying here, and instead wait for a promotional event."[2]

A third example: A leading mattress retailer says it offers the best mattresses for the lowest prices because the retailer can buy in volume.

---

[2] "Cracking the Code: How Not To Pay Retail," *The Wall Street Journal*, November 27, 2002: D1. "Shops . . . use price cuts to lure customers, who are in turn reluctant to buy without a significant discount."

The message seems to be, "I recognize that my prices don't convey the quality I offer, but here's my explanation."

The point here is that it's good practice on the part of senior management to make sure the company's marketers can articulate in words the message a numeric price is intended to convey. Perhaps that verbal message should always be presented alongside numeric price structures being crafted in marketing or pricing departments, so that there is no conflict with branding and promotion.

OTHER FACTORS: TIMING AND BIDDING PATTERNS

Timing can have a substantial impact on the message a price sends out. Most brands can support the occasional promotional or sale price—in most cases people will still believe the sticker price has some validity.[3] A sale every month would quickly destroy that belief. Similarly, industry knowledge that most customers have negotiated a material discount will erode the credibility of a price. Few things are worse than a salesperson offering a discount without an explanation because this sets most customers to wondering if there are other, or bigger, discounts to be had. If the discount was in response to a question from the customer, the message is even worse: "We only offer our best prices to our most aggressive customers." A similar problem can arise if there are too many discounts, and this gets worse if the sales representative seems confused by them.

Timing is even more important in an iterative price setting, such as a negotiation. Depending on the situation, rapid responses can be read either as "I'm decisive" or "I am under time pressure, therefore weak." Craig McCaw, the billionaire founder of Cellular One (now AT&T Wireless) used timing in an innovative way during the bidding for PCS frequencies in a government auction. In that auction the bids were public, and he was often bidding against large telephone companies.

McCaw's objectives were a bit unusual—for the most part he was not there to win, rather, he was participating to make sure that the other

---

[3] Of course, not all do. Tiffany & Co., the high-end retailer, never runs a sale, but reportedly has two warehouses full of older, unwanted goods that any other retailer would have liquidated.

bidders did not get the frequency rights too cheaply, as that would leave them with more money to compete against his existing services.

Several times, instead of placing a bid and then waiting for the opposing bid, McCaw came back and raised his own bid just before the Telcos offered their opposing bids. Because the Telco bidding process was labor-intensive, difficult, and slow, he hoped that by preempting their bids he could possibly distort their judgment and induce them to make higher bids each time so that they would not be topped by a surprise bid. In some ways his message was "When I bid $100, you might discover I really am at $120, so act accordingly." It appears to have worked, as the victorious bidders emerged cash-poor, and some of the independent bidders later went bankrupt.

Aside from the timing of bids, the pattern of bid levels also sends a crucial message. Take, for example, the development of the huge Atlantic City casinos. The developers, having bought up all the land they needed except for a final remaining plot, were faced with an elderly woman who was reluctant to sell out. They offered her a generous price, but she refused. A higher bid followed and was refused. A much higher bid followed, and another, each growing exponentially higher as the deadline for construction neared. This strategy was a mistake.

From the viewpoint of the seller, the escalating bid levels sent a clear message: "Don't take this bid because a much richer bid is sure to follow." Contrast this to the inverse pattern, where each succeeding bid would have been a smaller increment, or even a decrease. The message then would have been, "You have little to gain from holding on. Be careful, or you'll be left holding the bag." Sadly, because the developer sent the wrong message, both sides lost: The developer decided it had no choice but to build around the woman's lot, and the woman missed out on a windfall.

KNOW YOUR AUDIENCE

Product managers and marketers understand that price messages need to address a number of audiences—especially products or services being marketed to companies or other large organizations. Despite this, managers don't always envision how the message will look after it goes through various intermediaries or filters within the target organization—administrators, financial controllers, and others. The effect of filters can be to garble messages, or at a minimum translate them into specific actions. For example, if an information service is offered at a flat rate per month to a group of end users, a company's systems administrator will condense the terms and conditions of the contract into a short message along the lines of, "Use all you like." On the other hand, if the contract is linked to usage volume, the message might be, "Avoid unnecessary use." In our personal experience as users of various services, many times we've received a summary of a complex price as the much simpler message, "It's cheap" or "It's expensive." Similar simplified messages often go out concerning warranties, such as "It's covered" or sometimes "Be careful."

Some product managers react to the potential for garbling and simplification by saying the price message should be kept simple. However, the way to craft a simple message to a complex audience is to be smart, not simpleminded.

CRAFTING THE MESSAGE ACCORDING TO AUDIENCE OR MARKET SEGMENT

To craft the right message, it's worth drawing up an explicit list of your individual audiences and their agendas. As described in Chapter 4 on segmentation, not only does the agenda drive the particulars that matter to each audience—it also affects how these audiences will summarize your price structure. Figure 7.1 shows some typical examples of this.

Not surprisingly, each audience listens to a service or product description and the associated price with an ear to its own concerns. And because each audience has a different set of concerns and responsibilities, each audience is best addressed through a different message.

The good news is that rarely do all of these audiences matter equally. If you find yourself insisting that your case is different and your audiences do matter equally, it might be that you don't understand your market segments sufficiently well. We have found that any major mar-

Audience	Typical concerns
Business leaders	Will it grow the top line? The bottom line?
Operational managers	Is it proven? Does it run cheaper?
Sales managers	Does a purchase help me sell? Is it time-intensive? Will it fit into expense guidelines and budgets?
Financial controllers	Low risk of varying from budget? Correct invoices?
Administrators	Does it need to be actively managed, usage monitored, abusers spoken with?
End users (for example, truck drivers, students, machine operators, salespeople, or attorneys)	Is it expensive? Is it cheap? The president of a major trucking company says his fleet is exclusively Peterbilt trucks because the drivers know it is a premium brandóin other words, expensiveóand so they handle the trucks with kid gloves.
End customers or beneficiaries of the product or service	Did it improve the service or product? Did it materially affect my price?
Technical support staff	How good is it? How reliable is it?

Figure 7.1. Examples of audiences affected by price level and structure.

ket comprises multiple segments, and these segments have different price sensitivities and concerns (again, see Chapter 4). In each segment, a different group has primary interest and authority regarding purchases and price decisions. Think through the segments, and the message to each segment will be relatively simple and obvious.

An illustration from the world of computers: Most companies move through a series of evolutionary stages in how they communicate among their computers and computer users. Thus, as companies move into each stage, they comprise a distinct market segment for anyone selling enterprise computer equipment or applications. In the first stage, for example, a company typically starts with an all-IBM world, run by its IT or MIS department. Because these departments are judged by financial criteria, they focus primarily on the long-run costs of an equipment lease or software purchase, including maintenance and related costs. For this audience, a winning price message might be, "Total costs are lower over the long run." In the next stage, the operating units start building their own computer networks and giving department members their own computers. Often this is driven by a need for immediate results, and the long run is not of great interest. The right message for this segment might be, "Here is the highest MIPS per dollar right now."[4]

In a subsequent stage, costs frequently soar and the purchasing department is called into action to rein in expenditures. Often the purchasing department can't calculate long-run costs and isn't very much interested in capabilities or MIPS, so they focus on the initial purchase price. A good price message for this group might be, "Lowest price tag."

Finally, after the end users rebel, the whole problem goes back to the IT department, or else a combination of IT and operations. This can mean either a return to the original set of IT concerns or else a more sophisticated balancing of costs and price. The price message here might now be, "Best capabilities for the best long-term price."

As you can see, each of the evolutionary segments described above has its own unique concerns. The implications for vendor pricing are fundamental. In the disguised market example shown in Figure 7.2 involving two vendors to a pharmaceutical company, two prices with the same initial MIPS offer radically different matches to company needs.

Not surprisingly, Vendor A consistently won the business in the first evolutionary phase—it offered a lower present value of expenses to the IT department. But when the company moved into the next phase, Vendor B took over—it offered more MIPS per initial dollar spent. Although each vendor had a consistent offer, what mattered was how well the offers matched the criteria of the decision makers for each stage.

LISTEN WHEN THE CUSTOMER SPEAKS

Some management inquiries into the price desired by customers focus exclusively on price level, with only a secondary interest in structure, and even less interest in executional details such as billing. This is a short-term view, and it can be a mistake. As the example in Figure 7.2 shows, often there is no single "objective" price level. Price is in the eye of the beholder. If you don't pay attention to the price structure preferred

---

[4] MIPS is defined as Millions of Instructions Per Second, a standard measure of a computer's processing power.

Offer	Vendor A	Vendor B
Terms (80 MIPS, 5-year life)[1]	$80,000 plus maintenance at $10,000 per year	$60,000 plus maintenance at $20,000 per year
Present value of expense at 7% discount rate	$121,000	$162,000
MIPS per initial $1,000	1.0 (or $1,000)	1.3 (or $1,300)
Implicit message	Best long-term value	Best MIPS per initial dollar

[1]*MIPS is millions of instructions per second*

Figure 7.2. Two prices offer radically different matches to a company's needs.

by your market, you might not be able to deliver the right message to send to your decision makers and other audiences.

Rarely is the customer's reaction to your price message a direct counteroffer and dialogue on price. Instead, it usually consists of purchasing from a competitor, or requesting a refund. There are many ways to listen to these kinds of more subtle messages. For example, if you sell via a Web site, you can track customers' navigation and see where they abandon their shopping carts.[5] If you then discover that they typically abandon the cart when presented with delivery charges, you know the charges are a sticking point.

Even if you sell indirectly, you can establish ways to listen to customer feedback. For many years, Apple Computer had no way for customers to easily call and comment on the company's products, prices, or customer support: All of this was supposedly handled by its distributors. But after realizing that important customer feedback was being lost—including reactions to price—Apple established its own feedback process. The company promoted a customer service director to vice president, so that this new information was not only gleaned, but acted upon. Partly as a result, Apple saw its end users grow more loyal by the year.

Feedback is important because details that might seem peripheral to the product or service you deliver—for example, a bill that clearly

[5] "So Much Information," *The Wall Street Journal*, December 9, 2002: R4.

breaks out departmental or billing categories—might be crucial to customers who depend on those bills to charge back costs to the government or to their clients. In some cases the administrator who reviews and processes the bill might be quite junior, and so not appear to be an important audience. However, if the enterprise for which he or she works is dependent on a bill for charge back, concerns with a poorly presented bill will surely rise to a senior level sooner or later. A clear bill configured in ways helpful to the customer says, "We understand your business and are here to serve you." A bill assembled with little care or detail says, in effect, "drop dead."

SUMMARY

Speak the language of your customers. Price is something that most customers consider important, and it gets their full attention. Don't send them a message such as, "Only shop here when there is a sale," unless you mean it.

Every company should ensure that the information contained in its price structure is not self-contradictory or is not sending the wrong message. Price should reinforce the other messages your company sends in sales presentations and advertisements. If management does not speak the language of price, your price will not match your strategies and objectives.

Chapter Eight | Ways to Set Price Level

If this were a book on home repair, this would be the chapter devoted to the topic of hammers. Hammers come in a number of varieties, but there is some sort of hammer in every respectable handyman's toolbox.[1] Similarly, the question that most often seems to come up in pricing is: "How much should we charge for this?" This chapter describes different ways for making that determination.

The 15 methodologies described here do not, certainly, run the full gamut of pricing methodologies—that would take several (not very interesting) books. They do cover a wide range of pricing options, and so make a useful menu for management contemplation. Because they are both efficient and replicable, these approaches are often referred to as pricing engines, especially those that are primarily analytic in nature.

The 15 techniques or price engines are summarized in Figure 8.1. The rest of this chapter is devoted to describing each in turn. Feel free to skip around to look at those that might be of most use to you.

---

[1] Claw, Rip Claw, Ball-Pein, Milled Face, Framing, Bricklayers's, TiBone, Sledge, Finishing, Insulated, Mallet, etc.

Pricing technique	Advantage	Disadvantage
Matching competitors	Close tie to market, assuming quality is equivalent	May be slow, suboptimal, or impossible
Market trials	Highly accurate	Expensive or not an option sometimes
Value analysis	Customer perspective	Share of value can be difficult to estimate
Economic models	Highly usable and insightful Highlights points of leverage Key to real-time yield management	Need to create an algorithm or model for the market being priced
Demand curves	Useful for product planning	Sometimes difficult to construct
Supply and demand curves	Critical for capacity management Insightful	Significant effort involved to construct paradigm and systems
Tax and regulatory strategy	High return in some markets	Does not address customers and competitors
Conjoint analysis	Nice model for demand in established markets	Narrow range, limited view of possibilities
Expert opinion	Often very accurate	Need legitimate experts May be conservative
War games and scenario planning	Handles discontinuities well	Expensive and takes time
Price as signal of quality	Effective for some products, not others	Even in right market, may be way off
Cost-based pricing	Focuses on cost element of profits	Does not maximize revenues Potential îdeath spiralî
Negotiations	Key for unique assets and limited number of buyers	Can take time, and results uneven
Auctions	Transaction itself sets price, useful if seller cannot determine price	Expensive initial setup Some types of auctions less efficient
Historic price	Convenient to implement	Potential downward spiral Sometimes ignores segments

Figure 8.1. Menu of pricing techniques.

Different methodologies are appropriate to different markets. In some cases, your only choice is to match the competition, while in other cases there *is* no competition, meaning that price level can come from a methodology based largely on the value you provide to a customer. In some cases, a market trial would be good or reassuring, but perhaps your market is unitary (can't split out a part for trials) or you can't afford the expense. In that case, conjoint analysis, which is described in Method 8, might do. If you have little market information, you might need to rely on information provided by your buyers in the form of an auction. On the other hand, if (like the airlines) you have abundant information about responsiveness to price, then you might find that a computerized supply and demand yield-management system is indispensable. If change in your industry is radical and discontinuous, and the stakes are high, such as in computer hardware, then tools such as war games or simulation might best meet your needs. Lastly, some pricing activities cost more than others, meaning you might also need to consider the economics of your business and what you can afford.

Some of the methods listed here fall short of providing a precise number that goes on a bill of sale. In fact, most are meant to generate only a baseline price, prior to any tweaks for discounts, special promotions, or temporary market fluctuations. A baseline price is no mean thing, however, because it helps ensure that your company debuts a product in the right price range. Moreover, an appropriate price engine enables rapid recalculation of prices depending on demand, competition, and short-term considerations. This is the role of a price engine as seen in Figure 8.2.

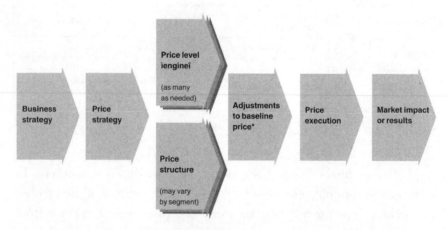

*There are many reasons for baseline price adjustments, including temporary market fluctuations, sales discounts, volume discounts, competitive responses, promotions, and trials.

Figure 8.2. Price engine in the overall system.

Thus, while the price engines in this chapter provide a fundamental service, you should recognize that very often other tools such as sanders and paintbrushes might be needed to finish the job.

METHOD 1: MATCHING COMPETITORS

The first methodology, and a commonly used one, is to set your price relative to competitors' prices. You can either match them directly or, if you think your product, service, customer set, or channel is different, you can match them with an appropriate differential.

The appropriate differential will vary by market segment, as it did for MCI in pricing against AT&T. AT&T had product, brand, and channel superiority for most of the 1980s in the residential and large business segments, so MCI had to offer a significant discount to those segments. However, for the small business market, MCI had a strong product set and channel capability, so here it could actually charge as much or more than AT&T.

Working off competitors' pricing is a pretty safe way to price, but it has some flaws. One problem is that this process is reactive, and sometimes the second mover cannot match the first mover. For example, many customers have finite budgets for particular purchases, so vendors in effect are not competing for one particular sale, but rather for the customer's budget dollars. If one vendor moves to use up these budgets—for example, if a publisher selling "must-have" books to legal libraries raises prices—competing vendors using a reactive pricing method might find they have been shut out.

Another problem is that competitors' prices are not always easy to understand or match. For example, one plastics manufacturer found that it was impossible to figure out its own prices, much less its competitors: By the time managers had stuck together all rebates, promotional specials, freight charges, warehousing arrangements, and financing, they couldn't calculate the true cost of any given order. Even if they had obtained the equivalent information about a competitor's prices, they wouldn't have been able to unravel those prices either.

When comparing your offer with that of competitors, you will often need to take into account differences in quality. For example, a Mercedes luxury sedan might cost more per car than a Ford sedan, but some fleet owners have found that in looking at total ownership costs per year and per mile, the Mercedes actually costs less due to its longer useful life.

In many cases the unit of comparison is tough to establish. For example, when charges are stated in dollars per hour, this is only half the story. If one competitor is twice as productive as another, you need a measure of output—for example, number of customer calls handled, lines of code produced, number of rooms cleaned, or students educated. We once found an example of this in software development, where one development shop was charging $23 per hour versus another shop's fee of $60 per hour. However, the second developer had coding and management techniques that made it six times more productive. Using a comparison of price per line of code revealed that the second developer was the better bargain at $1.17 per line of code, versus $2.25 per line of code for the first developer.

METHOD 2: MARKET TRIALS

Trials can be performed in a number of ways. For example, when testing the impact of reduced prices, special offers can be sent to selected customers, segments, or geographic areas.

The most certain way to experiment is to actually change prices. This is preferably done in part of the market, leaving another (ideally similar) geographic area unchanged, to serve as the control set. This provides you with a baseline so that if overall demand is up, or the competition undertakes something new, you can normalize the test market results to isolate and measure the price effect.

Unfortunately, while it would be convenient to rely on the results of promotions for market information, promotional trial results can be quite different from permanent results. Customers might stock up on a special offer, but longer-term demand might not be dramatically changed. On the other hand, if special offers are frequent, the special price can become the common price, with only time-constrained customers buying between specials.

Method 3: Value Analysis

This involves determining how much value is being created and seeing what portion you can then appropriate for yourself. For example, software developers in India enjoy total development costs of about 40 to 50 percent less than some U.S. software producers for certain kinds of software. These outsourcers in India know that offering savings to customers of 20 to 25 percent allows them to win the business, while keeping the extra 20 to 25 percent of the savings for themselves.

Method 4: Economic Models

This methodology is our favorite because it allows the greatest precision and insight into market prices. Every business has certain key economic principles by which it operates, but probably the area in which economic analysis has progressed the furthest is the financial industry, in part because the services are often highly comparable and the costs identical.

A use of modeling that touches all of us is yield management models for airlines, hotels, and other sellers of capacity. These models revolutionized the airline industry when they emerged. Before the 1980s, airlines used to change routes and run different-sized airplanes to accommodate the number of passengers who bought tickets—a procedure both expensive and laborious. Today, they run standard-size aircraft through hubs on regular schedules, because now they fill up airplanes by lowering prices as it becomes clear that there will be empty seats.

Even more impressive, these systems operate in real time. For example, American Airline's Sabre system adjusts prices for an airplane every six minutes. If you make a reservation on a plane for yourself, then 10 minutes later for a colleague, the price will have changed. Sabre notes when one more seat has been sold, and correctly concludes that the chances of selling out the airplane have gone up, and thus that it should charge you more for that next seat.

Although complex, the airline yield management systems are based on a simple idea: Try to match the price with the bargaining power open to travelers seeking a seat.

Another good example of pricing by algorithm is from the world of broad-lines retailing. If you are a retailer, the thing you typically care most about is inventory turnover. Turnover can be measured in any of several ways: for example, direct measurement, dollars in sales per square foot of retail space. Several firms offer software to optimize these calculations. These programs look at turnover rates, profit margins, carrying costs, and related costs such as training, or customer service, and then set an optimum price. To do so, these programs require a model for price elasticity—which is, of course, the sticky part. There is no magic elasticity number. It must be found through trial, or else estimated from historical data.

Parametric pricing is the marriage of statistics and economic modeling. Parametric models prescribe a way for pricing assets despite uncertainty and market volatility. A famous example is the pricing model for financial options called the Black-Scholes Option Pricing Model.[2] Variations on Black-Scholes are used thousands of times a day in all major stock and commodity exchanges to calculate option prices. Increasingly, the formula is also being applied in other contexts, such as pricing for electricity and other long-term supplies.[3]

Models demand a great deal in return for the insights they provide, however. They require a company to fully understand its price drivers and price elasticities, while pushing management to thinking about what can be done to optimize price. Models also require effort to build,

---

[2] The algorithm says that the present value of a call option on a share of stock is equal to the price of the stock now, multiplied by the cumulative probability that the stock will remain below the exercise price, minus the exercise price of the option adjusted for the risk-free rate of interest (continuously compounded), multiplied by the cumulative probability of the stock remaining below the exercise price. This is a rough statement of the algorithm; you can find the precise formula in R. Brealey & S. Myers, *Principles of Corporate Finance* (McGraw-Hill, 1981).

[3] A. Faruqui, K. Eakin, *Pricing in Competitive Electricity Markets*, Kluwer Academic Publishers, Boston, 2000.

and there are some markets that are too complex or too small to warrant this effort. Models are best applied when there is central control of price and marketing, a limited number of products, and a high volume of transactions. If these conditions exist, then we suggest you invest in developing an economic algorithm and using it for better pricing.

METHOD 5: DEMAND CURVES

Still another method for determining a price level is to understand the demand curve of your product. A demand curve shows the volume of product you will sell at different price levels. Typically it slopes downward, meaning you will sell few if your price is very high and sell a lot more if your price is very low. In most cases there are distinct plateaus along the demand curve. These result from distinct groups of users who value a product at a common level and are willing to pay a common price. Typically that group is a segment, and as you move out of that segment the number you can sell at that price falls precipitously. One sign of a genuine price demand curve, therefore, is that it isn't a straight line.

A classic example of how a demand curve can be useful was long-distance telephony in the early 1960s. AT&T found that if it lowered prices, its long-distance usage would go up faster than its revenues would decrease. And it then used the knowledge of this demand curve to dramatically lower prices. The resulting optimum price level was maintained until the breakup of the Bell system and the resulting price wars.

Some managers object to demand curves as being too difficult to construct. However, the degree of difficulty is typically less than might at first appear. In many cases you know from experience what the demand curve segments look like, and it then becomes simply a question of putting it on paper. If you don't understand what the segments are inside your market, then yes, you will have a hard time developing your demand curve—but without such an understanding you will have a hard time doing anything intelligent in your market. Assuming you know something about the segments being served and those being served by your competition, you ought to be able to construct a demand

curve of the entire market and learn from it what price levels correspond over the long haul with what level of business.

METHOD 6: SUPPLY AND DEMAND CURVES

A supply and demand curve is first cousin to a demand curve. The difference here is that you're less worried about demand inflection points
and more interested in figuring out what the overall industry price level
is going to be over time.

You can use supply and demand to figure out broader shifts in buying power or selling power in an industry. At one point during the late
1990s there was an expression that permeated the high-tech world, to
the effect that "content is king." Decoded, it meant that many thought
that content such as movies and other entertainment would be scarce
when compared to distribution media. If true, content owners would be
in a position to dictate terms to distribution companies—including
high prices. As a result of such thinking, cable companies, electronics
manufacturers, and telephone companies scrambled to buy equity or
make other arrangements with Disney, Time Warner, and other content
companies.

Yet, content proved not to be king over the following few years.
Instead, distribution companies paid large premiums in deals that
proved to be less crucial than most people believed. What happened
was that while channels of distribution (demand) increased, the supply
of content also went up dramatically. This was in part because digital
technologies had emerged that could produce new content more
quickly and inexpensively than the old, painstaking methods. These
technologies included video recorders and computer-generated anima-
tion. Thus a TV show such as *Cops* became a top-rated hit, even as it
cost far less to produce than traditional fare such as movies.

METHOD 7: TAX AND REGULATORY STRATEGY

You can also set price to optimize taxes or conform to a regulatory process. This occurs frequently in arenas such as electric power, cable tel-

evision, telecommunications, water, financial services, and some medical services.

A good example of a bundle serving tax purposes is the combination of books and online services. In many European countries, online services are subject to a Value Added Tax (VAT), but books are not. Thus, a bundle worth €100 could avoid tax on the €50 for the book, and pay VAT on the €50 for the online service. But if the book is valued at €99 and the service at €1, then the taxes will be lower for the same bundle. Naturally, there is a need to demonstrate that €1 is a legitimate price to the tax authorities, but that can be done in a number of ways.

Bundles are an adroit way of optimizing both shareholder and tax or regulatory goals, but other techniques have also proved effective. For example, many regulators are focused on accounting results, whereas shareholders focus on free cash flow, and this divide can be exploited.

METHOD 8: CONJOINT ANALYSIS

Conjoint analysis is a mathematical process by which a sample of people is polled about their preferences and relative weighting of different product parameters. One of these parameters can be price. Thus, if a group is asked to choose between automobile features such as speed, comfort, crash-worthiness, and price, participants must make hypothetical choices as to whether they prefer a car with one set of enhanced features versus another set or a combination of features.

One limitation of conjoint analysis is that it relies solely on respondent self-reporting, which is subject to problems. Another limitation is that it only tests for trade-offs specified in the survey. For example, a conjoint model cannot answer how a car that goes over 200 mph and costs $100,000 would do, when all the choices are for cars with maximum speeds under 90 mph that cost less than $40,000.[4]

---

[4] For more on conjoint analysis, see A. Gustafsson, *Conjoint Measurements: Methods and Applications* (Springer Verlag, 2001).

METHOD 9: EXPERT OPINION

Expert opinion is not a technique per se, but is nonetheless an important part of many more sophisticated pricing processes. Often the experts (price experts, sales professionals, buyers, and others) have a strong view as to price; often, these views are correct. Even when incorrect, expert views are still useful in gauging how ready the market, the channel, and other stakeholders will be to accept your ultimate price. If you are using conjoint analysis, it might set the bounds of your survey and the primary factors to be surveyed. If you are developing an economic model, experts are a very good place to start the process and to test the completeness and accuracy of a developing model.

A major problem with expert opinion is that experts often are reluctant to spend the time on pricing exercises. Experts tend to be highly paid salespeople who are expensive and difficult to pull out of the field. In addition, they can be biased according to the culture and objectives of their departments. Finally, we have found that experts tend to underestimate the degree of change in their markets. This is understandable because a radical but incorrect forecast can be remembered for a long time, and experts hesitate to damage their institutional credibility.

METHOD 10: WAR GAMES AND SCENARIO PLANNING

A war game consists of teams of managers playing the role of your company, competitors, customers, regulators, suppliers, and any other interested parties. Each group looks out after its own interests and plays out several stages in industry evolution. During the game, a neutral group keeps score by calculating the financial impacts of moves and in the end assesses who won.

War games allow insight into future markets and price elements. This technique is particularly suitable to one-off negotiations, broad bilateral price contests, the sale of major unique assets, or whenever management suspects that something fundamental about the industry is about to change. War games are relatively expensive, time-consuming, and cumbersome, but are often required (like war itself) when there is no other choice.

A leading cigarette manufacturer performed a war game in the mid-1990s to simulate moves that it and its competitors might make in that market. Given the economics of cigarettes (high margins, volume-crucial), government limits on advertising, and the relative share and channel strengths of the players, the war game came to a key price conclusion: It was highly likely that the market leader would drop its prices dramatically to win share and grow revenues. This forecast proved true with "Marlboro Friday," when competitor Philip Morris dropped prices on its brands. The war game allowed the other cigarette manufacturer to prepare its channels and costs for this event and to test potential strategies for dealing with the cost move.[5]

Another technique that shares some power with war games—at least if you have bright people doing it—is scenario planning. Shell Oil Company at one point had a brilliant strategic planning group, which correctly forecast the Arab oil embargo of the 1970s. As described by Shell's former head of planning, P. W. Beck, the planners saw a combination of circumstances that suggested an embargo was likely. These included an accumulation of wealth by OPEC countries well in excess of needs, concern about depletion of that resource, and increased consumption by industrial countries. The planning group's foresight allowed Shell to be better prepared for scarcity, higher prices, and governmental price intervention.[6]

METHOD 11: PRICE AS A SIGNAL OF QUALITY

Perception naturally plays a role in all the means by which price is set— but sometimes it operates as the dominant means. For example, perception is at the root of cosmetics pricing. If something is perceived to be

[5] R. Ackerman, G. Thibault, and A. Asin, "Wargaming as a Strategic Tool," *Strategy & Business*, 2d quarter, 1996.

[6] P.W. Beck, "Corporate Planning for an Uncertain Future," *Long Range Planning* 15:12–21 (August 1980).

desirable, if it has a cachet or is in fashion, price alone can influence that demand or move the product into a new demand category.

Price will drive behavior particularly when there is no objective standard or comparison. Comparisons among restaurants are highly subjective, and driven by image. Thumbing its nose at the idea of precision in restaurant pricing, Smith & Wollensky, a well-known New York steakhouse, once offered the "NASDAQ Lunch." This lunch was priced in conjunction with the stock market index. If the NASDAQ was at 1850, then your lunch cost you $18.50. If the stock index was at 1700, then your lunch cost you $17.00. Smith & Wollensky offered the tagline, "If your portfolio is down, we share the loss; if your portfolio is up, you can afford it." Of course there is no logical connection between the NASDAQ and your lunch, but it was appealing. Other pricing schemes, like one by LexisNexis that linked its price increases to the prime interest rate have also been well received.

The lesson to be learned here? If you have a class of goods in which pricing is based on perception, then think primarily about the message you hope your price will send, and the credibility of that message. An understanding of the branding dynamics is key.

Also worth mentioning is that sometimes prices alone drive value. In many U.S. cities there are choices of roads leading to the same place: a toll road and a freeway. In some cases, the toll road is privately financed, and the freeway is publicly funded. The simple addition of a toll will typically reduce traffic levels, and so improve the speed and ease of transit.[7]

---

[7] We have often thought this principle could be usefully extended to other traffic situations. The Triboro Bridge, leading to Manhattan in New York, features eight toll lanes, each charging $4 to cross the bridge. Imagine one lane requiring $20 per passage versus another charging $2 for the same. In all likelihood the more expensive lane would have shorter lines; the less expensive lane, longer lines. Despite populist objections, the system would benefit users: If you were late for the airport (or too wealthy to care), you would gladly pay the $20. On the other hand, if money were more important to you than time, you would use the bargain lane. Depending on usage rates, the bridge authority would probably take in increased total revenues while offering less-well-off users a lower price. (You could also add time-of-day tweaking to the scheme.)

METHOD 12: COST-BASED PRICING

The appeal of cost-based pricing stems from a few good reasons—but several bad ones as well. The good ones are that in many industries competitors are so similar that cost is a reliable indicator of what competitors will charge. Another reason is that it helps guide customers' actions—for example, if you charge more for rush orders to cover freight and extra scheduling costs, then customers will be reluctant to expedite orders when rush charges might be incurred. (See Chapter 6.)

You might want to follow a cost-based approach when there are too many goods to price, or when other pricing models might be expensive for many goods (although if sales are brisk, a model based on inventory turnover might work). Also, a cost-based approach might be appropriate in areas where there is an implied covenant with customers, ensuring them that they will not be priced aggressively. One such area is automobile spare parts that are not subject to after-market competition. Many automobile manufacturers recognize the strong link between customer loyalty and how fairly they are treated in repair work. Such a link has spawned longer automobile warranties, and even a display at a Volkswagen dealer promising fair prices on spare parts.

METHOD 13: NEGOTIATIONS

Negotiations are often the only way to price unique assets that have just a few interested buyers. This technique is very much subject to the relative strengths of buyer and seller and their respective negotiating skills. Hence, negotiations usually result in widely varied prices.

Management skill in negotiation can affect price and compensate for differences in negotiating power. *The Wall Street Journal* described one negotiated outcome as "radically different," attributing the difference to improved negotiating skills on the part of TRW as it was being acquired by Northrop Grumman.[8]

There are many books on negotiation, and most of their lessons apply to pricing. Fundamentally, negotiated outcomes are a function of

---

[8] "Skilled Negotiator Helped TRW," *The Wall Street Journal*, July 1, 2002.

expectations, planning, and motivations. For example, if one party has high expectations, and a second has lower expectations, the first party will probably have a successful negotiation. Timing and apparent negotiating strength can affect both expectations and results.[9]

METHOD 14: AUCTIONS

An auction is feasible only when there is more than one potential buyer. There are many possible auction structures: secret bids or public bids, rounds of bids or "sudden-death," price floors or minimum bids, conditional or absolute commitment bids allowed, and varying degrees of management by the auction managers.

Auctions fall into three types: English, Dutch, and reverse Dutch.[10] The type of auction you want will depend on your situation. If you don't know where the final price will settle, but don't want to leave money on the table, you want the Dutch auction. Here sellers (or those managing the auction) that bid above the clearing price get shares of whatever is being sold. Those that bid below the clearing price do not succeed in purchasing anything.[11]

With any auction, an important issue is the setup and variable costs. For a typical industrial procurement, a successful bid requires significant preparation. The bid specifications need to be carefully drafted and potential bidders identified and made aware of the pending auction. Often it is advantageous for the buyer to work with bidders to guide them in their offer and price terms.

---

[9] Dr. Chester L. Karrass, "Effective Negotiating" (Karrass, 1991).

[10] American auctions, as used for IPOs on Wall Street, don't really allow the market to set the price. A British auction sets price also, but then prorates allocated shares based on number of shares requested. Thus, if an auction is 2 times oversubscribed, and you bid for 100 shares, you will get 50. See R. Brealey & S. Myers, *Principles of Corporate Finance* (McGraw-Hill, 1981).

[11] Such a system benefits the sellers. In some situations, for example, IPOs on Wall Street, the investment banks that manage the sale resent this system because it doesn't benefit them as much. See "Hambrecht's IPO Method Is in Dutch," *The Wall Street Journal*, July 31, 2002.

If there is rancor among buyers, an auction method can be quite expensive. For example, Royal Caribbean Cruises spent between $10 and $15 million for lawyers and bankers in fighting with P&O Princess Cruises over an auction of a cruise line.[12]

On the other end of the spectrum there are high-volume, low variable-cost auction frameworks such as eBay. eBay is highly successful, having experienced explosive growth in annual revenues since its launch in 1995. Setting up this auction framework was not cheap: The online infrastructure, publicity, vendor rating system, and policing of auctions, among other things, are expensive fixed costs. However, once established, the incremental cost of each additional auction is very low. Compared to an industrial procurement there is high standardization and an ability to sell objects for some sort of market price, even when information on the object's value is not available to the seller.

METHOD 15: HISTORIC PRICE

A final means for setting price, and the most commonly used, is to continue with the historic price, or a percentage adjustment from the historic price. This approach has several advantages, which is why it is so commonly used:

- When market information is lacking (for example, no demand curve), continuing with a price is among the least risky approaches. Assuming the price adjustment is small, the consequences of changing from a proven base are relatively low risk.
- It's easy and institutionally less risky as well. A simple 7-percent price increase is easily understood by the sales force, implemented by the billing system, and incorporated into financial plans.

Most important, customers and competitors can easily understand and accommodate for the new prices. Customers can be trained to build

---

[12] "Carnival Puts a Price Tag on P&O Battle," *The Wall Street Journal*, April 16, 2002.

annual price increases into their budgets, and competitors will not react wildly, possibly provoking a price war.

Given all of the above, why would anyone ever use any other pricing method? In many cases, companies should not rock the boat if things are going well. Also, for brand extensions and derivative products, existing prices of existing products do make for solid starting points. And such a methodology is cheap and requires little senior management time.

If the outlook is not as rosy, however, then a different methodology is required. If revenues or margins are threatened, then new revenue opportunities are needed. If competitors are making inroads, perhaps they have a better price-to-benefit ratio, and customers are converting. Only by understanding customer economics, industry economics, and the segmentation that builds a demand curve can you see if more aggressive price rises might be possible in selected markets and segments, and how to go about implementing those prices in those segments.

SUMMARY

These 15 means of pricing don't cover the full gamut of options. Still, they represent a wide variety of methods, covering an equally wide range of needs. Each has its advantages and disadvantages, but should theoretically lead to a market price. In practice, however, the market price is like the "missing link" in anthropology: You can see some tendencies, but the actual prices rarely seem to conform to the theory. In one market study of a type of communications hardware called a PBX, a low-end competitor (Panasonic) actually sold for more money per telephone line for an entire year as the higher-quality, bigger-installation competitors AT&T and Northern Telecom battled for position

An absurd result in the PBX market? Perhaps—but prices sometimes demonstrate counterintuitive patterns. We believe this is usually a function either of diverse competitor goals, or of a lack of information among customers and competitors. The first factor cannot be corrected, but often customers, salespeople, and competitors can be educated.

Chapter Nine | How to Price New Services

Pricing is an important part of developing new services, just as it is for developing new products. This is so much the case, in fact, that when Whirlpool, the white-goods manufacturer, successfully overhauled its pricing in 2000, the company said it approached the project by thinking of *"prices themselves as* a product, much like a dishwasher."[1] This makes excellent sense because the process of launching a superior product is extremely similar to the process of launching a superior price and price structure in that it requires innovation and effort.[2] The price choices you make for a new service can help propel growth, lock in customers, frustrate the competition, smooth operations, and boost profit margins.

[1] *The Economist*, May 23, 2002. The italics here are added for emphasis.

[2] In the film *Austin Powers: International Man of Mystery*, the villain (Dr. Evil) contemplates various ways of terrorizing the world, but after objections from subordinates says, "Well, let's do what we always do: Steal a nuclear warhead and hold the world for ransom!" Not surprisingly, Dr. Evil fails to take over the world with this ad hoc strategy. Doing what your company has always done will not produce superior results, either.

Before continuing, let's clarify what we mean by a product versus a service, because these terms have become a little slippery. If we're being literal, a product is always a good, while a service is always an action performed on behalf of the customer. For example, the post office sells stamps as goods—therefore products in the strict sense—but it delivers mail as a service. However, the boundary between products and services has blurred to the extent that things like mail delivery are sometimes described as products. Most of the time in this chapter we'll refer to services and products as distinguishable entities. Occasionally, we might lump them together.

In the strict sense, then, pricing a new service represents a different and often more complex challenge than pricing a new product. Being intangible, services are harder to define and face a more variable set of customer demands. For example, counting units sold is more difficult with a service than with a product. To make a comparison, cars are nearly always sold by the vehicle, but online information services can be sold by a variety of measures—the minute, the Web page, or the search.[3]

Another issue is how to deal with the potentially immense variety intrinsic to services. An HMO must price its fees to handle tens of thousands of patients with a thousand different ailments over the next year. By comparison, a PC manufacturer sells only a handful of models and has no reason to care what happens to them once they're sold.

Here are some good questions to ask about pricing a new service:

- What's the underlying strategic purpose the price must support?
- What's the basic unit for charging? A minute? A task?
- What's the best price structure—one rate, or different rates for different activities?
- What message should the pricing send to customers?
- Is the price definition complete? Does it capture all the value offered?

---

[3] While carmakers do offer a variety of options, such as financing and warranties, at least the price can be anchored to the physical good. Even fleet sales and leases are priced per car rather than per ton, per wheel, or per horsepower.

- Is there a defined minimum amount of service? Can services be combined into chunks to make them more desirable to the customer? Are these chunks modular?
- How do we account for any variations in service quality?
- Are there implications for product pricing as well? Would any of our products be better marketed as services?

As services grow more complex, the effort required to successfully answer these questions is likewise growing. IBM in 2002 announced that it was shifting $1 billion of its R&D budget for the next three years away from traditional information technology and into research related to consulting and computer services. In a comment that reinforces the difficulty of pricing services, the IBM senior vice president in charge of research stated that his "organization [hadn't] worked out the details of how it will be reimbursed for work done directly for customers."[4]

STRATEGIC PURPOSE IN SETTING PRICE

Whatever the chief strategic concern for a new service or product, price should help address it. This is true no matter what that concern is—whether to achieve rapid penetration of the market, retain customers, protect margins despite uncertain costs, or reduce customer churn. In each case, the strategy should be reflected in the price.

For example, when MCI first challenged AT&T in long distance, the chief concern was gaining a competitive share of the market. Believing that lower price was the key to winning customers, MCI decided to charge by the minute, like AT&T—but unlike AT&T, defined its minutes so they were only about 57 seconds long.[5] This not only placed a burden of explanation on the AT&T sales force, but improved unadjusted minute-to-minute price comparisons in favor of MCI.

---

[4] *The Wall Street Journal*, November 20, 2002: B5. Note that had IBM been talking about launching a new line of computers, there likely would have been no uncertainty about pricing.

[5] MCI included "setup time," meaning the time before someone picks up the phone on the other end, in its minute. AT&T included only talk time. And MCI rounded up its call time, while AT&T rounded down.

An example of using price to reduce customer churn comes from the life insurance industry, which naturally enough wants to retain its customers for life. Products such as "whole life" insurance reflect this strategic goal: Prices are highest when insurance needs are greatest, as with wage earners raising young families, and lowest when those needs decline, as with retirees and customers on fixed incomes. (In fact net prices under this scheme can go so low they're negative, with the insurer paying the insured.)

Our final example comes from eBay, which needed to support an infinite number of highly diverse, often low-value transactions. The solution was to charge sellers by the transaction as well as a percentage of sales, but leave the retail price of the underlying goods to be set by auction. eBay's reward for this innovative use of price to support strategy was to grow from nothing to the status of major retailer.

DEFINING THE UNIT CHARGE

Although strategic goals might help with the broad outline of a pricing scheme, there often remain nittier, grittier issues to be addressed. One such matter is how to quantify services for billing purposes. This is known as the charging unit and can take many forms, some of which are shown in Figure 9.1.

Not all charging units will be equally beneficial for your company or situation—some will be better or worse proxies for value, costs, or sharing risk with the customer. Customers tend to be more accepting of

Charging unit	Examples
Flat rate	Billed per month, project, customer, lifetime, or year of warranty
Variable usage based on customer activity	Billed per use, minute of use, successful use, attempted use, mailing, successful sale, seat, customer mile, or visit
Variable usage based on provider activity	Billed per time (total minutes seller spends supporting a service including administration), team hours, assistance, cycle, mailing attempt, line of code, setup, employee mile, or hour on-call
User or asset	Billed per ID number, employee, recipient, IP address, building or site, or car
Share of value	Percentage of sales, share of revenues, share of awards

Figure 9.1. Some typical charging units.

charges when they see either a link to their benefits or a link to your costs and effort. Which linkage works best will depend on the standards and economics of the market. Typically, dentists charge by the delivered benefit: A dental crown is $375, regardless of how difficult that particular crown was to build or mount on the tooth. On the other hand, the meter in a taxi clicks over while sitting in traffic, regardless of the distance traveled because taxis charge by both time and distance. The apparent conclusion here is that there is less variability to teeth than there is to urban traffic patterns.

For a given industry, the charging unit is usually an enduring fixture, because changing it would require re-educating the customer. Thus, while the price per gallon of gasoline changes daily, gasoline retailers are likely to continue to use the gallon as their unit for a long time to come. However, competition can force such a change, if one or more competitors believe it would be to their advantage or if customers insist on it. For example, at one time attorneys charged only by the hour. Today, many charge by the case, or as a percentage of the award. These new charging units offer benefits to both clients and attorneys— some clients might not want to pay cash up front, and attorneys can now participate in large awards. Similarly, at one time long-distance telephone rates were set by time and distance, whereas now they vary by calling plan. The new unit scheme is better at reflecting telephone company costs. Car rental companies used to charge for mileage, but now generally charge by the day, as a way to match customer preferences.

PRICE STRUCTURE AND DIFFERENT RATES

The way you combine charging units, and set their rates, is the price structure. Almost never is there just one charging unit or just one rate. This would be simple, and some customers might appreciate it—but alas, it would rarely address all the seller's needs.[6,7]

[6] "Simple" is a word frequently used to describe prices in advertisements for cell phones, cars, high-tech products, etc. This suggests that simplicity has considerable consumer appeal. Whether or not it can represent competitive advantage is another question, however.

[7] See the seminal article by Andy Stern: "The Strategic Value of Price Structures," *Journal of Business Strategy*, Fall 1986.

Even where the service provided is uniform or identical, this rarely dictates a single price.[8] For example, although all passengers on an airplane will travel the same distance and arrive at the same time, airlines sell coach-class seats over an array of prices ranging from $170 to $1200 for the same flight from New York to Chicago. Technically, this is because as long as the demand curve slopes downward, a seller can obtain larger revenues by selling at different prices to different customers.[9] Nontechnically, we can observe that having different prices allows the airline to fill more seats and make more money: Without a $170 seat, one passenger might not fly to visit a friend in Chicago, while a $1200 seat price won't discourage another passenger from making a last-minute trip to close a sale in Chicago. As described in Chapter 4, one of a pricer's roles in life is to develop such different prices, and see that customers pay the maximum they can afford.

At a minimum, whenever you face a downward-sloping demand curve (as in the airline example, where you must sell a service at different prices or customers might drop out), it's useful to have two types of charges. The first is a fixed charge—that is, a flat fee for even a minimal level of participation—while the second is a usage charge. The classic example comes from theme parks: Originally, Disney developed a two-part tariff whereby Disney charged you to get into the park, then charged you for specific rides within the park. The more rides you went on, the more you were charged overall, even though your entrance fee stayed the same.[10]

---

[8] This applies to products also. For example, GE for many years charged different amounts for the license of some of its electric lighting patents, depending on the volume of the bulbs to be manufactured.

[9] The demand curve is a graph of what price would entice individual customers to buy a good. Each dot on a demand curve represents the number of customers who pay a given price. These points are arrayed cumulatively, highest to lowest, and generally form a downward-sloping line. The exception is for commodities: No informed user will buy a commodity for more than the standard price.

[10] Disney has since abandoned the per-ride charge.

SENDING THE CUSTOMERS THE RIGHT MESSAGE

When setting up a price structure, bear in mind the underlying business purpose, and make sure that the elements of the price structure serve this purpose. This is not always the case. For example, when introducing a new service, you typically want to encourage customers to give it a try, therefore, it's common to waive the fixed charge or offer an incentive for signing up.[11] However, what this really does is encourages people to sign up, not actually use the service.

A more effective approach might be to institute a price structure with a nonnegotiable fixed fee, from which a smaller amount is subtracted with each use. For example, an online service might charge a fixed fee of $210 per month, but subtract $10 from this fee for every day a user logs on. Companies using such a structure find that they can describe the service as *potentially* free (if users log on for every one of the 21 working days of the month), yet in practice still obtain revenues, because there will be many days when users fail to log on for one reason or another. More important, this system encourages the desired behavior of actually trying out the service.[12]

Another example of a precisely tailored structure is to vary the price by time of day. This is especially useful for limited-capacity services such as electricity, delivery services, trains, and television advertising slots. The message to the customer is clear: Use the service more during off-peak times, when there is less demand for the limited supply.[13] Naturally, each of these tariff structures will be unique to the service or product in question.

---

[11] Free trial offers abound. For a while in the late 1990s, long-distance telephone companies were mailing out $40, $60, and $80 checks to bribe residential subscribers into switching carriers.

[12] Such a structure could be highly effective in encouraging customers to do things that actually help control a company's costs. For example, HMOs find that the failure to take prescribed medications is a major contributor to illness among the elderly. In addition to other encouragements, HMOs could create a negative daily charge for every day a patient demonstrates that he or she has taken their medicine.

[13] Utilities haven't yet hit upon the idea of negative usage charges during low-load periods, but they have gone so far as to set up significant price differentials according to time of day.

In fact, if the price structure is *not* unique, then we can safely say that your company has missed an excellent opportunity to use price to its advantage. As advertising legend Patrick Thiede said when accepting the 1999 award for best European advertisement of the year, "If the picture exists, it's not a great idea."[14] By this he means that a truly great idea will be so new that existing stock photos won't be adequate. The same concept applies to pricing, as every pricing situation is different, and applying "stock" price structures won't produce outstanding results.

COMPLETING THE PRICE DEFINITION

Many kinds of charges might be necessary to fully accommodate the range of services demanded by customers. This helps limit those customer behaviors that increase costs, while doing a better job of reflecting added value where it occurs. Airlines not only charge for passengers—they charge for excess baggage, animals, special ticketing (for example, rush delivery), and alcoholic beverages. In a tribute to hard-nosed pricing, Southwest Airlines charges extra for obese travelers who need more than one seat.[15]

Even when the service or product appears straightforward, there might be important, intangible price questions associated with it. Do you have prices for warranties? For returns? How about for financing? For early payments and prepayments? For refunds, repairs, and shipping? For duplicate bills or special billing? For extraordinary customer service?

An ancillary benefit to many charge points is that it's harder for customers to compare prices (or for regulators to do so, for that matter). With many charging units, a company can modulate its pricing to reflect both customer priorities and its own cost structure. A single charging unit is like a guitar with only one string—it's hard to create an attractive composition.

[14] Remarks by Patrick Thiede, chief creative director of FCB Berlin, upon accepting the 1999 Euro-Best award.

[15] Southwest Airlines news release, June 20, 2002.

SERVICE MINIMUMS: COMBINING SERVICES INTO CHUNKS

What is the minimum set of services your company will offer its market? Obviously, a surgeon won't offer half an appendectomy. Universities require a minimum number of courses before they award a degree. Postal services don't offer to carry letters halfway—only to the final destination.[16]

This is an important point, and there is no one answer. Some service providers have been moving to offer smaller and smaller revenue services. For example, Dun & Bradstreet (now D&B) formerly set contract minimums to make it difficult to buy less than $2000 worth of credit reports. Today, anyone can buy a single credit report by using credit cards and the Internet. On the other hand, the minimum project being accepted by systems developers such as EDS and Accenture, or by high-end strategy consultants such as A.T. Kearney or McKinsey, has been steadily increasing.

In each case, the movement toward bigger or smaller minimums has been driven by a careful look at costs. For D&B, setup costs for identifying and delivering credit reports have declined through the use of information technology and the Internet. But for developers of custom systems and high-end strategy analysis, setup costs, including design and training, have increased with the growing sophistication of customer requirements. The minimum sale has therefore gotten bigger in these markets to accommodate this.

Thus we can see that you must calculate where your company's economic range lies, and set minimum purchases accordingly. If the range lies outside market requirements (that is, outside the market's price tolerance), then it might be time for some business process reengineering. For additional perspective, see Chapter 5, The Truth about Costs.

---

[16] Although billing might differ from the service. For instance the surgeon's bill might be rendered separately from that of the hospital, most universities charge by the semester, and postal services offer carriage with and without returned mail service. On the other hand, trans-Atlantic phone calls are handed off to foreign phone companies in the mid-Atlantic, but your bill just shows one charge.

Another major factor in determining the correct minimums for service offerings lies in whether or not you make your offerings *modular*. By modular, we mean that it's easy to mix and match one service or product with another, just as you can easily order different combinations of items from a restaurant menu. Modularity is especially important in cases where you require a great deal of customer self-service—for example, when offering services or products via the Web.

Modularity can also provide a way out of situations in which the rules of combining services have become too complex for customers to understand. For example, purchasing multiple magazine ads is so complex that many magazines' sales people have difficulty explaining the discounting rules to customers, or even understanding the rules themselves: duplicate coverage of target audiences among magazines, different reach and frequencies, and innumerable choices of ad position within publications, to name a few. For the same reason, automating such sales is difficult or impossible.

To create modularity, whether in magazine advertising purchases or any other market, there needs to be a logical underpinning to the price structure. More specifically, there needs to be:

- A price for every service a customer is likely to want
- Service elements that are viable on their own or that have simple rules for making useful combinations
- The ability to combine any service element with another service element, or else very simple rules for defining the combinations
- Minimum overlap among the service elements so customers do not discover that they have paid twice or more for the same part of a service

Having a realistic price for every service element is perhaps the most important requirement. At many companies, packages have become so much more important than the individual elements that meaningful prices for the elements are no longer available. In our experience, this lack of modularity makes it very difficult for product managers to confidently fashion new packages.

ACCOUNTING FOR VARIATIONS IN SERVICE QUALITY

Services are diverse to fit the diverse needs of clients.[17] This diversity means that results aren't likely to be uniformly successful, nor of uniform quality. In turn, this might result at times in significant customer dissatisfaction. How can pricing best reflect such variations in quality, so as to improve satisfaction and customers' willingness to make repeat purchases? One approach is to look at the risk of failure. If we do, we find useful questions to ask.

The first questions should be asked primarily from the customer's point of view: Just how bad can the outcome be? Do the possible bad outcomes outweigh the cost of the service? If your cable television service goes out and you're without TV for a few hours, that's not a major problem. If a surgeon is found guilty of malpractice, on the other hand, the consequences can run to many millions of dollars.

Another question is of importance both to customers and to the company offering the service: How frequently does failure occur? What constitutes "frequent" will vary according to the market, but usually the context will make this clear. Frequency not only affects customer perception, but also affects the economics of the provider, who must now mitigate or make good the customer's loss. The economic calculation should include the administrative burden on both buyer and seller.

Together these two factors—severity and frequency—form a framework for accommodating variations in quality. This framework takes the form of a matrix, as shown in Figure 9.2.

Bad outcomes, which are low in frequency and carry minor consequences (box C), are addressed most easily. A warranty is the most common cure because the economics are usually favorable and the cus-

---

[17] We suspect that services are more diverse than products in their needs and outcomes. This is difficult to demonstrate, but manufacturing has historically been oriented toward the mass production of uniform-quality goods. We recognize that actual performance might not always be uniform, but the report that a French mainframe computer manufacturer found that one out of three of its mainframes did not work—ever—is shocking. By contrast, a two-out-of-three success rate for a dating service or for advertising campaigns would be world-record breaking.

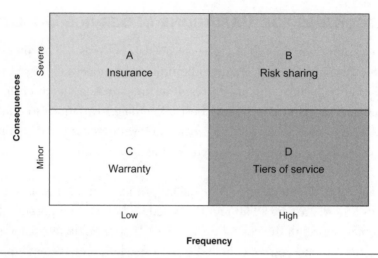

Figure 9.2. Pricing response depends on consequences and frequency of the problem.

tomer sees it as reasonable.[18] For example, if a restaurant serves an unappetizing meal and the customer complains, the meal is then free.

Bad outcomes that carry minor consequences but occur frequently (box D) are more troublesome. A warranty won't make customers feel better because of the effort they must undertake to exercise the warranty (an effort shared by your company). While it's not a bad idea to offer a warranty, nonetheless, some additional price tactics should be considered to improve the situation:

- If lower-quality transactions can be predicted in advance, create two tiers of service: higher quality and lower quality. This not only allows you to adjust price to value, but also acknowledges to customers ahead of time that the effort required on their part might be greater than usual.

- Define the unit of payment so that it reflects the lower value received by the customer. If the payment is defined as a share of

[18] See W. Earl Sasser, *Management of Service Operations* (Allyn & Bacon) for a discussion of the purposes of warranties. Professor Sasser says that not only does a warranty make customers happy, but also it aligns the organization to improve service and provides a clear measure of customer feedback.

the value created, then the customer is more prepared to believe that you gave it your best effort and that she is not being exploited. Attorneys do this with their contingency fee arrangements.

- Finally, where possible, sell the service in "chunks" that are statistically likely to include both high-quality and lower-quality outcomes. This makes each purchase more predictable, and therefore easier to price. It also ensures that the customer experiences some fraction of the best outcome. For example, many newspapers won't sell classified ads for a single issue. They require a certain multi-issue minimum, since they know from experience you're more likely to get answers to an ad (and sell what it is you're selling, or find what it is you're looking for) if the ad runs several times.

It's important to define in exact terms how failure or variance in quality can affect your customers. For example, for a firm that provides credit reports, two types of failure are possible. First, a report on a potential borrower or credit customer could be incomplete and therefore not informative. In that case, the customer has spent $45 and gotten nothing—a relatively nonsevere consequence. The second possibility, however, is that the report is wrong or out of date and mistakenly suggests a company is creditworthy when in fact the company is a credit risk. In this case, the customer stands to lose far more than the cost of the report by lending or extending credit to a poor risk—a severe consequence.

When there is potential for a severe quality problem, typically many times the price of the service, but the frequency is low—as in box A of the matrix—insurance is likely to be your best answer. Customers who are particularly concerned about the possibility of low quality or failure can be given the option to buy insurance and thus have some protection in the event that failure actually occurs. An additional benefit to you is that if customers fail to purchase insurance, they now share some of the responsibility for any potential loss. An example of this is telephone companies that offer "inside wire" insurance. The inside wires rarely fail, but many subscribers are willing to pay a small monthly fee to ensure that they never pay the more expensive repair fee. When the chances for failure are low, but the likelihood for failure is *perceived* to be high, acting as an insurer for customers can be quite lucrative.[19]

Here's an example of an inappropriate response to failure: When an airline flight is canceled, most airlines offer to refund your ticket or schedule you on a replacement flight. Yet for many of us, the inconvenience and cost of a canceled flight is greater than the ticket price— therefore we find the offer of a refund (which would have been appropriate for a box C situation) both inadequate and annoying. Insurance would be a more appropriate response in this case.

When failure will result in major consequences, and the frequency of occurrence is high—as in box B of the matrix—you've got a real problem, because such situations tend to push hard on the economics of a business. Examples of businesses that regularly deal with these nasty situations include litigation, complex and risky surgery, commercial satellite launches, and oil-field fire-fighting. Insurance tends to be unfeasible because of the frequent payout required.[20]

The best answer here is some form of risk sharing. An example is contingency fees charged by recruiters to be paid only if the candidate remains in the new job for a year or more. Another example is contingent fee pricing by attorneys. This helps focus the price discussion on the best-efforts nature of the service. Another example is a joint venture between two companies that wish to enter a new market: Neither company is confident it can enter the new market alone, and so they jointly pay for the resources required. Likewise they expect to share the rewards should the venture succeed.

Assessing and developing the right price strategy for service warranties is key not only for pricing, but also for branding. Few manage-

---

[19] Note that you don't have to be an insurance company to benefit from this. One Telco obtains a referral fee for referring call-center customers to a specialty insurer that does the actual underwriting.

[20] On the other hand, something called "liquidated damages" can be helpful. This is a legal term that means the parties involved have agreed to an amount of financial compensation if things go wrong.

ment decisions are more important to building a premium brand than the choice of how to deal with product or service failures.[21] While many companies handle their failures on an ad hoc basis, this often results in uncertainty and delay in handling customer grievances. This can be very damaging to a brand, as demonstrated by the fall in Audi sales after the supposed failure of the Audi 5000 model, and the fall in sales of Nestlé baby food formula following the debacle in developing countries.[22] The appropriate price strategy will inject certainty and speed redress, and this is the best action to preserve the brand also.

IMPLICATIONS FOR PRODUCT PRICING

Much of what we've discussed applies to the pricing of products as well as of services. Many products naturally have two-part price structures— for example, a water filtering device with both a one-time charge for the basic apparatus, and recurring charges for replacement filters. Cars represent a one-time charge, yet with recurring usage-based charges for replacement parts.

In many cases, pricing offers companies the opportunity to expand their offerings from products to services. For example, software producers are moving from the one-time sale of software to leasing it for discrete lengths of time. Similarly, the producers of light bulbs for streetlights have moved from charging for the sale and installation of discrete bulbs to flat-rate service contracts where they maintain lighting for contracted areas. This is priced without explicit reference to the number of bulbs required during the term of service. Because this encourages the contractor to use longer-lasting bulbs to keep costs down, this can be a win for municipalities as well.

Sometimes a move from product sale to service lease can be very profitable, as has proven to be the case in software. Microsoft's Windows XP, for example, comes with a license program that commits customers to purchase upgrades every two years. Although unpopular, this

---

[21] See David A. Aaker, *Managing Brand Equity* (The Free Press, New York, 1991), 176–181.

[22] Ibid.

has proven profitable because it ensures that customers will buy upgrades they wouldn't have otherwise. In addition, Microsoft charges rental fees up to 85 percent of the cost of a perpetual license.[23]

SUMMARY

Given that services are intangible and can have a wide range of outcomes, they are often more difficult to price than products. As we've seen, it pays to take the time needed to think through the price structure. Think also about how to ensure customer satisfaction despite differences in outcome. Treat price development with the same methodical care as normal product development. And don't be afraid to get creative—for example, adapting the idea of a negative-usage charge to situations where you want to encourage trial and usage, not just purchase. There's a lot of opportunity here.

[23] Professional Pricing Society, *The Pricing Advisor*, February 2003: 3. Note that most software users consider a perpetual license a purchase.

Chapter Ten | Tiering, Bundles, and Solutions

When is the value of an offer greater than the sum of its parts? How do you price a suite of products so that customers pick the most expensive one? How can you create new value by combining existing products, or products and services, and how do you then capture that value?

We've come to the third in our trilogy of chapters that address value. In Chapters 2 and 4, covering the nature of prices and segmentation respectively, we discussed value primarily in passive terms, as the embodiment of customers' needs. Now we shall consider creative ways of reshaping products and services to better serve those needs—in some cases, to serve needs customers might not yet know they have, simply because an offering that would crystallize those needs hasn't yet been presented to them. We look at three related approaches to creating such new value:

- *Tiering* presents customers with a range of quality options and explores the difference in customers' willingness to pay for a product or service. Given the context of higher and lower quality choices, customers will often switch to a higher-tier product (up-tiering), and spend more with your company.

- *Bundling* creates one-stop shopping for customers through improved overall functionality, or through making products and services simpler and easier to use. A single bill and single point of contact can contribute to customer convenience.

- *Solutions* take bundling a step further by creating greater customer value through a complete customer outcome. Examples of solutions include guaranteed improvements in the performance of the customer's business processes, such as process-yield improvements or turnkey systems. Solutions make a customer's problem go away. The vendor meanwhile uses value-based pricing to monetize the solution, increasing profits.

TIERING

The idea behind tiering is to offer customers a coherent choice of product and service options that offer progressively higher value at progressively higher prices. The tiering framework must convincingly demonstrate these differences in value, no matter how subtle or intangible they might be.

An example comes from the multi-billion-dollar funeral industry, which is in the process of refining its tiering of coffin prices. Formerly, many of the 22,000 funeral homes in the United States neglected explicit tiering of their offers. Customers were shown only a few coffins and could learn prices only by talking to morticians, who were often vague on the details. The typical coffin price ran between $2500 and $4000, with a minimum gap between tiers of $1,000—a big jump for any buyer contemplating moving up to a better coffin.

Through improved tiering, the average coffin purchase increased by more than $300 per customer. The new showrooms display 30 or more sample sections of caskets, priced in $200 to $400 increments. There are explicit price tags, and coffins are arranged from cheapest to most expensive. The developer of this new approach to coffin presentation said the advantage to the seller is that, given a clear understanding of their options, most people "want to be in the middle . . . like the Honda Accord LX."[1] At the very least, the approach provides customers with an explicit context and reference for their choice.

Tiers can be created without building a better product. For example, GE Americom offers three tiers of leases of satellite communications channels, or transponders: gold, silver, and bronze. There is no difference in the actual transponder; rather, the difference consists of the right of continued usage. If a bronze customer's transponder fails, she might be switched to another one, but only if it is available. If a gold customer's transponder fails, on the other hand, he will be assigned another transponder no matter what—even if it means displacing silver and bronze users. Naturally, gold transponders can cost more than twice as much as bronze transponders, but to many customers the price is worthwhile. The result of such tiering is that GE enjoys higher overall revenues.

Higher-price tiers can be created in most markets through better products, warranties, preferred service priority, preferred sales venues, or other means. Regardless of the mechanism, the key is to have the tiering reflect the market. Coherence is also crucial: price, offer, channel, and promotion must all go together.

A classic example of ineffective tiering was described by a well-known retail guru who visited a popular New York department store. During her visit, she discovered a display with $500 hats mixed in with $39.99 hats.[2] She characterized this as an example of incompetent tiering, for four reasons:

- The $500 hats needed to be sold, not just displayed.
- The $500 hats didn't look obviously different than the $39.99 hats, so the fashion value didn't speak for itself.
- There was no thought given to the context. Instead of being next to $39.99 hats, the expensive hats should have been among $800 handbags.

[1] "Cold Comfort: Breakthrough Product Visits Funeral Homes," *The Wall Street Journal*, January 7, 2000: A1.

[2] Comments by Ursula H. Moran, who is also author of "Managing Hybrid Market Systems," *Harvard Business Review*, November–December 1990.

■ The more expensive hats would inevitably become shop-worn because of their easy accessibility to customers' fingers and would turn into $39.99 hats in no time, relegated to a remainders bin.

Tiering requires an understanding of the brand and quality propositions. Some managers link tiering to price but are surprised to discover that the basis for tiering isn't that higher levels of service cost more. For example, a leading manufacturer of printers prices its laser printers on how many pages each can print per minute. Ironically, however, the less expensive printers actually have additional costs for certain selectively added components that slow them down.[3] Similarly, Professor Hal Varian, in his seminal article on versioning, mentions that FedEx's second-day service (significantly cheaper than its standard overnight service) arrives at the destination FedEx depot at the same time, but is simply held another day to distinguish it from standard overnight.[4]

Varian also relates a historical example of the relationship between costs and pricing in his account of French railway carriages in the nineteenth century:

It is not because of the few thousand francs which would have to be spent to put a roof over a third class [railway] carriage, or upholster the third-class seats, that [railroads have] open carriages with wooden benches. . . . What the [railway] company is trying to do is to prevent the passengers who can pay the second class fare from traveling third class; it hits the poor not because it wants to hurt them, but to frighten the rich.[5]

---

[3] All of the company's laser printers work off the same "engine," which is purchased from overseas suppliers. For its less expensive models, this company adds chips that slow down the engine. The more expensive printers have no such chips.

[4] "Pricing Information Goods," Hal R. Varian, University of Michigan, June 15, 1995. In his paper, Prof. Varian gives numerous other examples of degrading products to create versions. These include the Intel 486SX chip, which is the faster 486DX chip with the coprocessor disabled, and a financial services firm that sells access to its portfolio accounting system at $50 per month for real-time access and $8.95 for the same information delayed by 20 minutes.

[5] Dupuit (1849), ibid.

BUNDLES

Bundling is an important way to increase customers' convenience and persuade them to buy a group of related products and services. These products and services typically have a previous independent existence, and the bundling is a post hoc way of linking them, with the goal of increasing revenues or customer loyalty, or perhaps amortizing channel costs. For example, land-line telephone service has now been successfully bundled with cellular telephone service, after each was sold individually for many years.

Products and services can be linked into bundles by one of four means. We're all familiar with the first—the physical linking of products. For example, cars commonly packaged with radios is an example of two independent products that seem to go well together.[6] In this case, car manufacturers charge a premium on the radio when combining the two.

The other means for creating bundles are to link the product or service to any of the other three marketing "P's": place (that is, channel), promotion, or price. Examples of channel linkage include an airline reservations agent asking if you need a rental car after you have made an airline reservation, or the Starbucks employee who asks if you want a bagel to go along with your coffee. A sophisticated example of channel links is *Amazon.com*'s cues recommending another book based on the one you have just chosen.

Promotional links, the third of the four ways to create bundles, can consist of advertisements that suggest a set of products. For example, Bell Canada Mobility ran advertisements recommending that customers who purchased Bell Canada's Internet service also purchase call forwarding and a cell phone, so that when the land line is tied up by the computer, calls are forwarded onto the customer's cell phone. Another example of promotional links is the inclusion of samples of fabric softener inside detergent packages.

---

[6] For more than 40 years the two did not go well together, until a new company called Motorola came up with the way to isolate the radio from the car's electrical interference.

Here's a powerful example of bundling from the financial services arena: Early financial bundles included links between previously separate savings and checking accounts. Later, credit cards were linked through promotions and channels to checking accounts. Next, the Merrill Lynch CMA® (cash management account) brought together these services *plus brokerage*. This bundle was a huge success, seizing more than $300 billion in banks' business over time. Belated efforts to match this bundle by banks and others have not made much headway. Today, Merrill Lynch is trumpeting its WCMA® (includes working cash and online business banking), and its RCMA®, which helps manage the assets of a retirement plan.

In retrospect, the CMA might appear to be a logical extension of previous bundling, one with obvious appeal. But in fact when Merrill's then-CEO Donald Regan pursued this strategy, it was a bold move. The CMA offered Merrill modest cost savings, but cost a great deal to create, therefore Merrill needed to recoup these extra costs through a big increase in volume.

This is true for many bundles: The up-front costs are such that the bundle will be profitable only if commensurate with a significant increase in volume. The risk of not achieving this volume is greater the longer market followers wait after the bundling leader acts. And the risk to followers is greater still if the bundling leader is also the market-share leader, because the followers might not be able to convey an equal degree of legitimacy for their bundles. For other bundles the operational savings of the bundle itself will rapidly pay for the up-front costs—for example, offering customers a credit card along with your product can often reduce billing costs by encouraging customers to pay through automatic credit card charges instead of waiting for a paper bill.

Price is the fourth and last way to link two products into a bundle— and such is its power that the strongest bundles typically rely on price in addition to one of the other "P" elements. In many situations, customers expect a bundle discount. Their rationale is that because bundles often result in savings to companies, they expect to share in these savings. In consumer goods, bundle discounts can run from 5 to 45 percent off the sum of the parts. However, in cases where the savings on a bundle are difficult for consumers to calculate, companies have offered negligible or even negative savings. Customers sometimes wise up to the fact they're getting charged more for a bundle than the combined price of the individual services, and when they do, both trust and brand are badly damaged.

TIERING AND BUNDLING TOGETHER

Tiering and bundling can work well together. In the specialized world of structured finance, for example, tiering creates huge value. Structured finance starts with the acquisition of many low-quality debt obligations or bonds. Individually, each obligation is high-risk, and so poorly rated. However, based on the total income stream from many bonds, a fairly secure income stream can be obtained. (While any one bond might default, it's unlikely that all will default.) Thus the formerly low-rated bonds can be repackaged as a set of AA-rated bonds, some intermediate bonds, and finally some very insecure bonds that pay only after the higher-rated bonds have been paid out.[7] The key here is that the value of the repackaged obligations is higher than the cost of obtaining the many low-quality obligations. The restructured whole is more than the sum of its parts. The value created is purely a function of tiering and bundling.

To be more explicit, the source of the value is that the risk profile of the resulting structure is a better match for market demand. A similar process of retiering and rebundling to redistribute risk can be found in arenas besides high finance. Auction houses such as Sotheby's, for example, take estates and retier and rebundle the estate pieces for resale. Similarly, Health Maintenance Organizations take groups of doctors offering medical services and bundle them into HMO provider groups. They also tier the service based not on the quality of the doctors, but on the type of membership. This has proven very profitable in some cases.

---

[7] The nickname for these obligations on Wall Street is "toxic waste" after the residual fuel from nuclear power plants. Even so, there are customers for such obligations.

SOLUTIONS

Many business-to-business vendors today have taken one step beyond bundling: They are defining and delivering complete *customer solutions*, with the goal of creating even greater value for the customer and increased profits once this value is monetized. While we acknowledge that solutions is an overused term, in this book the term "solutions" refers to an expanded offer that:

- Addresses the total cost of ownership for the customer and optimizes the performance of the customer's overall business process.
- Focuses on the desired customer outcome, rather than on functional characteristics of the product or service.
- Is structured in such a way that the vendor assumes and manages the risk related to guaranteeing performance. Typically this leads to a tiered pricing structure with both usage fees and performance-based fees.

An example of a solution is Johnson Controls. Traditionally a supplier of systems integration services and HVAC management, it now offers facilities management solutions.[8] Customers want efficient and secure facilities, but often lack the skills and expertise to achieve them. Johnson Controls offers its customers HVAC, fire safety, security access, and closed-circuit TV. Customers that sign on reduce their operations costs, improve productivity and the bottom line, and do it all while staying focused on their core business. In 2002, services and solutions represented 65 percent of Johnson Controls' revenues from controls.

Similarly, EDS' introduction of its mobile connected office (MCO) underscores the value of integrating hardware, software, and process components into an operational end-to-end business solution. IBM offers a supercomputing on-demand solution.[9] The idea is that clients

---

[8] "Johnson Controls 2003 Outlook Presentation—Final," *Fair Disclosure Wire*, October 9, 2002.

[9] IBM press release, January 9, 2003.

are more interested in getting timely results rather than where the computing platform is located. Thus, IBM's networked computers are located in data centers around the globe. Clients have the option of buying computing power on demand. So they get the power they need during particularly busy business cycles such as when new products are being developed. IBM takes on part of its customers' risks, guarantees availability and processing power, and offers flexible pricing packages based on customers' usage, power, and transactions.[10]

CREATING A SOLUTION

Defining, developing, and—most important—managing a customer solution requires you to assume significant operational risk. Naturally, you expect to be compensated for this increased risk through premium pricing and improved profit margins.

Value is won through reductions in the cost of the customer's business processes, increased revenues, and improved customer satisfaction. The price for the solution is a share of this total value.

A simple approach, in concept. Begin to implement it, however, and you immediately confront a number of fundamental questions:

■ Some sources of value are more difficult than others to quantify. Will the customer agree with your definition of all the sources of value?

■ What is a fair split of the overall value between the supplier and customer, and what is the maximum price the customer is willing to pay?

■ The value of the solution can differ substantially by customer segment and individual customers. How can these differences be accounted for to optimize pricing?

■ What pricing structure will enable you to share the upside potential while monetizing the value of the solution in an optimal way?

[10] Bob Parker and Dana Stiffler. "IBM Global Financing: The Engine of On Demand," *AMR Alert,* January 22, 2003

A four-step methodology addresses these questions and provides an effective value-based pricing strategy. The first step is to define value ceiling parameters—in other words, decide what customers will gain through the solution. Step two is to refine value parameters for customer segments, that is, decide how to measure the value so that the customer is persuaded. Step three is to determine an equitable value split—how much can we get? And step four is to use pricing structure to capture value.

APPLYING SOLUTIONS PRICING IN HIGH TECH

One high-tech company developed an advanced call-center solution, and then used a thorough solutions pricing approach to extract the most value from its innovation.

This high-tech company, based on the East Coast, developed an automated call-center solution that featured advanced speech recognition, a natural customer interface, caller-intentions recognition, and the ability to automate more calling. It was far better than any existing products on the market. The challenge: how to price the solution.

Determine the ceiling price. The first step was to determine the absolute total value being created, because this establishes a ceiling (maximum) amount that could be charged for its product. To do this the company quantified all potential sources of value—in other words, it had to determine how the solution would help clients cut costs, increase revenue, and improve customer satisfaction. The analysis showed that the call-center product would significantly reduce labor, which typically represents from 70 to 80 percent of all center operations. Other benefits followed from reducing labor, because fewer staff meant reduced facilities costs, technology costs, and management overhead. These items made up the other 20 to 30 percent of costs, but were not a primary source of recognized cost saving because they do not always immediately follow headcount reductions.

Create customer segments. The potential for value creation varies from customer to customer, and on a more macro basis, from customer segment to customer segment. The high-tech company found four distinct customer segments for its call-center product. The basis for the segmentation was customer technological sophistication, current level of call automation, how pressing the need was for incremental automation, time to realize value, and propensity to purchase bundled offers versus integrating individual best-of-breed solutions. The company then developed a business case to illustrate the value creation potential. For a health-care customer, the product would reduce 40 to 46 percent of its call-center operation costs.

Determine an equitable value split. The high-tech company assessed the features and functions of key competitor offerings and quantified their potential for creating value. Based on the analysis, the company found that competitive alternatives allowed customers to achieve—at best—a 35-percent ROI. On the other hand, the company's solution would create roughly 50 percent more value for customers. The high-tech company, therefore, was able to establish its own value split, going a step above competitors—allowing customers to realize a one-year payback and 35- to 45-percent ROI.

Use pricing structure to capture value. The company then developed a pricing structure to help capture and monetize the value of the call-center product. It chose a three-element pricing structure: a somewhat smaller up-front fee than the industry norm, a monthly usage fee based on number of calls, and a gain-sharing quarterly fee based on the number of future automated calls. For a large call center, the cost savings could approach $50 million, and the company would command a superior profit margin.

Some additional comments on steps three and four: When it comes to deciding how to split the value between you and the customer, there are two major considerations: the customer's purchasing criteria, and the incremental value of the solution over the customer's next best alternative. In most cases, customers have well-defined capital investment rules that govern their purchasing or investment decisions. Knowing these rules is essential for determining a range of acceptable value splits, and consequently, a price range acceptable to the customer. This information can often be obtained by examining customers' historical investment decisions and conducting carefully designed interviews. As for step four, a good pricing structure should reinforce the notion that payment is linked to performance and that the customer pays only for the incremental value delivered by the solution.

Chapter Eleven | Turning Value into Money

Recently the minister at one of our local churches asked her congregation for donations.[1] She explained the forthrightness of her request by recalling that back when she was still newly ordained, she believed that if a church did good deeds, then donations would naturally follow. As a senior minister, however, she came to realize that good intentions weren't enough. Hence she had developed a stewardship program to actively solicit donations from parishioners, in addition to her frequent direct appeals.

Similar to a good church, your company probably has a plan to deliver the superior value your customers want. Yet like the minister in our story, you might be surprised to learn that serving your customers well doesn't necessarily produce cash. A monetization strategy is how a company intends to use pricing strategy and related tools to extract cash from customers. The minister in Wilton had developed an effective monetization strategy. Can you as a senior executive say the same about your company?

[1] The Wilton Congregational Church, Wilton, Connecticut.

Distinguishing monetization from value creation is important because value alone is neither as liquid nor as stable as cash. It can't meet payroll, pay for a new factory, or pay dividends. Only money does this. Once we understand value in this light, we can focus on the alchemy of transforming into cash not only superior value, but such related intangibles as customer loyalty and favorable market position.

There are several means of achieving monetization. We'll start our discussion with those most commonly used, after which we'll turn to a conceptual approach we prefer. Our approach not only supports an integrated monetization strategy, but places its development properly in the hands of top management.

THE CONVENTIONAL APPROACH: LAST-MINUTE MONETIZATION

Most P&L managers think about monetization only on an ad hoc basis, typically at the end of a quarter when results have lagged expectations. It should come as no surprise that the tools resorted to in such haste are those requiring little advance notice—namely, manipulating financial reports and accelerating billing and collections. With a slightly more distant time horizon, a manager might dig a little deeper in the tool chest and emerge with something along the lines of tactical pricing (for example, discounts given out to new customers) or general price rises.

These at-the-ready tools can produce good results, but they can also have significant downsides when done to excess. For example, raising prices too high is detrimental to any business. In some industries, the negative results are so immediately obvious that management doesn't play this game.[2] But in other industries the damage lags the benefits, allowing management to travel a long way on the road to ruin before anyone notices. For example, a leading publisher of professional materials knew from experience that while its subscription lists were

---

[2] In industries with low switching costs and high transparency, erosion is rapid. For instance, in the airport car rental market, Hertz can see erosion of share within 24 hours of being 5 percent higher than Avis. This market does not allow even brief over-pricing.

highly price-elastic, subscription cancellations lagged price increases by 18 months. Hence a price rise allowed management increased revenues for the fiscal year even if, in the longer run, market share declined steadily.

Similarly, getting overly tough on sales discounting might not be a good way of boosting revenues. Only if the discounting system is out of control, offering a discount where none is needed, will stricter discounting be beneficial. A better means to increase cash is an intelligent discounting plan. Sales discounting is not a sign of a "spineless sales force," as was suggested by the CEO of a Fortune 100 corporation during a bad quarter with heavy discounting. Discounting serves a perfectly valid purpose: It adjusts for the differences in price sensitivity among accounts.

Being overly conservative on discounts in a competitive market will result in share loss as price-sensitive segments look to alternatives. In one information services market, inadequate discounting to smaller companies resulted in stagnant growth in that segment. After the right discounting criteria were established, growth increased to 6 percent and net margins grew. This was getting smarter, not tougher.

The other common short-term tactics of accelerated billing and collections, and changes in financial reporting practices, are irrelevant to a sound monetization strategy, and so not discussed here.

A SUPERIOR APPROACH: USING THE LAUNCH CYCLE TO DISCOVER MONETIZATION OPPORTUNITIES

It's true that revenue and profit shortfalls sometimes come as surprises. In such cases, P&L management is completely justified in pursuing short-term measures. But in many other cases, management knows at the beginning of the year that achieving goals through conventional, value-oriented measures will be a big stretch. Suppose you know this upcoming year will be a tough one for the company—what are your options?

Our preferred means of envisioning the monetization choices available to top management is simple—the service or product launch cycle, displayed in Figure 11.1. The salient idea here is that opportunities for monetization naturally occur throughout the cycle, if only we think to take advantage of them.

Let's now examine the most crucial steps of the launch cycle as far as pricing is concerned, in order to diagnose the corresponding opportunities.

What Product or Service Will Produce the Most Cash?

At the very beginning of the cycle, the left-hand side of Figure 11.1, we have the decision of what service or product will produce the most cash. Some services and enhancements will be easier to monetize than others. For example, the electronics superstores Best Buy and Circuit City make virtually no profit selling the thousands of products on their shelves (although they do try). Instead, they make all their profits—and

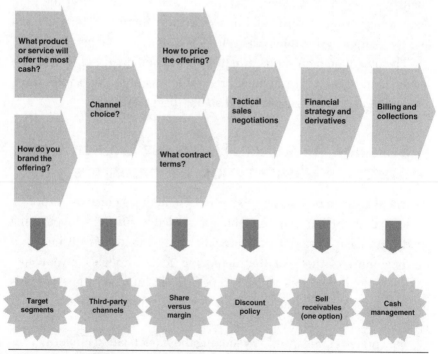

Figure 11.1. Management monetization opportunities.

more, to cover losses in retail operations—from selling extended service warranties. This probably isn't how their customers see the utility of the superstores, but it is a profitable monetization strategy just the same. Similarly, at least two major airlines make their money from ancillary activities, such as ticketing systems and the sale and purchase of aircraft, rather than from selling seats to passengers.[3]

Often, the issue of monetization arises when companies are considering adding a new feature, ancillary product, or service to their existing offers. What additional cash will it raise? Such a decision might be supported by tools such as conjoint analysis, but often, it's a matter of judgment and negotiation. This is especially true when the incremental offer is inseparable from the main product. An example is the computer-generated yellow first-down line used in network broadcasts of the National Football League. How much is such an enhancement to the television coverage worth? The value created is the incremental enjoyment of viewers who appreciate this visual marker, but that doesn't begin to tell the story of how dollars came to be ascribed to the yellow line.

If the networks had developed the yellow-line software, we suspect they would have accounted for it on the basis of its costs amortized over a season of use. Perhaps they might have estimated value by the incremental viewership ascribed to the enhancement, if that were possible. Either way, the dollars assigned would have been low. But as it happened, the software was developed by an independent company that negotiated hard with the networks to obtain more than $2 million per year. This number was clearly shaped by the monopoly on NFL football, and the oligopolistic competition for network sports broadcasting in the United States. Networks saw the program as a factor to winning the highest audience share, and hence assigned a high value to it. Thus we see that monetization of value depends not merely on the product, but on who owns it, to whom it's sold, and how it's priced.

---

[3] It's not easy to make money in passenger air transport. More than 130 carriers have filed for Chapter 11 since the industry's deregulation in 1978. Industry cash flows are billions negative.

Similarly, Procter & Gamble's recent decision to sell some of its manufacturing know-how resulted in instant monetization. Previously, P&G kept its formidable production capabilities a closely held secret. However, P&G apparently decided it had more to gain through monetization of those capabilities than from retaining their exclusive use. Hence it now offers consulting services to other manufacturers that want to learn from P&G.

How Do You Brand the Offer?

Segmentation, which is inherent in product choice, brand, and channel, is always a monetization choice for products and services. Even if you offer only one product or service and one market, don't ignore monetization. Any market of significant size has multiple segments that vary dramatically in their ability to generate cash—put simply, some customers will part with cash more easily than others. If your segments don't show this sort of distinction, you have the wrong segmentation.[4]

Choice of brand is a powerful monetization tool. On occasion, automobile manufacturers have chosen to monetize their brands. One means of doing so is to offer a less desirable car under a more prestigious nameplate. Examples include Cadillac's decision to offer the Cadillac Cimarron, a car with the same engine and body shell as the Chevrolet Cavalier. Another is Infiniti's decision to offer a spruced-up version of the Nissan Altima. Both offers generated profits because the cars commanded more money than the car platform alone would have suggested. However, some observers suggest that the Cimarron offer might actually have damaged the Cadillac brand and long-term corporate value. This is an example of the trade-offs that must be considered by management when thinking about monetizing brand.

Channel Choice?

Although channel choices represent clear monetization options, they are rarely considered to the fullest degree possible. Third-party distribution

[4] Frank, Massey and Wind, *Economic Principles of Market Segmentation* (Prentice-Hall 1972).

sometimes allows monetization, albeit with implications that go beyond monetization. For example, selling prepaid telephone cards offers cash to telephone companies months in advance of when it would be accrued by normal telephone calling cards. Often, the savings in direct channel costs exceeds the discounts required to allow third-party distribution, which adds to the monetization appeal. Other examples of the opportunity for accelerated cash through channel choice are the collection of franchise fees or the decision to sell wholesale only.

What Contract Terms?

Contract terms also offer significant potential for monetization. In the mid-1980s, for example, IBM decided to convert its business model from leased base to direct sales and customer ownership. The result was an explosion of earnings as long-term leases were converted to immediate cash payments. It was also a good decision in light of the upcoming free fall of dollars per MIPS, because it prevented IBM from being shackled with old technology. In the course of this migration, the stock market rewarded IBM shareholders with huge gains over three years.

The choice of offering customers shorter- or longer-term contracts can also dramatically improve monetization. Which is better depends on your view of the future, as well as your customers' view of the same.

Moving customers to longer-term contacts can preserve margins and cash in a period of falling volume or decreasing market prices. For instance, due to some strategic missteps by Lexis in the mid 1990s, senior managers in 1998 realized that their core user set (that is, recently graduated law students) would overwhelmingly choose their competitor's product. To forestall massive erosion, Lexis initiated the "Lock and Block" program, which locked customers into multiyear contracts for discounts that were far less than expected share loss. Because user preference did in fact fall as severely as had been forecast, the Lock and Block program served to stabilize and monetize Lexis's value before the fall in user preference.

Longer-term contracts can also offer other advantages. With a predictable cash flow from a stable customer base, various financial plays become feasible. One of these is the selling of receivables—a popular choice among many consumer companies and financial services providers. Selling of receivables is often pursued for motives related to financing and collections, but it has the additional benefit of promoting monetization.

This leads us to another fruitful subject. Selling receivables, including future receivables, is a form of what financial markets call derivatives. A derivatives strategy is often a good tool for monetization.[5] Such a strategy can stabilize the value of your assets, either desirable in its own right or useful as a means for borrowing money against cash flows. Even more directly, the derivatives themselves can be sold for cash.

A good example of how derivatives stabilize value comes from the pooling of shares. If you hold a disproportionate amount of your wealth in one company's shares (for example, the family business) and wish to diversify, you can trade those shares for shares in a pool of shares from people in similar positions. Because there are several hundred different stocks in these pools, investors are trading in a single stock for a broad portfolio. The broader portfolio is generally more stable than the individual stocks, and this stability is a step closer to monetization.[6]

Derivatives needn't be built on financial instruments—they can also be based on the products you sell, or on the cash flows you generate. The electric utility industry has provided significant examples of creating derivatives based on their own products to achieve monetization. As one example, Georgia Power profits from derivative sales to its customers.[7] Customers can buy energy from the power company

---

[5] A derivative is a financial contract with no physical product delivery associated with it. The most common type is a "fixed for floating swap." In this case one side of the swap is assured steady cash flows; the other is making a bet that prices will increase. In almost all cases, however, the derivative's initial value is related to the expected cash flows from the original asset, and when actual results vary from expectations, then the purchasers of the derivative will either make or lose money.

[6] "A Tax Break for the Rich Who Can Keep a Secret," *The New York Times*, September 10, 2002: C1.

[7] A. Faruqui and Kelly Eakin, ed., *Pricing In Competitive Electricity Markets* (Kluwer Academic Publishers, 2000), 298–305.

according to market rates (spot rates), or buy it in advance via forward contracts. Going one step further, Georgia Power also allows its customers to sell back forward contracts, thereby creating a liquid market.

What are the benefits to Georgia Power in developing such derivatives? The company is monetizing future use. (It could also do this with prepaid subscriptions, but it isn't clear whether or not customers would be interested in purchasing subscriptions.) The derivatives shift the risk of fluctuations in price and demand to the power company's customers, who don't mind the risk because they're in a better position to control their own electricity demand. In addition, it appears that many customers are able to make money on the trading of the futures and so are happy to support this form of monetization.

Financial Strategy

By now you might have concluded that monetization has many of the attributes of financial strategy. This is correct. A business can make decisions on how and when to monetize its value in the same way it might decide whether to build up or liquidate an asset, or capitalize an expenditure, or undertake a capital improvement project versus experience the increased cost of older equipment. Yet this is not CFO turf. Although a CFO should take an interest in these decisions, rarely will he or she be in a position to comment on brand, channels, and other essential factors in monetization strategy. This is pricing turf.[8]

The path from corporate business plan to value creation, and from value creation to monetization, can be traced along two dimensions: liquidity on the one hand, and stability of value on the other—that is, risk. At the end of the trail lies cash, which is by definition perfectly liquid and generally regarded as risk-free, inflation and crime aside.

Low liquidity and low stability of value—represented by the bottom left corner of Figure 11.2—are both present when a company first builds and offers a product or service. It isn't clear that anyone will buy the product, nor is it clear that the product will retain whatever value it

---

[8] In some cases, the chief pricer will be the CEO.

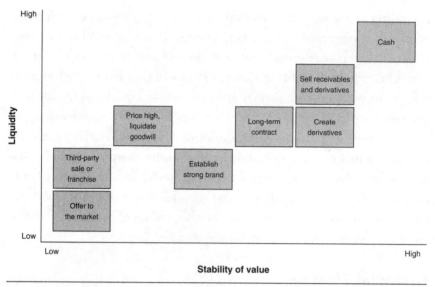

Figure 11.2. Stages of monetization.

might possess at the moment of its birth. How then should management choose to monetize this potential new asset?

One choice is to immediately liquidate the product. For example, the company could turn its inventory over to a third-party distributor, which, depending on the terms, might either pay cash or else take the product on consignment and sell it through its distribution channels. Another choice would be to enhance the perceived value of the good or service, perhaps by building up the offer's brand equity. This helps stabilize the value of the good or service. If management believes that investing in brand through advertising, offering generous value for the price, or other brand-building activities will result in a long-lasting price premium, then this might be a prudent decision.[9]

Another example of forgoing cash to build value is in the realm of initial public offerings, or IPOs. With some exceptions, companies

---

[9] An example is soap. Liquidators such as Dollar Tree Stores often sell off-brand soaps such as Lifebuoy (which has long since lost its brand strength) for a dime a bar. The reason you don't see Ivory or Neutrogena in these outlets is because their brand strength allows those manufacturers more profitable ways to clear excess inventory.

offering stock will underprice the initial stock offer relative to the expected market value. This results in a first-day or initial run-up of the stock relative to its issue price. Such run-ups can range from nil to 100 percent or more. The purpose of selling something below its ultimate price is a belief by issuing firms that the momentum thereby achieved will help the price in the long term by making for contented shareholders and happy underwriters. Often, the price of the IPO shares isn't of primary interest to issuers—rather, the price being maximized is the ultimate price of those shares not sold during the IPO. Some companies and commentators doubt that such a tactic actually does increase the ultimate value, but many do believe it, and this belief explains many IPO prices.[10]

Although in a cash society the natural tendency is to want to monetize value more or less immediately, there are many reasons to invest as part of a longer-term plan to build a greater ultimate value. Activities such as creating a better service or product through R&D or creating customer loyalty through strong channels or branding might not create immediate liquidity, yet in the long run they obviously can be worthwhile. This is why monetization should be looked upon as having two dimensions: liquidity on the one hand, and long-run stability of value on the other.

By asking how a business unit will achieve the evolution from value to cash well in advance of year-end, you can consider the options for monetization while you still have time to act. This reduces the likelihood of monetization choices that destroy shareholder value.

WHO OWNS MONETIZATION?

We have seen how the product or service launch cycle yields multiple opportunities for monetization. Some of these means can be easily monitored by a corporate headquarters, but some—including such powerful

---

[10] For instance, a leading retailer priced its 1999 stock offering exactly at the market, resulting in no run-up. R. Brealey and S. Myers, in *Principles of Corporate Finance* (McGraw-Hill, 1981), comment on page 298 (with sarcasm) about the desire to sell shares below their market value.

options as brand, channel, and contract choices—can be implemented by operating divisions well under the radar screen of corporate monitoring. Thus a company that has spent hundreds of millions of dollars to build a brand might be dismayed to discover that this very same brand has been damaged in order to meet a budgetary shortfall. The danger is all the more real in that there are generally few checks or deterrents to restrain line management from meddling in monetization where it shouldn't.[11]

For this reason alone, you as a top manager should demand an explicit plan for your company's monetization strategy. Monetization can be done wisely, or it can be done with a shortsightedness that destroys customer loyalty, brand value, channel integrity, and possibly the business model as well. Beyond simply avoiding catastrophe, another reason to get involved is the skill set: Monetization requires pricing skills that are a cross between marketing and finance and are a worthy focus for top management's efforts.

---

[11] Two measures that can detect the overly aggressive liquidation of value and brand are customer retention data and market share. With a lag of one to two years, the wrong monetization program will manifest itself as higher customer churn as customers realize they have been sold an empty promise. Similarly, market share is another measure, because squandering value for disproportionate monetization will generally deteriorate share over time.

Chapter Twelve | # Special Considerations: Lawyers and Other People's Money

I n this chapter, we discuss two wrinkles that offer unusual pricing opportunities. These special considerations fall outside the framework assumed in our other chapters—that is, pricing opportunities focused on competitors, brand, and creating value for customers.

First we provide an overview of the legal issues associated with pricing in the United States—more pungently, we give you the ability to talk back to overly cautious counsel. And second, we look at pricing situations in which the purchaser of a good or service doesn't own the money that's being spent—in other words, the use of other people's money.

LEGAL CONSTRAINTS ON PRICING

For those who have been thwarted by conservative legal counsels, this section should provide you with the ammunition to argue for (and implement) more aggressive pricing practices. As a preview of the main discussion points, Figure 12.1 sets out a list of common concerns that counsel might have for not pushing pricing practices to the legal limit,

What your lawyer may argue	Suggested rebuttal
Price discrimination is illegal	Not really. There are so many loopholes that it is not clear what is *not* allowed. For example, price discrimination is legal when: ■ Market conditions fluctuate over time ■ Selling services ■ Goods are not identical (highly differentiated or customized) ■ Practiced among noncompeting customers ■ It occurs between end consumers ■ It reflects differences in cost of serving different customers ■ Selling deteriorating perishables, obsolete seasonal goods, and other goods whose markets are subject to fluctuation ■ Used to meet the more favorable price of a competitor ■ The same preferential price is offered to all customers
Promotional discrimination is illegal	Not really. As with price discrimination, there are loopholes: selling services, practicing promotional discrimination among noncompeting customers, and offering the same promotion to all customers on proportionally equal terms.
Price fixing agreements with our competitors is illegal	True. But, we may be able to accomplish similar results through other means, such as information exchanges with our competitors in trade associations.
Practices facilitating tacit collusion and price signaling are legally risky	Not necessarily. Tactics such as matching competitors' prices, most-favored-nation clauses, meeting-competition clauses, and advance notices of price changes are not easily observable and not necessarily illegal. They are mostly risky in highly concentrated industries such as airlines.
Predatory pricing is illegal	True. But, it is very difficult to distinguish from healthy price competition, and so, difficult to prove. Predatory pricing can help eliminate weaker competitors.
Resale price maintenance (RPM) is illegal	True, in theory. In practice, RPM is okay if there is no explicit contract between you and your retailers. It's also okay to provide financial incentives to encourage retailers to maintain a minimum suggested price.
Exclusive territories are illegal	It depends. Companies in several industries have successfully argued their pro-competitive aspects, including automotive sales and service, beer, fast food, and soft drinks.
Exclusive dealing is illegal	It depends. It's okay if competitors have reasonable access to the market through other distribution or retail channels. You can also provide financial incentives to discourage distributors from carrying competing brands.
Tie-in sales are illegal	It depends. There is no legal issue if the market power of the tying product is not high enough to restrain trade in the tied product. It's also a defensible strategy if tied products function better when sold as a package.
Transfer pricing laws do not allow much flexibility to avoid taxes	False. For example, by setting up subsidiaries in low-tax jurisdictions to hold intagible assets, companies can reduce their tax liabilities.

Figure 12.1. Top 10 arguments lawyers make and suggested rebuttals.

as well as our suggested rebuttals to those arguments.[1] We hope that by the end of this section, you'll be primed on the relevant laws and have a roadmap for working within these laws to your advantage.

[1] Neither this table nor the remainder of the section is meant to provide definitive legal analysis or advice. The law and its interpretation are inherently dynamic and therefore subject to change.

Price Discrimination

As discussed in Chapter 4 on segmentation, setting different prices on the same product to different groups of customers is more profitable than selling to all at a uniform price.[2] Although price discrimination has been the object of much legislation, the law is nonetheless subject to numerous qualifications, exceptions, and defenses. The total effect is to permit price discrimination in all but a few, well-defined circumstances. If you understand these exceptions, you'll more than likely be able to price discriminate as needed to optimize profits. Let's look at each exception in turn. We phrase them in the positive, rather than the negative.

Price discrimination in services is perfectly legal. The laws on price discrimination only apply to bundled goods and services when the value of the goods in the bundle dominates. If you sell a mix of goods and services (or only goods), the implication is to create bundled offerings in which the value of the services component prevails (for example, information technology where the value of ongoing maintenance services can be significant).

Price discrimination is okay when products are not the same. If you routinely tailor your products to particular customer groups, it's difficult to be attacked on legal grounds. More fundamentally, if you currently sell relatively undifferentiated goods, you can escape legal scrutiny by customizing your products or adding ancillary services.

Price discrimination is allowable if it doesn't cause "competitive injury." The most common type of competitive injury results when your discriminatory pricing inflicts harm on your customers. However, for the discrimination to be illegal, the two customers must

---

[2] Much of the discussion in this and the next section is based on Donald S. Clark, "The Robinson-Patman Act: Annual Update," in a speech before the Robinson-Patman Act Committee Section of Anti-Trust Law, Forty-Sixth Annual Spring Meeting, Washington, D.C., April 2, 1998, and other Federal Trade Commission documents on the Robinson-Patman Act, notably Guides for Advertising Allowances and Other Merchandising Payments and Services, 16 CFR 240.1 (also known as the Fred Meyer Guides).

themselves be competitors. In other words, it is perfectly acceptable to price-discriminate between customers that don't compete with each other, for example those in different geographic areas. Even more fundamentally, you're not prohibited from price-discriminating to individual end consumers because these consumers don't compete with one another. Hence, if you're a retailer selling to the general public, you're exempt from the laws on price discrimination.[3]

Price discrimination is permissible if it reflects differences in costs. In other words, quantity discounts are perfectly legal if they reflect differences in the cost of manufacture, sale, or delivery to two customers. In addition, two goods that are functionally identical (for example, a branded and generic pharmaceutical product) can still be sold by the same manufacturer at different prices, because the two products typically have different sales and marketing costs. You should be prepared to show through fairly rigorous customer-level accounting that the price differential doesn't exceed the cost differential.

Price discrimination is allowable if it compensates customers for particular functions they perform on your behalf. For example, if one of your customers performs sales and marketing functions for you, it is acceptable to reward that customer with a lower price. Again, you should be prepared to demonstrate that the discount is linked with either your costs or your customer's costs.

Price discrimination over time is acceptable, particularly in markets that are highly volatile. For example, many agricultural products are subject to the vagaries of climate. Selling the same commodity at two different prices before and after a major drought would be permissible.

Price discrimination is perfectly legal on perishable and seasonal products. In addition, goods sold through bankruptcy proceedings or "going out of business sales" are included in this category.

---

[3] Of course, retail price discrimination is limited by other factors, such as the extent to which resale opportunities between high- and low-priced markets can profitably be exploited, the retailer's market power and ability to identify distinct customer segments, and its public relations strategy.

Price discrimination is okay if it's necessary to meet a competitor's price. Acceptable ways of meeting your competition include territorial price differences, introductory discounted prices for new customers, loyalty discounted prices for established customers, and matching a rival's bid in an auction or request for proposal process, even if you don't know the rival's exact bid.

Price discrimination is allowable if the lower price was available to all buyers. In other words, you can't be sued for price discrimination if your customers failed to take advantage of a favorable price that you made available to all.

At the end of this long list of exceptions to the laws on price discrimination, you might wonder what is *not allowed*. To answer that question, you should consult your legal counsel. However, the message is pretty clear: More often than not, price discrimination is perfectly legal, and you should encourage legal counsel to take full advantage of the exceptions.

Promotional Discrimination

Because price and promotional discrimination can be used interchangeably to achieve the same result—differentiation in the net prices paid by different customers—promotional discrimination is also prohibited. However, as with price discrimination, there are many qualifications to the law.

Promotional discrimination occurs when you as a manufacturer provide different incentives to different customers to promote the *resale* of your product to final consumers. Such incentives could come, for example, through cooperative advertising, product demonstrations, catalogs, displays, prizes and contests, and special packaging.[4]

While there are many similarities with the law on price discrimination (for example, promotional discrimination in services is perfectly legal), there are also three important differences. Two of these make

---

[4] Promotional discrimination excludes the price concessions that you provide to motivate your customers (the resellers) to buy your product in the first place. These concessions are covered under the price discrimination laws.

promotional discrimination more legally risky than price discrimination, while the other makes it less risky. The choice between price and promotional discrimination (or some elements of both) will therefore depend on your particular situation.

The definition of "competing customer" is more expansive in the law on promotional discrimination, reducing your flexibility to discriminate among customers. Promotional discrimination is prohibited not only when you are selling to competing customers one level down in the value chain (that is, direct buying retailers), but also when you are *indirectly* selling to competing customers two levels down in the value chain (that is, competing retailers buying through wholesalers). You must provide promotions to all resellers of your product, even those that buy through intermediaries.

There are fewer legal defenses to allegations of promotional discrimination. The only defense against promotional discrimination is the meeting-competition clause.

The requirement that discriminatory policies be "available" to all competing customers allows more flexibility under promotional discrimination. Specifically, you are required to make promotional services and allowances available to all competing customers on *proportionally equal terms*, a requirement that gives you significant latitude to achieve effective promotional discrimination.

For example, you can give greater promotional discounts to larger customers, to customers that spend more on promoting your products (for example, national versus local advertising), and to customers that engage in activities that are relatively more valuable to you (for example, a sales force dedicated exclusively to your brand rather than one that serves multiple firms).

Price-Fixing among Direct Competitors

Often companies would like to soften price competition with their closest competitors. As you probably already know, however, explicitly agreeing with competitors to fix prices or cooperating to reduce competition and output is illegal.

Mergers are a less direct method to improve pricing. As described in Chapter 2, by reducing the number of competitors, you have the potential to raise prices. So mergers are worth contemplating, particularly in industries suffering from overcapacity or price pressure.

Another option is to share information with other members of your industry under the auspices of a trade association. Such exchanges permit firms to gather intelligence on the competitive landscape, and might serve a useful signaling role (see below). Under the law, these associations are gray areas. Although they often collect information valuable to their members, they could easily be used as a vehicle for price fixing.[5] If your industry is fragmented, however, you're relatively free to use this method of exchanging information with competitors.

Tacit Collusion and Price Signaling

If neither of the two legitimate price-fixing methods already discussed fits your circumstances, you might want to consider tacit collusion or price signaling. Not only are such activities less observable, the courts have agreed that these activities do not necessarily imply wrongdoing, nor do they have anticompetitive effects.[6]

For example, it is not illegal for you to simply observe your competitors' prices in the market and match these unilaterally, even though this has the same effect as fixing prices by prior agreement. Nor is it illegal for you to employ a host of practices that tend to facilitate collusion. These include the use of most favored nation (MFN) clauses, meeting-competition clauses, and posting advance notices of price changes.

MFN clauses assure a customer that he or she is paying the lowest price charged to any customer. Such clauses encourage your customers to be on the lookout for price cuts and, therefore, raise your cost of trying to steal a customer from a rival: Any price cut must be passed along to all existing customers. If both you and your major competitors use such clauses, it is easier to collude on price.

---

[5] Dennis W. Carlton and Jeffrey M. Perloff, *Modern Industrial Organization*, 2d ed. (HarperCollins College, New York, 1994).

[6] Carlton and Perloff (1994), op. cit.

A meeting-competition clause is a guarantee to your customers that if another firm offers a lower price, you will match this price. To the casual observer, meeting-competition clauses appear designed to promote competition. However, they actually motivate your customers to inform you of the lowest price in the market, making a price-cutting strategy by your competitors easily detectable and therefore ineffective in the long run. Again, if both you and your major competitors use such clauses, it is easier to collude on price.

Another method to facilitate collusion is advance notices of price increases. In the time between your announcement of the increase and its effective date, your competitors can decide whether or not to go along. If your rivals decide not to go along, you can rescind the price increase. In such circumstances, you need never find yourself selling at different prices in the market, which removes your deterrent to raise prices in the first place.

Predatory Pricing

Predatory pricing is difficult to prove in court, so if you have been itching to quash an annoying competitor with low prices, chances are you won't suffer any legal consequences from employing such a strategy. A successful plaintiff would require not only evidence of pricing below cost (and cost has been difficult to define), but also evidence that your predatory strategy was credible: you must subsequently have been able to recoup the losses you sustained as a result of the predatory strategy. In general, the courts have had great difficulty labeling pricing behavior as predatory, rather than evidence of healthy competition between rivals.

For example, even in the post-deregulation airline industry, the government has had difficulty finding any evidence of predatory pricing. A recent case alleging that American Airlines used predatory pricing to drive out rivals such as ATA, JetBlue, and Ryan International from its key Dallas-Fort Worth hub was dismissed on the grounds that "[American] played by the traditional rules. . . . It competed with the low-cost carriers on their own terms. . . . There is no doubt that American may be a difficult, vigorous, even brutal competitor. But here, it engaged only in bare, but not brass knuckle competition."[7]

Resale Price Maintenance

Resale price maintenance (RPM) is the agreement of minimum resale prices between a supplier and a retailer. If you are a manufacturer of branded products, you no doubt recognize that RPM motivates your retailers to increase their selling efforts. When minimum resale prices are established, retailers are more inclined to compete on nonprice dimensions such as advertising, showrooms, quality of the sales staff, service, and inventory. Of course, it helps that RPM has historically sustained higher prices, often by as much as 20 percent.[8]

At the moment, U.S. courts tolerate RPM, as long as there is no explicit agreement or contract to this effect between the supplier and the reseller. In other words, you can "suggest" that your product be sold at a certain minimum price and refuse to sell to any reseller that does not comply.

To encourage retailers to adhere to minimum prices, you can provide them with financial incentives or discounts for expenses such as advertising. For example, Nine West, the branded shoe manufacturer, provides promotional assistance to the major department stores that carry its shoes in exchange for following minimum prices.[9]

Exclusive Territories

Exclusive territories—the practice of assigning distinct geographic areas to each of your dealers and prohibiting other dealers from locating in the same area—are also applicable to manufacturers of branded products. As with RPM, the rationale is to provide your dealers with the incentive to promote your branded product, and to prevent one dealer from free rid-

[7] United States v. AMR Corporation, et al., U.S. Department of Justice, April 27, 2001, at "Conclusion."

[8] Lawrence Shepard, "The Economic Effects of Repealing Fair Trade Laws," *Journal of Consumer Affairs*, 12: 220–36, in Carlton and Perloff (1994), op. cit.

[9] "Treading a Contentious Line: Shoe Store Owners Battle Nine West over its Pricing System," *The New York Times*, January 13, 1999.

ing on the promotional efforts of another. Of course, reducing competition among dealers also supports the price that can be charged to end consumers. There is currently considerable legal latitude if you wish to employ exclusive territories, and examples abound in markets such as automobile sales and service, beer, fast food, and soft drinks.

Exclusive Dealing

Exclusive dealing prevents your distributors from selling your competitors' products. As with RPM and exclusive territories, it prevents free-riding. But in this case, between competing manufacturers rather than competing distributors. For example, if you conduct an advertising campaign to entice consumers to go to your distributor to buy your product, a competing manufacturer might benefit from the increased flow of customers without having expended a similar degree of selling effort.

Legally, you can freely engage in exclusive dealing as long as your competitors have reasonable access to the market through other distribution or retail channels. For example, in the early 1990s, Double Rainbow, a manufacturer of ice cream, was unsuccessful in blocking Haagen-Dazs' practice of requiring its distributors to carry only Haagen-Dazs products.[10] As an alternative to outright exclusive dealing, you can also provide financial incentives to your distributors to discourage them from carrying competing products.

Tie-In Sales

As discussed in Chapter 10 on tiering, bundles and solutions, tie-in sales can often improve your company's profitability. If you're contemplating a tie-in sales strategy, you need only be concerned if you have significant market power in the tying product, and this power has a significant effect on the market for the tied product. For example, if you're Microsoft and enjoy significant market power, and if you then force customers to purchase your Internet browser, you might be accused of foreclosing the business of independent browsers.

---

[10] Arthur I. Cantor (2001), "Tying, Exclusive Dealing, and Franchising Issues," Presentation to the 42 Annual Anti-trust Law Institute Practicing Law Institute, page 66.

However, even if you *do* have the remarkable market power of MS Windows, you might still be able to justify the tie-in. You can argue that as the operating system owner, you're in the best position to provide repair services, or else that the two products in question work in tandem and are necessary for the proper functioning of an overall unit.

Transfer Pricing and Taxes

If different divisions of your firm are located in multiple tax jurisdictions, then you might have an opportunity to shift profits from the high-tax to the low-tax jurisdictions. This is one way to minimize the total amount of corporate tax. Think about transactions involving intangibles, such as trademarks, patents, and corporate branding. Retailers such as Toys "R" Us, Limited Brands, and Burger King have set up subsidiaries to hold their intangible assets (such as corporate trademarks) in low-tax states such as Delaware. The subsidiaries then collect royalties on the use of these intangibles from other parts of the firm or from partly owned subsidiaries. The subsidiary is established in a low-tax jurisdiction so that the royalty payments are subject to very little tax. At the same time, the divisions that pay the royalty reduce their taxable income through this expense—effectively transferring part of their income out of relatively high-tax jurisdictions. Limited Brands moves $300 million per year in such fees to its subsidiary in Delaware.[11]

Recently, variants of this strategy have been employed by several large U.S.-based companies to reduce their taxes on U.S. profits to as little as 11 percent, from an average effective rate of 21.5 percent.[12] Unlike individual Americans, U.S. publicly traded companies are taxed only on their U.S.-source income, so they have every incentive to shift this income to offshore tax havens. Similarly, a U.S. based company collecting royalties on intangibles can help reduce taxes for foreign subsidiaries in countries with higher taxes.

[11] "Diminishing Returns: A Tax Maneuver in Delaware Puts Squeeze on States," *The Wall Street Journal*, August 9, 2002: A1.

[12] David Cay Johnston, "Tax Treaties with Small Nations Turn into a New Shield for Profits," *The New York Times*, April 16, 2002.

Still, although these tax minimization schemes can be highly profitable, they might also be short-lived. Governments everywhere are continuously working to block transfer pricing practices that reduce tax revenues. Therefore, strategies that are profitable today might not be tomorrow.

Legal Constraints on Pricing Summary

In summary, despite the apparent ubiquity of the law in pricing, firms retain an enormous degree of flexibility when making pricing decisions. The scope of the law is rarely all-encompassing, neither is its application usually black or white. Therefore, it's useful to have a good understanding of the scope of legal pricing opportunities, in case your counsel seems to focus too much on the seeming constraints.

THIRD-PARTY PURCHASING, OR OTHER PEOPLE'S MONEY

Our second wrinkle is purchases by people acting as agents on behalf of the ultimate payor—"other people's money." Up until now, we've assumed that the party making the purchase decision also owns the money being spent. Yet examples of companies spending other people's money aren't at all rare. They include health care institutions and patients spending insurance company monies, and fund managers buying and selling on behalf of their clients or government agencies.

What's interesting is that spending other people's money can actually make the decision makers—that is, the spenders—behave differently than if the money were their own. Depending on the degree of accountability, the spending party might be either freer with the money, or much more conservative. In either case, where behavior changes, there's opportunity for better pricing. Two examples:

Charge-Back of Expenses

Professional services firms such as law firms and consultancies often include the costs of items such as travel and research in the total fees they charge their clients. However, quite commonly, not all clients are willing to pay for such costs. These hard-negotiating clients might exclude certain expenses from those eligible for reimbursement—in which case, the professional services firm will suddenly care a lot about such costs, coming as they must out of the firm's pocket rather than the client's. Also getting a lot more attention will be the previously immaterial issue of charge-back allocation—that is, which client pays for what.

For example, suppose a law firm incurs $100 per month in expenses for its research, which it then attempts to charge back to its clients. Now suppose that this particular month, the firm engages in two research sessions, one for Client 1 and one for Client 2. Client 1 is willing to pay for its research sessions, but Client 2 is not. If both searches are for Client 1, 100 percent of the costs will be recouped, whereas if one of the searches is for Client 2, only 50 percent will be recouped.

An insoluble dilemma? Hardly. The solution is to consider the client's willingness to pay for searches and charge accordingly—that is, to reallocate. Returning to the example above, Client 1 might be willing to pay $99 per search (probably a fat antitrust defendant), while Client 2 might be unwilling to pay anything at all. In this case, $99 of the $100 monthly research fee can be charged to Client 1. By charging on the basis of its clients' respective price sensitivities, the law firm almost doubles its recouped costs for the two searches relative to the pro rata allocation, and it lessens or even removes variability in the amount it can expect to recoup. This is the better pricing result.

Not-For-Profit Organizations

Another example of the use of other people's money comes from the world of not-for-profit institutions, in particular performing arts centers such as the Lincoln Center or the Kennedy Center. Because many of these institutions are not directly concerned with their patrons' finances, their approach to ticket pricing is often suboptimal.

Suppose that an arts center offers a six-performance subscription for $60, which translates to $10 per ticket. Now suppose that *single* ticket prices are $20 per performance. Many season-subscribers find that they can't attend every performance, and can't give away the tickets either. So some not-for-profit organizations, including the Greenwich Symphony Orchestra, offer patrons the option of calling in to "donate" their tickets back to the performance center so the ticket can be resold. The donor gets a $10 tax deduction, and the performance center gets extra revenues if it can resell the ticket.

It's been pointed out, however, that this system doesn't properly account for market value.[13] Season-pass holders are donating *single* tickets, not their entire season subscription. Thus the performing arts centers should accept the donation at the single ticket rate of $20, because that's the market value—not the $10 rate. This approach would give donors a higher tax deduction and encourage more tickets to be donated. It might also allow the center to increase prices for subscriptions, as these would now have higher value.[14]

Taking a hard look at market value comes naturally to most of us when selling goods we own, for our own benefit. When we sell our house, we're acutely aware of the distinction between the current market price and our purchase price. However, when handling other people's money, this attentiveness is often lacking. Simple mathematical allocations are often employed because they're relatively easy to administer and explain. The flaw is that they usually also ignore real distinctions, such as cost and market price, and are suboptimal for many of the parties involved.

OPPORTUNITY KNOCKS

Management focuses on mainstream pricing issues—how to maximize profits in situations where buyer and seller are attempting to optimize the outcome at the other's expense. In some cases, such as those highlighted here, there are wrinkles in this scenario. The law might constrain the players, or the buyer might behave differently than if she were negotiating and deciding on her own behalf. These can be opportunities for blunting competitors or improving profits—cards worth keeping up your sleeve for when the occasion arises.

---

[13] "Earned Income," white paper published by Linda Sullivan Associates, Silver Springs, MD, 2003.

[14] In the more hard-nosed world of stocks and bonds, this would be obvious. One of the authors recently made a charitable donation of stocks he had purchased for $16, when their market value was $80. Of course he got a deduction for $80.

Part Three

How to Manage Ongoing Revenues

Chapter Thirteen | Getting Started: Fundamental Questions for Senior Management

You are a senior manager who has moved into a new P&L with an assignment to improve results rapidly—an increasingly common event. While very often your primary focus is on pruning costs, you should also look at pricing. This chapter offers a quick overview of some pricing questions to ask incumbent managers.

The list is short, with only 10 questions, however, we believe these 10 questions cover (or uncover) most major pricing issues and touch on branding as well. We also devote some attention to how to verify whether the answers you receive are accurate, or in some cases use different definitions than you would use.

Question 1: What is the basic unit price for our primary product or service?

Issue: A surprising number of management teams do not know the realized price ("pocket price") of their principal product or service. Without this knowledge, it is impossible to evaluate competitor prices, discounting efficacy, or sources of margin.

Litmus test: If you have good unit-sales figures, multiply them by the purported average sales price and see it if matches revenues. (You might also ask for the average spend by customer. If average spend multiplied by the number of accounts does not roughly equal revenues, then further explanation is required.)

Role model: Despite having complex fare structures and numerous package deals, airlines know their yield (for example, price-per-passenger-mile, price-per-passenger) to the fraction of the penny. You too can know your prices this well.

References: Chapter 5, The Truth about Costs; Chapter 2, The Secret Life of Price.

Question 2: Which is higher priced—our products and services, or our competition's?

Issue: Surprisingly, many management teams are not really sure if their competition is priced higher or lower. Most believe they know which markets are lower priced and less profitable, but often they are wrong. Sources of misunderstanding include hidden costs that management might not be aware of—for example, differences in transportation cost, or by segment. Often it's not clear what the correct unit of comparison should be.

Litmus test: Are they quoting anecdotal evidence from the sales force? How does this match with customer perception? Customer perception might be wrong, but often it's right. Get actual hard data—documentary, in the form of competitor invoices. These are usually not hard to obtain, either from the sales force (offer a reward) or from common customers.

Role model: Financial services firms generally know exactly what terms are being offered by competitors, through common funding sources and alert lenders and brokers.

Follow-on question: Does our company or the competitor offer a higher-value or higher-quality product or service? This is a softer question than dollars per unit, but necessary to evaluate the price question. Higher price plus lower quality requires a sophisticated defense strategy, including making prices as opaque as possible.

References: Chapter 9, How to Price New Services; Chapter 16, How to Use Price to Penetrate Markets.

Question 3: What segmentation scheme is being used? Is it adequate? Are there appropriate data tags in the customer database, or are we resorting to proxies for segmentation?

Issue: To see if your management team has developed a real versus window-dressing segmentation scheme, and whether or not the scheme is really being used. You need a solid basis for segmentation to improve pricing.

Litmus test: If management has chosen some piece of operationally necessary information or a governmental classification as a proxy for segmentation (for example, geography represented by zip code, or product represented by SIC code), this usually signals the need for new segmentation and the potential for material revenue improvement through pricing. On the other hand, if management has demand curves that show different segments, then you can be sure the team understands its markets.

Follow-on question: Have the customer records been tagged with specific segment codes, or do we have to use an algorithm each time we need segment-specific data? (Tags are usually a good sign.)

More follow-on questions: What are the target price points for each segment? How big is each segment? Answers to these questions will show how frequently segmentation is used, because without knowing (for example, the size of each segment), segmentation cannot be used for market planning.

Still more follow-on questions: What is the average price by channel? By geography? By product or service type? How does that compare with costs, for example, with acquisition costs by channel? Are there customer-apparent price differences (that is, conflict) among channels, geographic areas, or in other areas? Usually conditions differ sufficiently to warrant price differentials, and it's usually fear and lack of capabilities that inhibits such differential pricing.

References: Chapter 4, Segmentation: Beauty Is in the Eye of the Beholder; Chapter 21, Sales Channels; Chapter 22, Pricing Technology—Vapor or Value?

Question 4: How do we react to competitor price initiatives? How quickly?

Issue: The rule in responding to competitors is to hurt them more than we hurt our own company. Because competitors will tend to initiate price changes in areas where they have less to lose, it's important to be able to respond in ways that hurt them without damaging your position—and this can require a very fine instrument.[1]

Litmus test: Do you use system "workarounds" to react to competitor price initiatives? In other words, do your systems support a range of price tactics, or are workarounds used to fool the system into partially meeting market needs? Are other constraints, such as the sale force compensation system, preventing rapid and efficient responses?

Role model: When Kiwi airlines lowered prices for a major route, United Airlines lowered prices on all flights on that route. Continental reacted by lowering prices only on flights leaving at the same time as Kiwi flights.

Follow-on question: In the event of lower competitor prices, can we react on an account-by-account basis or some similarly narrow focus?

References: Chapter 4, Segmentation: Beauty Is in the Eye of the Beholder; Chapter 21, Sales Channels.

Question 5: What do our customers particularly value in our products or services? How is this reflected in our price structure? What specifically charges for, or reflects, that value?

Issue: To see if pricing captures the value created for customers, and to find out if major costs, such as transportation costs or special orders, are reflected in our price structure.

Litmus tests: How many charging points are there? Is there at least one flat charge plus a variable charge for usage? If not, there probably

---

[1] You can also respond to competitors in other areas, but the danger is that they will not see the action as connected to their own price action. This can result in missed signals and a price war.

should be. How does that compare to the sales force compensation plan? Are they rewarded for extracting the most value?

Role model: Sam's Club, Costco, and others have a multipart price structure in which they charge an annual membership fee and then enjoy a small markup on all goods sold.

Follow-on questions: Do you warranty your services to reinforce the value proposition? How much do warranties cost us? If the warranty costs are high, what does that say about our quality?

References: Chapter 2, The Secret Life of Price; Chapter 8, Ways to Set Price Level; Chapter 9, How to Price New Services.

Question 6: What do we give away for free?

Issue: When products or services are initially launched, customer support, spares, and education are often a necessary part of introducing them to the market. Over time, however, such product and service integration is less necessary for many customers. Thus, eliminating or charging for the ancillary services represents revenue opportunities in an advanced market.

Litmus test: If the answer is "nothing," then management hasn't thought through the range of ancillary efforts associated with the sale of core products. Ask about calls to customer service, extra billing detail, and delivery. Note that it might be appropriate that some services are offered free, but this should be done consciously and deliberately.

References: Chapter 9, How to Price New Services; Chapter 3, Branding for Profit; Chapter 11, Turning Value into Money.

Question 7: Who sets list price? Who sets discount categories? Who sets discount levels? What discounts do we offer? Who is in charge of the after-market?

Issue: Someone must have an overview of the prices actually paid by customers, and there should be few or no unintended price outcomes. This can only happen when there is clear, delegated authority, as well as a logical overall structure to prices.

Litmus test: Managers should have available a one-page flow chart showing decision flows from origin (for example, sales or marketing) to decision point, and from decision point to execution. They should also be able to produce a table showing responsibilities and approval levels. If there is truly someone overseeing the process, then they should be able to answer the follow-on questions below:

Follow-on question: What is the process for the periodic price increase? For responding to requests for proposals (RFPs)? For pricing the after-market? For setting discounts?

Another follow-on question: What is the maximum discount we have ever offered? The average price spread?

Still another follow-on question: What is the total amount we forego due to discounting? How are price changes communicated internally? Externally?

Role model: Markets that call for centralized pricing (online services, universities, airlines, financial institutions) have a clear delineation of pricing authority. In complex, decentralized markets, IBM and the better retailers such as Home Depot feature effective blends of central and local control. IBM has excellent price oversight: For major accounts, all invoices and announcements must cross the sales representative's desk—ensuring that errors are corrected before they reach the client.[2]

References: Chapter 20, A Supporting Organization and Process; Chapter 15, Discounting and the Price Stack; Chapter 23, Building a Price and Brand Powerhouse.

Question 8: How do we price new products? When was the last time we changed our list prices for our main product or service?

Issue: To assess how actively management uses price to react to changing market circumstances.

---

[2] The role of the sale representative at IBM is an admirable one because he or she enjoys a central role, with access to information and lines of communication within the company.

Litmus test: Ask how a particular price was determined. If the answer is "competition," examine the competitor's price history, and also ask to see the paper records on the decision. A lack of records would suggest a very ad hoc process, which in turn usually signals a lack of analytical rigor.

Role model: Many professional services firms build a custom price for every assignment using sophisticated estimation methods. Airlines change their prices every six minutes.

Follow-on questions: How has our pricing changed as our market share has changed? Where there is a pattern of market share loss over time, pricing is often a culprit. For example, management might be inflating margins by pricing too high and accepting share loss if it's not measured in their incentives.

References: Chapter 14, How to Raise Prices; Chapter 8, Ways to Set Price Level; Chapter 16, How to Use Price to Penetrate Markets; Chapter 22, Pricing Technology—Vapor or Value?

Question 9: Do We Bundle Our Products? Our Services?

Issue: Determine if management is open to making use of bundling to expand markets, test new prices, bring new offers to market. Sometimes bundles are among the quickest ways to launch new offers and move prices.

Litmus test: The number of bundles launched in the past year. There are always obstacles to launching bundles, but ad hoc bundles are essential to assessing the market appetite for bundles.

References: Chapter 10, Tiering, Bundles, and Solutions; Chapter 19, Quick Hits.

Question 10: How Do We Leverage Our Brand? Coordinate Price with Brand?

Issue: To find out if management focuses its branding efforts to improve revenues, pricing, and profits. Although many companies spend on overall brand, often this isn't buying them anything in terms of improved revenues or profits.

Litmus test: Are branding managers measured by how their company's products and services are priced relative to competitors? Can they point out specifically where brand is supporting higher prices?

Follow-on question: Do objectives and measures overlap among branding and pricing managers? How do these two groups, along with marketing, coordinate their focus? What are the reporting connections?

References: Chapter 3, Branding for Profit; Chapter 20, A Supporting Organization and Process.

SUMMARY

The vast majority of businesses can do a better job of managing price levels to reflect the overall market, market segments, and price drivers. The questions we have discussed in this chapter should provide both a diagnostic tool and an indication of how to improve pricing, branding, revenues, and the required processes.

Chapter Fourteen | How to Raise Prices

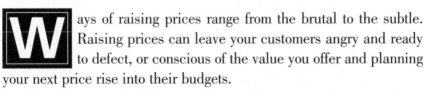**W**ays of raising prices range from the brutal to the subtle. Raising prices can leave your customers angry and ready to defect, or conscious of the value you offer and planning your next price rise into their budgets.

There are at least seven basic approaches to raising prices, with myriad variations and ample room for creativity. These approaches are:

- Brute force—simply insist on a higher price
- Increase the value, increase the price
- Price more completely—charge for incidentals and previously free services
- Adjust the roles of buyers and sellers in the marketplace
- Leverage your price structure so that customers grow into a higher price level
- Improve your segmentation to better capture total value
- Link offers for goods or services

Each of these approaches requires a solid understanding of customer value and economics, for by raising prices you are attempting to change the relationship between the money you're asking for and the value you provide. Many—perhaps most—buyers do not want to change that relationship. For example, Wal-Mart makes it very difficult for manufacturers to raise the prices of goods in its stores. The Wal-Mart rationale is that it offers the best value possible to its customers, and that prices should remain stable so that customers remain confident of finding what they want at a price they can afford.

BRUTE FORCE

Brute force increases succeed in the same manner as street crime: You demand a rise and if the customer has no better choice, he pays. Like street crime, this technique for raising prices can be effective. The key question is, do customers have an alternative? If there are literally no viable alternatives, or if alternatives exist but cost as much or more for the same value, or if the cost of switching is prohibitive, then in fact they don't have a choice.

A good way to understand likely customer behavior and choices is to observe past behavior by segment and market position. For example, in the women's hosiery market there are premium brands (Calvin Klein and Silk Reflections) and nonpremium brands (No-Nonsense, L'Eggs, and generics such as CVS brand). During one period in the 1990s, the price elasticity of premium hosiery was 0.9, while the price elasticity of generics was 2.0.[1] This clearly suggested that the premium brand could profitably take a price increase while the generics could not afford to do so. In fact, the premium brands *did* take a price increase by ending promotional sales, coupons, and other discounts.

As shown in Figure 14.1, the average purchase price then edged upwards for a year, leading to reduced sales (presumably as women waited for the next coupon, which never came). After that it recovered to previous levels—a successful example of a brute-force price increase.

An example of a failed brute-force increase was an attempt by Continental, Northwest, and United Airlines to raise ticket prices in the

---

[1] Price elasticity is the percentage change in volume divided by the percentage change in price, thus if volume falls 9 percent due to a 10-percent increase in price, then the elasticity is −0.9, which is conventionally noted as 0.9.

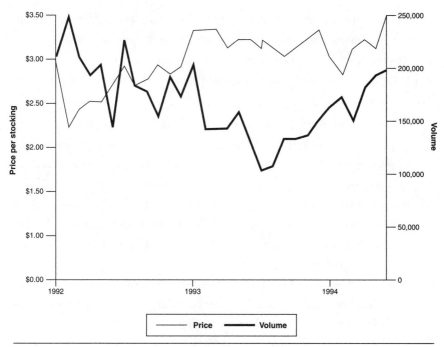

Figure 14.1. Premium hosiery price versus volume.

spring of 2002, mainly by reducing the number of routes and the availability of lowest-price seats.[2] Unfortunately for these three carriers, not
all other airlines went along. America West in particular cut prices on
unrestricted tickets and eliminated Saturday night stay requirements,
sparking a price war. In reaction to America West, several larger carriers slashed fares and made more bargain seats available. The result for
all carriers was a net revenue hit. America West was hit particularly
hard as competitor reactions cut its previously brisk share of traffic to
a dribble.[3]

---

[2] "America West Slashes Unrestricted Fares," *The Wall Street Journal*, March 26,
2002: A10, and "Buy Your Ticket Now; Cheap Seats May Be Going," *The Wall Street
Journal*, April 18, 2002: A12.

[3] Before the price war, AmericaWest carried half the traffic between Des Moines
and Phoenix, but afterwards this fell to single digits. "America West Sparks Price
War," *The Wall Street Journal*, April 22, 2002.

Brute-force price increases succeed or fail based largely on the market power of the seller, but there is an important caveat: This approach appears to work less well if no explanation or change in value is provided to customers or competitors, or if it comes as a surprise. This is because:

- Customers want to be treated fairly and tend to see the existing price level as fair or at least acceptable. A price increase with no explanation or apparent cause violates this expectation of fairness.
- In industrial purchasing situations, the purchasing organization needs to be able to explain or defend a price increase to its internal clients. If it can't, it might need to start looking at alternatives to justify its existence.
- Many customers take past as prologue. If a price increase occurs without apparent rationale, they feel that to accept it would be to tacitly accept future arbitrary increases as well.

In many markets, customers have been educated to believe that regular price increases are fair. For example, in industries where technological sophistication increases yearly, prices are expected to rise.[4] Going further, we find that customers can be educated by sellers to acquire expectations of price rises where none previously existed. An example comes from the retail sales of electronic devices and computers: Although the price of a home computer had been dropping an average of $211 per year from 1996 to 2001, such devices (including palmtops) subsequently increased in price about 25 percent between November 2001 and mid-2002. Consumer reaction to the new increase was moderate, in part because manufacturers were able to attribute it to increased costs for memory chips and flat-screen displays.[5] We can see that there is little effort involved, and much to gain, in offering cus-

---

[4] Examples of this are publishing, automobiles, gasoline, pharmaceutical, and medical services.

[5] "Tech Companies Are Raising Prices of Electronic Gadgets," *Asian Wall Street Journal*, April 18, 2002: A7.

tomers an explanation for a price increase, along with a promise that future increases will be reasonable.

INCREASE THE VALUE, INCREASE THE PRICE

A good way of persuading a customer to pay more is to persuade him that you are offering more value. Greater value deserves higher prices, right?

Value is in the eye of the beholder, or more specifically, in the eye of the decision maker. In some cases customers are willing to pay a premium for better quality. The past few years have seen gradual improvement in toothbrushes—improved handle for better grip, variations in bristle shape. These improvements have allowed Johnson & Johnson and others to increase prices from $1.99 to $3.99 or more. The cost of implementing these improvements averaged little more than $0.50 per brush, so as a value-based strategy, it was a good one—especially because it encountered little consumer resistance and increased volumes.[6]

The flip side of this approach is to decrease the value offered but keep the price the same. An example is Band-Aids and its competitors in the adhesive bandage market. While the price per box has held constant over several years, the box and the number of bandages have not. Cardboard boxes replaced metal ones, and the new boxes hold fewer bandages. The result is more boxes sold, more revenue generated, but no sticker shock from higher price tags.

Another tactic is to shift some of the burden of providing a service to the buyers. Retailers have moved increasingly to self-service, placing upon their customers the burden of selecting goods, bringing these goods to registers, and increasingly, checking themselves out.[7] This evolution can be seen in grocery stores, airports, and at computer equipment facilities. For example, Lucent allows customers to configure and reconfigure the software in its communications equipment,

---

[6] To obtain this increase, Johnson & Johnson focused on "customer-apparent improvements." However, there is little or no claim of reduced cavities.

[7] While this might not raise the total price, and might even be accompanied by a lowering of the total price, it is almost always a strategy for raising the price for the remaining services performed by the seller.

even as it moves down the assembly line, through a direct interface to the manufacturing process. In some cases the seller offers a discount to buyers for taking up part of the production burden, but in all cases the seller obtains an improved ratio of price to cost of service.

How well the customer accepts increases in price and value depends, of course, on the market, and even on the segment within that market. Among retailers, high levels of service are expected and paid for by customers of luxury stores such as Nordstrom and Saks. On the other hand, Sears has reduced the level of service available on its sales floors over time: A Sears spokeswoman says, "Our customer has told us that she is not willing to pay for a higher level of service."[8]

Not all changes in value come from a company's actions. Some come from changes in fashion, as when Merlot wines fell "out" of fashion while Spanish red wines came "in" fashion.[9] This suggests an opportunity to raise prices if your product happens to be "in"—the increase can always be justified by citing more demand. Even in markets less susceptible to fashion, increases in perceived value can lead to disproportionate increases in price, as the value surges past the alternatives. For example, increases in the usability of voice recognition systems led to prices increasing from zero to seven digits, as such systems suddenly became capable of replacing expensive call-center staff.[10]

PRICE MORE COMPLETELY

In still another approach, companies have turned formerly free aspects of their service into chargeable events, thereby increasing revenues without increasing base prices. Because the charge has a distinct rationale (whether a cost or a benefit), these companies have found customers willing to pay for the formerly free items. Some examples:[11]

---

[8] "Layoffs Can Have Downsides For Companies," *The New York Times*, December 26, 2002: C4.

[9] *The Wall Street Journal*, December 27, 2002: W10.

[10] Although many of us find such devices stupid and annoying.

[11] "Fees Hidden in Plain Sight: Companies Add to Bottom Line," *The New York Times*, December 28, 2002, p. A1.

- In certain areas, Domino's Pizza now charges extra for delivery as compared to pick-up at the store
- AT&T Wireless now charges a fee for unanswered calls if the phone rings for more than 30 seconds
- Intuit now charges $14.95 for customer service calls
- Some hotels charge $1 per night for in-room safes
- Some airlines are reinstating long-ignored charges for extra or oversized luggage
- A brokerage firm has instituted a $2 fee for every trade confirmation that goes through the U.S. Postal Service
- New York Broadway plays now charge an additional facilities fee to pay for theater restoration

A key operational requisite, of course, is to inform customers of the new charges at the appropriate moment in the sales cycle. Without such mention, a higher price will correctly be seen as a violation of fair play—that is, of the implicit agreement between buyer and seller. Keep in mind that the more a new charge varies from previous such agreements, the better job you must do to communicate both the change and the reasons for it. If the change is *too* great from the past, however, customers are likely to rebel no matter what your explanation.

Some companies have indeed gone too far in this respect, charging for actions that customers perceive to be part of the normal course of business. BankOne at one point tried charging for access to human tellers and met with considerable resistance because this was viewed as an integral part of the business. Similarly, at various times airlines and rental car companies have tried to charge for canceled reservations and met with limited success. Over time, however, efforts such as these might succeed as markets change: IBM for many years included free training with the purchase of its mainframes, but is now able to charge for much of the cost of training, separately from equipment costs.

This strategy of moving to more complete pricing offers several advantages. For one thing, no change in list price means less scrutiny from customers who focus on such prices. For another, customers can choose if they want the newly priced adjunct service without necessarily having to give up the basic purchase. Finally, this strategy avoids automatically subsidizing customers who use expensive adjunct services at the expense of those who do not.

ADJUST THE ROLES OF SELLERS AND BUYERS

It's easy to think of sellers and buyers as locked in a zero-sum game, with a resultant limit on prices. In many cases this is true—however, creative thinking can sometimes open up the relationship and allow for higher prices.

One tactic is to see if another party can pay for the goods or services you are providing. There are many segments of the economy that operate as pass-through agents for suppliers. For example, attorneys purchase legal research from providers such as Westlaw or Loislaw, and bill it back to their clients. Doctors order procedures and tests for patients, who then pay through insurance. Travel and hospitality industries serve customers who are then reimbursed by employers. Advertising agencies purchase ad space on behalf of their clients. Members of stock exchanges buy and sell stocks on behalf of their clients.

Increasingly, sellers have become more sophisticated at manipulating these third-party purchasing arrangements to achieve higher prices, higher volumes, or other goals. An impressive example is a deal cut between Pfizer and the State of Florida, wherein Pfizer agreed to help Florida limit the costs of Medicaid for the poor, primarily by controlling drug costs for the very highest-cost patients. The catch was that Pfizer also effectively controlled which drugs got approved for Medicaid. All of Pfizer's drugs were naturally on the approved lists, but competitors were forced to cut prices or have their drugs rejected. As a result of the agreement, "doctors who treat patients insured by the state's Medicaid program for the poor can prescribe Pfizer medicines routinely and without hassle."[12]

---

[12] "Pfizer Ducks Pressure On Prices By Helping State Save On Medicaid," *The Wall Street Journal*, July 9, 2001: A1.

Another innovative way of raising prices, particularly when selling unique goods or goods of limited quantity, is to increase the number of potential buyers. To illustrate this point, let's go back to our earlier example about Northrop Grumman's acquisition of TRW. In Chapter 8, we discussed the takeover in terms of TRW's fabulous negotiating skills. But there was also an impressive role adjustment taking place between buyers and sellers. When the Chairman of TRW, Philip Odeen, considered Northrop's initial offer price too low, he quickly found another buyer for a key part of the business, thus forcing Northrop to increase its bid by 27 percent.[13]

LEVERAGE YOUR PRICE STRUCTURE

Price structure can be used to reflect your cost structure and so reduce the chances of customers acting in ways that dramatically increase those costs. It can also be used for operational convenience, as when you charge more for night service calls because you have fewer repair staff available then. Still another function of price structure—from the point of view of profitability—is to increase your price levels and total revenues over time.

Price structure can seem independent from price level when a snapshot of both is taken.[14] Over time, however, price structure moves price levels up or down. The trick is to tie your structure to some aspect of the environment or customer usage that is surely moving in a direction to increase revenues from your market. For example, if use of your services or goods is going up, then it's to your advantage to have usage-based prices. Say you sell computers and know that your customers will inevitably require more memory capacity: It might be desirable to price

---

[13] "Skilled Negotiator Helped TRW Get Higher Offer From Northrop," *The Wall Street Journal*, July 1, 2002: Section C.

[14] Example: If two car rental companies offer the same car, one for a flat rate of $100 per day, and the other for $1 per mile, and if customers drive an average of 100 miles per day, the structures are different but the price levels identical—for the moment. Note also that price structures tend to last longer than price levels: Levels might change day to day, but price structures can be in place for years.

initial installations inexpensively but exact a premium on memory upgrades.[15]

The basis for using structure to leverage price is a better understanding of the market—or of your product and its likely use—than your customer's. Being rational, customers often can estimate their future usage. However, they rarely possess the same degree of product knowledge, facts concerning their own usage patterns, or confidence in the product, as you, the seller. As an example, cell phone users often believe their usage will remain within the monthly flat-fee terms, but then go beyond those terms and incur expensive per-minute charges.

One Internet Service Provider (ISP) crafted its rate structure in three parts as shown in Figure 14.2. In this case, the provider divided the customer base into three categories: 1) Neophyte users who were unsure of how much they valued access to the Web and did not expect to spend much time online, 2) inexperienced users who were spending more time online and found the Internet valuable, but knew little of alternative ISP prices, and 3) experienced users who were well aware of the market price for Internet access.

The ISP's price structure set appropriate prices for each of these segments. Neophyte and highly price-sensitive users were allowed access to the Web for very low cost. Users spending an increasing but still moderate amount of time on the Web were charged above-market rates because they could be relied upon to remain ignorant of competitors' prices. Finally, experienced, high-usage users were retained by competitive prices. This pricing scheme resulted in the addition of more than 600,000 subscribers in the first eight months of the plan.

IMPROVE YOUR SEGMENTATION

Any significant market will have multiple segments, and price sensitivity will differ by segment. Because of this, improved segment pricing will bring in incremental revenues.

---

[15] This is precisely what HP, Sun, and IBM do in their midrange computers, where typical lifetime-cluster needs are well understood. Sales of additional memory, cabinets, and power units is highly lucrative because they can't easily be substituted by other vendors.

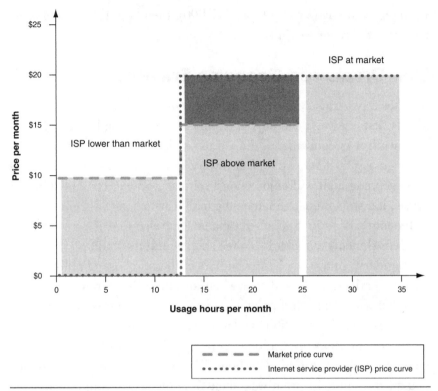

Figure 14.2. Three-tier price structure for an Internet service provider.

By way of illustration, a geographic price structure can be effective in raising revenues where there are geographic differences, such as in newspaper advertising. A structure in which rate cards break up the total circulation of the newspaper into regional editions will improve revenues.[16] Suppose a newspaper serves two geographic areas, both addressable through an ad price of $15,000 per column inch. This would be fine for a national advertiser that perceives its value is in reaching this total audience at $17,000, but would be too much for a local advertiser whose business is confined to only one geographic area and perceives its value closer to $11,000. If the newspaper were to create two editions, each priced slightly below their respective advertisers'

---

[16] Regional editions also tend to have region-specific local content—but the primary motivation for most publishers is price, not editorial improvement.

willingness to pay ($15,000 and $17,000), then both the local and the national advertiser would buy.

LINK OFFERS FOR GOODS OR SERVICES

Another way to raise prices is to tie two or more services together.[17] The idea is that one good can enjoy not only higher pricing but also greater volumes if it is conveniently linked to services or goods that currently enjoy greater customer volume or loyalty. For example, smaller retailers in a shopping mall will enjoy higher volume, and can command higher prices, if a strong tenant anchors the mall. Customers will come to shop at Bloomingdale's or Filene's Basement, but also find it convenient to buy refreshments at a nearby coffee shop within the mall.

Similarly, in a study by the authors of the purchase of online information services, we found that when an umbrella search engine was included within an information site, it raised both the volume and the price for *all* the information available at that site, regardless of whether the information was high volume and easy to find elsewhere, or low volume and difficult to find elsewhere. For the high-volume files in particular, the uplift in price was about 7 percent. The implicit linkage between these two different forms of information was accomplished through hyperlinks and pointers in search engine results.

PRICE MANAGEMENT

All seven of the above techniques can be useful—however, there is more to good pricing (and to raising prices) than technique. If you haven't already done so, consider creating a specialized pricing organization within your company. Such an organization must have authority or strong influence over all prices charged to customers—list prices, discounts, and realized prices. The focus is on bringing discipline and expertise to pricing decisions, with an emphasis on profit margins rather than on

---

[17] Under antitrust law, it is illegal to tie one good to another that enjoys monopolistic power. However, where there is no monopolistic power, tied goods can be perfectly legal.

revenues or costs. You're not seeking merely higher prices in isolation, but better pricing overall.

One study of the pharmaceutical industry showed that a formal pricing department had a marked impact on pricing. Companies with a pricing department discounted less and had very narrow price spreads for a given product, compared with companies without such a department.[18] Companies without formal departments had wide price fluctuations (that is, large discounts), as well as ad hoc competitive price responses.

Pricing organizations have a place in almost all industries, but in some more than others. They are important to airlines, where pricing must be centrally controlled. Airlines are special cases, however, because all relevant information (capacity, competitive prices, and demand) can be assembled centrally. Thus they typically have scores of price managers and impressive IT resources.

In other industries—where competition is locally dispersed, there is a variety of products, and the sales process is negotiation intensive— a price organization can't play as central a role. It can, however, inject price expertise into key product pricing decisions such as new product launches and negotiations. In some cases, such expertise can raise the price obtained by 25 percent or more. It's worth considering.[19]

SUMMARY

Raising prices by simply changing list prices is possible if your firm has the market power to do so. When customers have alternatives or the power to say no, then more sophisticated means are needed. Ideally, your company should be exploring all of the initiatives discussed in this chapter at any given time.

If there is actual improvement in the effectiveness of pricing, then price increases can be significant to the point that the process of improvement creates new product categories and price ranges. For

[18] Aimee L. Stern, "The Pricing Quandary," *Across the Board*, May 1997: pp 16ff.
[19] *The Wall Street Journal*, July 1, 2002, ibid.

example, Clearasil has successfully made the migration from a $3.50-per-tube acne medicine to a $6-per-tube, multitube skin-treatment line. Clearasil has been able to persuade young women that this new product line offers a range of advantages not present in the old Clearasil. The result is an increase from $3.50 a tube to $35 for a set.

Discounting and the Price Stack

Discounting is the recognition that one size does not fit all, and that a list price is not ideal for all situations and customers. Discounts can help address fluid market situations and individual customer needs, and help lubricate the selling process.

The other side of the coin is that discounts are the single-most abused tool in the pricing toolbox. Dangers of discounting include destruction of price levels, customer confusion, and damage to brand. Sometimes, giving discounting authority to salespeople without clear and intelligent guidelines is like giving inmates the keys to the asylum.

In this chapter, we define the purpose of discounts, illustrate how they can be used to handle swings in demand, describe a leading-edge way to set discounts, and then describe the organizing principle known as the "discount stack." Armed with these foundations, your company should be able to avoid unnecessary discounting, while ensuring that discounts do occur where they're actually needed. As a bonus, we touch on international pricing, an area that often requires discounting or differential pricing.

THE PURPOSE OF LIST PRICES

Discounts take up where list prices leave off. The precise division is a matter of practicality. We know one manufacturer that has list prices geared to the size of its customers, and another manufacturer that uses a size-based discount structure based on a single list price. Despite the apparent overlap, list prices have some fundamental aspects that distinguish them from discounts.

A list price is your stake in the ground as to the value of a service or product in the market. In many markets, list prices influence customer behavior because they're what companies actually charge as well as advertise. List price in this context serves as a contractual certainty. For example, health insurers insist that health providers offer their policyholders the best price available, thus no discounting below that level is possible—list price becomes the de facto price. Even where list prices don't serve as absolute prices, companies and customers still expect them to stay relatively constant, especially in relation to discounted prices. This permits most competitive signaling to be done with list prices rather than with the harder-to-observe discounts. Finally, list prices also serve an important role internally for market planning.

Sometimes, discounts become so prevalent that list prices begin to lose their symbolic value in the market. This is a problem if it leads every customer to insist on a discount, or on a bigger discount than generally offered. In addition, the sales force can no longer debunk customer anecdotes of underbidding by rivals. Finally, in service industries, where usage measures are frequently neither standard nor obvious (see Chapter 9), list price dollars sometimes serve as a stand-in for this purpose. If these prices become discredited, price negotiations are more difficult for sellers because the measure has now lost its meaning. For example, initially competitors in the long-distance market compared their prices to AT&T's list prices, but as AT&T started moving off a tariffed price to various discount programs, this comparison lost its meaning—good for AT&T, bad for the competitors.

DISCOUNTS FOR FLUCTUATIONS IN DEMAND

Many goods and services experience obvious price fluctuations and go through price cycles. In some cases it makes sense to change the official price, as when wheat is sold through exchanges: The price will definitely rise in the winter and definitely fall in the spring. In other cases, however, a list price can't be so easily changed. Here is where discounting steps in to provide this flexibility.

Clothing sold in department stores is a good example of seasonal discounting. Again, the reason we use discounts in this situation, rather than change the list price, is that the list price has meaning: Customers can use it as a reference point for the quality of the discounted goods because enough of the clothing once sold at list price to preserve meaning for that measure.

The discounts appropriate for a line of clothing are purely a function of one, the projected price sensitivity of sales volumes, and two, the economics of selling versus keeping or disposing of the clothes in the off-season.[1] Hence the retailer must optimize discounts by balancing foregone revenues against increased volume. To a retailer at decision time T_D, this means the following (pardon the equation) :

Set Discount % at T_D such that it Optimizes: (Increased Number of Unit Sales $\times$ Discounted Price) $-$ (Normal Number of Sales Without a Discount $\times$ Discount $\times$ Price) $-$ (Expected Number of Leftover Units at End of Season T_E $\times$ Disposal Value)

Thus, if management anticipates some degree of elasticity, the discount will increase toward the end of the season because fewer clothes can be expected to sell at normal prices. In addition—and not included in the above formula—floor space will be increasingly in demand for the next season's clothes.

---

[1] Clever use of hybrid channels minimizes this problem, where feasible. Instead of selling all of its end-of-season goods at a discounted price, a high-end merchandiser can quietly begin to transfer inventory to discount outlets as the season draws to a close, thus reducing inventory by means other than globally discounting.

This sort of discounting strategy is useful for any industry facing a predictable decline in value at a particular point in time—seasonal Caribbean resorts, flowers, foodstuffs facing an expiration date, or PC chip manufacturers expecting a new generation of faster chips—all do or should make use of a model similar to this one. Discounting in advance of expected changes in demand and price level is an ideal use of discounting. It requires an understanding of price elasticities and an understanding of costs, but offers significant value.

COUPONS AND REBATES

Other instruments for discounting include rebates, which serve the same purpose as point-of-sale discounts, but can offer operational advantages: They're usually processed directly by the manufacturer or service provider and so don't rely on the retail channel. This can lower costs while providing more information about customers. Other advantages are that rebates rarely equal 100 percent of eligible sales, so you save here as well. And finally, in the event of price controls, similar to those imposed in the early 1970s by President Nixon, rebates might be immune from such a freeze.

Discounting through promotional coupons and rebates isn't a strategic tool, however, but merely a tactic. More specifically, many world-class marketing companies contend that promotions merely motivate some low-loyalty, price-based buyers and existing customers to stock up—in other words, they don't induce enough customers to switch from competitive brands.

EVERYDAY LOW PRICING VERSUS HIGH-LOW PROMOTIONAL PRICING

Discounting is also known in retail circles as High-Low Promotional Pricing, or HLP. As it happens, some retailers, most notably Wal-Mart, prefer a strategy with a different acronym—Everyday Low Pricing, or EDLP. Under EDLP, the retailer maintains lower prices on an everyday basis, with relatively few promotions or discounts.

Proponents of EDLP argue that its simplicity and consistency make for a compelling price and value message to customers, a theme we emphasized in Chapter 7, "Price as a Language to Customers." It also has the potential to lower operational costs by reducing expenditures on advertising and in-store promotion. For example, Wal-Mart advertises on a monthly basis, rather than on the weekly schedule used by most of its HLP competitors. Inventory and warehousing costs can also be reduced because demand is more stable and easier to forecast. Finally, because merchandise is repriced less often and there are fewer special displays, these costs decline as well.

Despite this potential for savings, EDLP has failed to find a home with most retailers.[2] Apparently, the switch to everyday low prices doesn't bring in enough new volume to compensate for reduced profit margins from existing customers.[3] In addition, EDLP doesn't make for a lot of promotions—and retailers like promotions because they generate additional store traffic and can prompt customers to buy not only the promoted products, but also other higher-priced, nonpromoted products. This is especially important for products in seasonal categories (fashion goods and produce), in the growth phase of their life cycle (newer types of wines), or for products that are prone to impulse purchases or variable patterns of consumption (snack foods).[4]

So how does Wal-Mart succeed with EDLP where others have failed? First, Wal-Mart applies EDLP on a selective basis; it is not the lowest-priced retailer on all products. In its monthly circulars, Wal-Mart promotes a few high-visibility items that offer customers savings and reinforce its low-price image. On the vast majority of items, however, Wal-Mart's prices are only as low as they need to be to maintain

---

[2] This applies only to the U.S. retail market; in the United Kingdom, by contrast, all three of the major supermarkets (Tesco, Asda, and Safeway) have recently adopted some variant of EDLP. See articles on these three retailers in *The Grocer*, June 22, August 3, and September 14, 2002.

[3] Stephen J. Hoch, Xavier Dreze, and Mary E. Purk, "EDLP, Hi-Lo, and Margin Arithmetic," *Journal of Marketing*, October 1994.

[4] Jolyon Roe, "EDLP or Promotions," AC Nielsen Consulting Group (UK), April 2002.

this image. Often the price differential between Wal-Mart and other retailers is only a few cents, and for many products, Wal-Mart might well be higher priced. Wal-Mart can get away with this because consumers typically rely on a relatively small number of items to form an impression of a store's price image.[5]

SALES DISCOUNTS: THE GOOD, THE BAD, AND THE UGLY

Discounts can also be used to address the fact that every customer in a market has a different price sensitivity. This price sensitivity will change in different circumstances, such as the presence or absence of a credible competitive bid, but the key point is that no two customers will have exactly the same ideal price point. Discounting can thus win sales that otherwise might have been lost, but the process is frequently abused on all levels. Hence we need tools and strategy for intelligent sales discounting.

For the sales force to achieve better pricing through discounting, two tools are required: First, a better and more sophisticated compensation plan, and second, a "discounting scorecard" that tells sales reps when they need to hold firm on price and when they need to offer discounts, based on a careful analysis of price drivers.

Let's take the compensation plan first. In any negotiation, the side with a better strategy and a stronger motivation to win tends to emerge victorious. Unfortunately, with a typical sales compensation plan, the buyer is usually more motivated to obtain a good price than your sales representatives. This is because revenue-based compensation plans put more weight on the volume of sales rather than their profitability. The result is that sale representatives tend to fare better with a high vol-

---

[5] "Mike Troy, "Drop EDLP, Continue Promoting the Value Message," *DSN Retailing Today*, March 11, 2002.

Sales scenario	Quota percent	Average discount	Compensation
A	80%	37%	90%
B	100%	38%	100%
C	110%	39%	90%

Figure 15.1. Sales-force incentives.

ume of low-margin sales, rather than a lesser volume of high-margin sales.[6]

To remedy this state of affairs, the compensation plan should be redesigned to encourage sales representatives to be as tough on price as the customers are. One leading computer manufacturer has exactly such a plan: It measures both the average discount given by the salesperson and the total revenues achieved. The plan includes an expanded matrix similar to that shown in Figure 15.1. You can see that merely selling above quota won't result in meeting target compensation; neither will selling too small a volume at higher-than-average profit margins.

Even when properly motivated by a good compensation plan, sales reps still don't have enough information to intelligently offer discounts tailored to the account or to the circumstances. They need to know what drives prices in the market, but this takes considerable analytic effort. Without this knowledge, discounts will always tend to be a reflection of irrelevant factors, or of the relative negotiating skills of sales represen-

---

[6] As an example, take a product that sells for $100, but flies off the shelves at $90. If the company involved compensates its sales force at 5% of sales, it's telling its sales force it would rather sell three widgets per month at $90, rather than one per month at $100. This will be the case even if the company's total variable cost per sale is $90, and the more successful sales person will see the company into bankruptcy. This problem is somewhat tempered by a responsible rep's desire for the company to do well; in addition, higher levels in the sales organization are likely to have at least a few performance measures related to profitability and margin; stock options also serve this function. Nonetheless, under most compensation systems no good pricing deed goes unpunished, and discounters are rewarded no matter what.

tatives versus customers. If they know the drivers, on the other hand, both sales reps and management can resist customer requests for discounts with confidence and organizational support.

Enter the "discount scorecard," a means of controlling discounts by setting explicit rules for what discounts are appropriate under what circumstances. These rules are based on an analysis of current price drivers. A disguised example is shown in Figure 15.2.

Let's suppose that our sales representative is negotiating with a potential customer with an AA credit rating, who is located within 25 miles of the factory and who is unable to produce a lower competitive bid. Using the scorecard, such a customer is entitled to no more than a 5-percent discount. The customer can argue for a bigger discount, but armed with the scorecard, the rep doesn't have to give in. He or she knows that the 5 percent is in line with the drivers for this customer and will likely be accepted in the end.

One appealing aspect of scorecards is that they can induce sales reps to offer discounts to customer profiles that traditionally have resisted penetration. This is because in ordinary circumstances, sales reps

Account characteristics	Score
A. Competitive Bid (more than 20% below list price) • Yes = 10% • No = 0	
B. Number of miles client site is from our service center • Above x miles = 10% • Less than x miles = 0	
C. Credit rating of customer • Rating BBB or above, 0% • Rating B or BB, 5% • Rating CCC or below, 8%	
D. Subtotal (A+B+C)	
E. Additional sales force discretion–add 5% if needed (If D > or = 30%, then skip to F)	
F. Maximum discount suggested (not to exceed 30%) (D + E)	

Figure 15.2. Sales force discount "scorecard."

sometimes ration their discount requests in the face of hostility to discounting from sales management, finance, or P&L. Such rationing can translate into lost sales at small but profitable accounts, or at accounts where traditionally the company hasn't been successful. The scorecard reverses this self-rationing by giving salespeople permission to offer appropriate discounts to *all* accounts, including those that fall into the small or tough category.

The results of scorecards have been impressive. At one company, they resulted in an almost instantaneous reduction in discounts by 35 percent and increased penetration of smaller customers. The overall result was a 12-percent increase in revenues. The scorecard in question was similar to the one illustrated in Figure 15.2. Although some initial training was required, as well as auditing to prevent cheating on scorecards, overall the new system was low maintenance because sales managers bought into the concept. Once managers know the key price drivers, discussions on discounting become much more focused.

COMPLEXITY AND THE DISCOUNT STACK

Over time, managing discounts can become a major problem—one that most companies fail to deal with properly. One by one, discounts are added ad hoc—discounts for prompt payment, cumulative volume, multiyear contracts, frequent shoppers, trade-ins, overstock, bundles, new customers, discretionary discounts—the list keeps growing. At some companies, we've counted more than 26 categories of discounts.

After seven or more major discount categories, companies begin to lose control. Management begins having problems forecasting sales revenue, and sales representatives become boggled to the point of amnesia by the sheer number and variety of discounts available. Almost as important, the complexity of the process limits automation and precludes customer self-service.

Complexity is not only due to the numbers of discounts offered. There are other factors as well, including the number of decision makers involved and the number of rules required to control discount combinations. As these combinations become more numerous, they become more dangerous. Taking the number of decision makers first, suppose that we have a mere eight categories of discounts (far fewer than at many companies). These categories are administered by different managers in finance, sales, marketing, and strategic pricing. Because discounts are developed iteratively, discounting decisions typically involve repeated reviews. A little math shows that if decision makers for all eight categories must be consulted to arrive at the total discount, then in theory as many as 84,672 conversations might be required.[7]

The result is that at most companies, discounting (like other pricing decisions) is implemented with insufficient interdepartmental communication. A vice president of marketing from a respected consumer-goods firm explained it this way: "In real life, no one talks about pricing. Marketing usually is the group that sets the price, and it just has to live with the discounts pre-established by finance and others." Very often this situation is at its worst at those companies where a great deal is made of the need for coordination.[8]

Naturally, bad things happen, such as accidental discount combinations that give away a product or service nearly for free. Also naturally, most organizations do nothing to correct this until the very end of the marketing process. Hence the failures of different organizations to coordinate their discounting become apparent on the order form, in the form of innumerable rules that burden the sales force. A typical rule might be that no promotional discounts are allowed in conjunction with bundle discounts, or that the discount is only 10 percent when selling to an association because of the association discount. The more dis-

---

[7] More explicitly, in this example, there are $7 \times 6 \times 6 \times 6 \times 7 \times 8$ permutations of decision makers possible. For instance, finance might have to talk to six other departments up to seven times, if a discounting decision happened to involve all eight categories. Naturally, intelligent use of meetings should allow this process to be collapsed, but it will take a lot of meetings to collapse it to manageable proportions. More likely, decisions will be made without the full participation of all interested parties.

[8] One sign of this is when otherwise intelligent managers repeatedly begin meetings by saying, "We need to make sure we're closely coordinated in this." Such a mantra is not, in fact, a means for building genuine coordination in an organization; see Chapter 20 for some approaches that are more meaningful.

count categories you have, the more rules they spawn—but there can never be enough rules to guarantee that something will not go wrong.

Fortunately, there is a better solution. To regain control of discounting and reduce the burdens on staff and systems, the company can create a *discount stack*. A discount stack is nothing more than a rational way of organizing the interactions of different categories of discounts. It defines the *order* in which discounts are applied, giving the entire process a single direction.

Figure 15.3 shows a discount stack as it might apply to our hypothetical company with eight categories of discounts. Notice that the stack has been arranged so the most important decisions are made first, at the bottom of the stack. Typically, such decisions are those with the biggest discount range. From then on, all parties with an interest in a particular type of discount are brought in already knowing the previous decisions. Thus they need only decide if the discount as it currently stands serves their purposes also. To anticipate any incremental discounting decisions that might come afterwards, a decision maker need only look up the stack to the next higher layer, never down.

The differences between this and an unstructured discount process are the following: There is a clear order to the process; key decisions

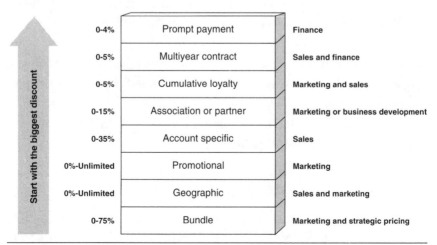

Figure 15.3. Discount stack.

are made first, so as to clarify the emerging discount profile sooner; there should be fewer revisions and negotiations; and it makes ownership of specific discounts clear. In addition, when combined with a clear timeline and a "speak up or step aside" decision process, it makes for faster decisions and a shorter process.

INTERNATIONAL PRICING

Given that the United States is a relatively wealthy country, U.S. companies seeking to add sales in other countries often find that simply translating U.S. prices into local prices results in prices that are too high. This can cripple sales, despite the overall attractiveness of building incremental revenues and margins through these markets. How then to price?

Often we suggest constructing a supply-and-demand chart that compares local levels of income and competition. Where there are fewer competitors and a high standard of living, for example, prices can be higher. Where there are more competitors, prices should be lower. Figure 15.4 illustrates the supply-and-demand conditions for one manufacturer, and the resulting target price levels. Further, it categorizes the world into four levels—above, similar to, below, and far below the United States.

Looking at the figure, you can see that this manufacturer adjusted its export prices to increase prices to Switzerland and other "above U.S." countries, while lowering prices to Chile, Israel, and other "below U.S." countries. For countries *far below* the United States, it adopted a skimming strategy and kept the U.S. prices.

Often, countries worry about goods (or even services) exported with a discount finding their way back into the United States or other premium-priced countries. This is a real issue, but usually the economics will suggest specific tactics to thwart arbitrage, rather than moving back to a one-price-fits-all policy.

ALL ABOARD FOR MONTREAL

Within pharmaceuticals, price discrepancies between the United States and many (if not all) other markets have been a lightning rod

---

Country	Demand (annual widget purchases per capita)	Resulting demand multiplier	Price of $1000 widget with demand multiplier	Supply (number of competitors, adjustment % to United States)	Resulting comparative price	Strategy category
Norway	$132	1.570	$1,570	2 (+ 0%)	$1,570	Tier 1 Above United States
Germany	$119	1.420	$1,420	3 (+ 10%)	$1,278	
Belgium	$105	1.250	$1,250	2 (+ 0%)	$1,250	
Switzerland	$100	1.190	$1,190	3 (- 15%)	$1,012	
United States	$84	1.000	$840	2 (+ 0%)	$1,000	Tier 2 Similar to United States
Denmark	$76	0.900	$900	2 (+ 0%)	$900	
Sweden	$70	0.830	$830	2 (+ 0%)	$830	
France	$55	0.650	$650	1 (+ 15%)	$748	
Netherlands	$71	0.850	$850	3 (- 15%)	$723	
South Korea	$53	0.630	$630	2 (+ 10%)	$693	
United Kingdom	$62	0.740	$740	3 (- 15%)	$629	
Ireland	$56	0.670	$670	3 (- 15%)	$570	
Italy	$45	0.540	$540	2 (+ 0%)	$540	
Chile	$42	0.424	$424	1 (+ 15%)	$488	Tier 3 Below United States
Czech Repub.	$40	0.396	$396	2 (+ 0%)	$396	
Israel	$26	0.310	$310	1 (+ 15%)	$357	
Argentina	$35	0.345	$345	2 (+ 0%)	$345	
Slovak Repub.	$27	0.270	$270	1 (+ 15%)	$310	
Colombia	$25	0.250	$250	1 (+ 15%)	$288	
Brazil	$23	0.230	$230	1 (+ 15%)	$265	
Hungary	$25	0.247	$247	2 (+ 0%)	$247	
Ecuador	$17	0.171	$171	1 (+ 15%)	$197	Tier 4 Far below United States
Estonia	$17	0.168	$168	1 (+ 15%)	$193	
Peru	$17	0.168	$168	1 (+ 15%)	$193	
Romania	$17	0.166	$166	1 (+ 15%)	$190	
Latvia	$10	0.097	$97	1 (+ 15%)	$112	
Lithuania	$10	0.097	$97	1 (+ 15%)	$112	
Pakistan	$10	0.120	$120	3 (- 15%)	$102	
India	$6	0.071	$71	3 (- 15%)	$60	

Figure 15.4. Supply and demand global price index.

for criticism of the industry. The situation exists due to differences between the U.S. health-care system, which is a free market with multiple payers, and that of most other nations, whose governments provide health care. Outside the United States, governmental approval of drug prices is common, and as the "single payer" these governments are anxious to keep prices low in order to minimize the cost of drug therapy.

By contrast, in the United States, companies are free to set prices based on market forces. And while some government-funded markets such as the military, Medicaid, and Veterans' Affairs mandate price concessions through legislative initiatives, these discounts are based on the product's average wholesale price (AWP), which is set by the manufacturer. So in response to (or in anticipation of) unattractive prices within other markets, prices in the United States are set much higher, causing U.S. buyers to shoulder a disproportionate share of the industry's costs and profits.

As a consequence of this phenomenon, cross-border trade has become an increasingly common approach for U.S. buyers to reduce prescription costs. While many approaches are used, including mail-order pharmacies and cross-border bus trips (many people head for Montreal), this trend is of increasing concern to pharmaceutical companies. The pharmaceutical companies typically rely on the U.S. market (and associated price premiums) to drive at least half of their sales and a greater proportion of their profits.

As these practices extend beyond nuisance levels, drug companies are considering ways to limit such activities. At the time of this book's publishing, several manufacturers have threatened to eliminate shipments to Canadian wholesalers that permit cross-border trade. Additionally, because the Food and Drug Administration (FDA) requires that drugs purchased in the United States be produced in FDA approved facilities, some companies are considering use of nonapproved facilities for products intended for sale in other markets, thereby limiting unintended importation. Practices such as limiting shipments to the exporter and using tracking devices are also under consideration.

Chapter Sixteen

How to Use Price to Penetrate Markets

To penetrate new markets, you can lead with price, product, channels, or promotion. Each can be the basis for a successful invasion—but price is particularly potent, whether you want to penetrate the low or the high end of the market.[1] Why so? Because in general, market penetration occurs when an invader offers customers a superior combination of price and value. Customers compare value propositions, contemplate the risks of adoption, and weigh the switching costs. And at every point, price is integral to their decision making.

We'll get into actual invasion tactics shortly, but first we need to understand a few fundamental customer behaviors that have particular importance in this context.

To start with, it's generally true that more potential customers will purchase a good or service as it becomes cheaper. However, when it

---

[1] By low end of the market, we mean those segments within a market that are most price sensitive, and the high end are those segments with higher willingness to pay. You could also define market strata by the quality of the goods and services purchased.

comes to penetrating a market, for most services and products there's an optimum trade-off of price and volume. Determining this calls for two specific analytic tasks: first, finding the optimum revenue, and second, determining the best trade-off between price and speed of adoption. You'll need to predict not only *how* different segments within the market will react to different prices, but *how quickly* they will do so. Both customer price sensitivities and the effectiveness of your sales channels are important.

In fact, both price sensitivity *and* speed of adoption vary dramatically depending on the market segment, driven largely by customer economics. For example, companies such as Caliper have developed tests for job candidates that, by some measures, can improve accuracy in predicting actual job performance by 47 percent over traditional interviews.[2] For most low-end jobs, the improved accuracy isn't worth the added cost of nearly $1000 per candidate—but for high-end jobs such as senior positions on Wall Street, it would be a small price to pay.

Another important factor driving customer acceptance is the "reference price"—that is, the mental comparison conducted by potential customers. Consumers have different price expectations based on past prices they have experienced, as well as on the circumstances and context of the sale. A client visiting a lawyer with a plush waiting room expects to be charged more than a client sitting in a threadbare office. Customers buying goods at an upscale retail store are more accepting of higher prices than they would be at Wal-Mart. Such reference prices, past and present, can speed or slow the acceptance of new offers. Be careful of these contexts, regardless of which end of the market you're seeking to enter. Moving upscale in particular requires close adherence to expected reference price cues, such as well-dressed salespeople, personal service, and customization. In many high-end markets, it is the absolute capability or quality of the good that propels market success, not the ratio of price to performance. This is also the case when—as with the employment testing service—the potential stakes are vastly higher than the immediate cost of the product or service. Test fees

[2] "Improv at the Interview," *Business Week*, February 3, 2003: 63.

would have been trivial compared to the benefits had they weeded out some of the players in the late 1990s trading scandals at Kidder Peabody and Barings Bank.

ATTACKING THE LOW END

By comparison, moving downscale requires a more careful price calculation to convey a compelling price-to-value relationship. And because your prices often must be lower than the existing alternatives, on the one hand, or the customer's reference price, on the other, you now face the additional challenge of being profitable. You in fact have four balls in the air: price, performance, costs, and profits. Moreover, in low-end markets, competitors constantly eye each other's prices and cost profiles with the attention of hungry Raptors in a dinosaur movie. Thus you must look for ways to make this juggling act easier, in the process thwarting competitors.

There are at least three proven strategies for using pricing to invade the low end: exploiting obscure price-to-cost relationships, segmenting better than incumbents, and reconstructing bundles so they become more compelling. Let's look at each of these in turn.

Exploit Obscure Price-to-Cost Relationships

A strong price strategy under these circumstances should take advantage of market dynamics, yet not invite immediate imitation by competitors. Hence the logic of using cost structure as your point of attack. Ideally, your company finds a market segment that has a lower cost-to-serve than other segments, yet is priced higher and doesn't attract new competitors. And, in fact, such a happy coincidence of factors occurs with regularity in many industries. One famous example comes from the insurance industry.

The Progressive Insurance Company noticed that its competitors were shunning younger drivers with poor driving records. Using the philosophy that "there are no unprofitable customer segments, only unprofitable business models," the company examined loss records and offered coverage—at raised prices—to drivers that other insurance companies had rejected. The result is that in contrast to the average for auto insurance of negative 3-percent margins, Progressive's underwriting is highly profitable.[3]

Another example of cost being used as the basis for superior pricing is the steel manufacturer, mentioned in Chapter 2, that faced immutable production bottlenecks in its blast furnace and rolling facilities. Dofasco realized that despite the industry's focus on certain kinds of steel production as the basis for profit—a focus derived from standard costing—it was better off focusing on those customer segments that offered the most profit per ton and per minute of facilities use. The result is that the steelmaker has experienced better prices and limited competition, while penetrating the most profitable segment of the market—and continues to do so despite a recent downturn in overall demand for steel (see Figure 16.1).

Because bottlenecks are common, other industries can make use of this kind of analysis. In professional services, there are always too few experts for the hottest new segments—for example, the dynamic areas of tax law. And in financial services, some customers require many times the administration than others do in the same revenue or risk category, an insight that can lead to improved segmentation and thus improved profitability.

Geography is also a frequent basis for successful market entry. A leading consumer products company in 1996 conducted a study of major metropolitan areas in the United States and made some interesting discoveries: not only did prices vary significantly and consistently between cities, but transportation costs didn't always explain the differences. Further comparison of prices and transportation costs suggested pricing "sweet spots" in Atlanta and Chicago, as shown in Figure 16.2.

This understanding allowed this company to focus on these intrinsically profitable markets, offering better pricing in these markets. Ulti-

---

[3] Progressive Insurance Company description, plus comments on the profitability of customer segments, based on D. Rosenblum, D. Tomlinson, and L. Scott, "Bottom Feeding for Blockbuster Businesses," *Harvard Business Review*, March 2003.

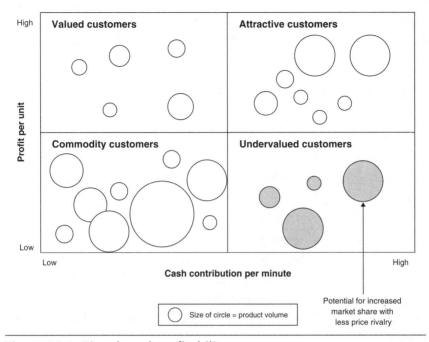

Figure 16.1. Time-based profitability.

Geography	Local price/unit (A)	Freight (B)	Net variance (A-B)	Potential
Atlanta	0.7%	(5.6%)	6.3%	Very High
Chicago	(1.8%)	(6.4%)	4.6%	Very High
Los Angeles	(2.6%)	(2.9%)	0.3%	High
Kansas City, MO	(2.4%)	(2.4%)	0.0%	Medium
Houston	(4.5%)	(0.1%)	(4.4%)	Low
Tampa	(0.0%)	8.0%	(8.0%)	Low
Denver	(5.5%)	14.9%	(20.4%)	Lowest

Figure 16.2. Local variances in price and cost (relative to U.S. average).

mately its competitors performed the same analysis and responded by building new factories close to the sweet spots, but this took some time, and the company enjoyed a highly profitable situation in the meantime.[4]

Segment Better than Incumbents

As we know, any significant market is composed of many segments, each with different price sensitivities and price structure preferences. Even so, many incumbents are volume oriented and unable to price-discriminate by segment, either because of limitations in IT or lack of market knowledge, or out of sheer corporate inertia.

This is the basis for a price-based invasion of their markets— particularly if these incumbents have allowed cross-subsidies to take root. The classic example from the telephone market dates back to the 1980s, when MCI mounted a price-based attack on AT&T to entice its long-distance customers, thereby undermining AT&T's historical practice of subsidizing Bell System local telephone service through long-distance charges.

During the early years of this price-led attack, MCI and companies like it experienced explosive growth, due to a strong value proposition and superior segmentation. MCI's objective for the first 15 years of its existence was to capture the top 25 percent of long-distance users, leaving AT&T with the remainder. To do this, it identified a rich variety of demographics that represented the highest-revenue customers: frequent fliers, Asian-Americans, mobile technical experts, truckers, students, and others.[5] Innovative pricing was another important element of this attack: MCI's "Friends & Family" program, mentioned earlier, handed MCI a rich set of new, high-value customers, while due to system limitations, AT&T couldn't match this program.

---

[4] One leading cigarette manufacturer used to have signs posted in its headquarters, "Volume is our business."

[5] The brilliant architect of this program was Helen Manich, who made sure that MCI captured markets with exclusive agreements such as the American Airlines-MCI partnership. See R. Docters, R. Katz, and C. Junquiera "Strangers in Their Own Land," *Telephony*, July 31, 1995

A key element in such low-end price attacks is price transparency—in other words, customers must be able to easily judge for themselves the price they currently pay for a good or service. Without transparency, customers can't judge whether or not a new offer represents an improvement. Incumbents, on the other hand, prefer price *opacity* because it allows them to avoid widespread discounting and the costs associated with developing price segmentation.

Reconstruct the Bundle

Bundles are another key tool for penetrating the low end of the market. In some cases, a bundle makes a product or service feasible because of the marriage of price with functionality. The growth of the personal computer has largely been a function of lower computer prices and bundling computers with useful software (initially VisiCalc, later word processing software, and finally email and Internet service suites). Before such bundling, the PC was only a minor adjunct to larger systems.[6]

Similarly, the bundling of service contracts with cell phones has allowed cell phones to become a mass-market item. Service contracts allow cell phones that cost $600 or more to make to be sold by service providers for as little as $1, with the assurance that this loss-leader can be recouped over the course of the service contract. This is crucial to penetrating the consumer mass market, where absolute price is so important.[7] Thus, bundling has helped propel cell phone market penetration.

Some markets can be better penetrated through the unbundling of existing bundles. For example, airlines have progressively retrenched from earlier incarnations as conglomerates—with a firm grasp on rental cars, hotels, in-flight food service, elaborate hub-and-spoke systems, and billing systems—to become much smaller entities, focusing only

---

[6] In 1980, DEC founder Ken Olsen said there was no reason ever for a household to own a computer. The same year, IBM had offered a computer similar in functionality to the Apple II, but priced for more than $9000. By the early 2000s, computer penetration had achieved more than 50-percent penetration of U.S. households.

[7] Many experts refer to $400 as the mass-market threshold point for consumer electronics. Goods above this price have, with some exceptions, a hard time finding mass-market acceptance.

on cost-effective fares for very limited routes.[8] Similarly, the life insurance industry moved away from whole-life plans (combinations of insurance and investment services) to simple term insurance. It appears that some bundles are simply not worth the trouble.

Whether a bundle proves useful in penetrating a market, or merely a burden for the incumbent, depends in large measure on whether or not its elements can be isolated by competitors. If a combination increases the value of its components beyond their combined individual value, such as with PCs, then bundling remains attractive. But if one element not only creates the most value but can be sold in isolation, you might need to undo the bundle yourself. Otherwise, competitors will exploit the high-value product or service by undercutting prices on it alone.

INCUMBENT RESPONSES

New markets usually feature an incumbent that views the market as its turf and tries to guard it accordingly. Such incumbents possess certain natural advantages, including existing customer relationships and occasionally even customer loyalty—but they often have some major disadvantages as well. For example, typically they fail to fully segment their markets. A smart newcomer can offer lower prices to selected segments, while the incumbent frets that it can only lower prices to *all* customers.

If you're an incumbent in this situation, the right way to minimize loss of share is twofold: First, by all means react to the new price, sending a visible signal that incursions will not be tolerated. Second, segment the market and your pricing so that future price responses needn't be global. Granted, this approach might not fit

---

[8] United Airlines sold Hertz and Westin in 1987. Food service for coach was broadly discontinued in 2000. Sabre was spun off by American Airlines and became a profitable stand-alone concern in 1993. See "Even as the Big Airlines Struggle, Computer Booking System Prospers," *The New York Times*, February 10, 2003, C1. See also "The Age of 'Wal-Mart' Airlines Crunches the Biggest Carriers," *The Wall Street Journal*, June 18, 2002.

well into a quarterly budget—but prudent managers can make it work, especially because most low-priced invasions can be predicted well in advance of the quarter in which they occur.

Estee Lauder is a good example of a smart incumbent with highly strategic responses, whether to competitive threats or market opportunities. Lauder regularly launches or purchases brands that either combat newer, less-expensive entrants, or address customer needs in ways seemingly inconsistent with their "classic" Lauder, Clinique, and Aramis brands. For example, Lauder's Prescriptives brand represents innovative products, its Origins brand addresses a distinct lifestyle and cosmetics orientation, Donna Karan and other brands address the fashion-conscious, and *jane* focuses on the teenage market.

As you might guess, each Lauder brand has distinct promotions, product characteristics, and prices. The purpose here is to build an impregnable thicket of powerful brands with nonoverlapping demographics and nonoverlapping price bands: Classics and fashion command a price premium, natural lifestyle products command somewhat lower prices, and teenagers command still lower prices. While Lauder might wish that all its products were equally profitable, its management understands the tough reality that it must create its own competitive brands and prices, or watch someone else beat them to it.

ATTACKING THE HIGH END

The high end can be approached in one of two ways—the crucial factor being whether or not the high and low ends of the market are linked. If they aren't—if the high-end purchases are stand-alone—then success depends primarily on the quality and presentation of the service or good. If, however, the high-end purchase is part of an interconnected suite of services or goods, then the total value of the package is important, and the overall better value might prevail.

Examples of stand-alone high-end goods include houses, entertainment, automobiles, some forms of travel, and various professional services. A high-end builder gains nothing from constructing low-end buildings. Similarly, because a Broadway theater can offer only one hit play, it needn't concern itself about supporting a set of off-Broadway productions. Engineering and distribution economies aside, a high-end automaker needn't make its product compatible with lower-end cars.

What truly defines the high end is the greater focus on benefit as opposed to price. Price no longer leads market strategy, but instead supports value and brand, as well as the contextual cues so important in this segment. Even so, the attraction of the high end is that very small increments in value can justify significant increases in price. The key is to avoid sending the *wrong* price signal—either far too high or else too low.

Let's look at high-end cars as an example of this supporting role for price. The high end of the automobile market is a rarified world involving low sales volumes in conjunction with high prices. In gingerly approaching the market for the $300,000-plus car, Mercedes-Benz has decided its own name is too downscale. It has therefore begun offering its cars under the Maybach label (a prewar name). Mercedes has further decided that this car should not be sold by mere dealers, as this undercuts the value proposition. Rolls Royce offers a similar $325,000-plus car, and the interesting thing here is that only 15 percent of the purchasers of this car ask the price beforehand.[9] The implication is that at these rarefied altitudes, price indeed plays only a supporting role.

Even in less exclusive upscale markets, price is still secondary. When selling to aficionados of upscale coffee and upscale coffeehouses (a segment that constitutes about one-third of the out-of-home coffee market), price seems to have little impact on choice. Despite an economic downturn from 2000 to 2003, Starbucks, the industry leader, has maintained a 27-percent compound growth rate and moreover hasn't lowered any prices. Interestingly, independent coffeehouses with a distinct ambiance and better coffees have thrived while raising their prices, often as a result of close proximity to a Starbucks. Those coffeehouses that fail to upgrade are often the ones that fail. It appears that the high end of the out-of-home coffee market is rela-

[9] "Got $300,000? These Cars Are For You," *Fortune*, January 20, 2003.

tively price-insensitive, and instead, more concerned with quality and presentation.[10]

The situation changes where there are links between high-end and low-end products. Now a pricing strategy becomes more important, and companies must take into account relationships between market strata.

For example, Nikon came from behind to surpass high-end camera manufacturers Hasselblad, Leica, and others, by creating an overall system encompassing both its less-expensive and more-expensive products. In this system, almost all Nikon lenses work on almost all Nikon bodies. A relatively low-end user can start with an inexpensive body, and then upgrade without having to purchase a new set of lenses. Similarly, a professional can buy additional Nikon camera bodies without having to spend thousands on new lenses. This makes switching costs among brands very high, because most serious photographers have a large supply of lenses that constitutes the bulk of their investment. To move to a new brand would require a major investment to achieve the various combinations possible through existing equipment.[11]

We can generalize from this example and say that switching costs are crucial wherever there are links between high-end and low-end products. For example, Timeplex, the high-end multiplexer manufacturer, belatedly discovered that its networks were being eliminated as customers switched to a competitor, Newbridge. Why? Because although the Timeplex machines were competent in isolation, what customers really valued was unified network monitoring, management, and maintenance—in other words, they were better off moving to all-Newbridge networks. In this case, the low end had surrounded the high

[10] "Despite the Jitters, Most Coffee Houses Survive Starbucks," *The Wall Street Journal*, September 24, 2002, and Starbucks company reports.

[11] Interview with Dan Caligor, photography expert. Mr. Caligor observes that Nikon got its big break with the advent of 35mm film. Also Nikon, unlike Canon, has licensed its mounting architecture to digital camera manufacturers and so will continue to prosper.

end on all sides. By the time Timeplex figured it out and offered its own low-end multiplexer, it was too late.

LIMITS TO PRICE

As we've seen, price can be a powerful weapon in penetrating new markets—however, it has some distinct limitations. For a service or product to gain share, it must offer either superior performance or a superior price-to-value relationship. And such a value proposition can only begin to work if key threshold requirements are met. For example:

- Upstart airlines can charge less, but they must have the precise routes that travelers actually need
- Insurers might possess superior actuarial insights, but they must meet regulatory requirements before they can begin to capitalize on those insights
- Despite its other advantages, the Internet wasn't able to win over information professionals such as librarians from proprietary information systems—not until it achieved the same degree of efficiency as the older systems

We can't emphasize enough that price moves must be coordinated with other elements of the marketing mix. Here's our closing example to this effect, one involving rivals Firestone and Goodyear. After a spate of bad publicity and a recall of Firestone tires fitted to Ford Explorers, Goodyear thought it would be able to gain share at Firestone's expense. In addition, Goodyear thought it could monetize its more favorable consumer perception rating by raising prices. But the price rise failed, and after a year prices returned to their old levels—this, despite a boom in car sales. What had gone wrong? The answer is that Goodyear had failed to meet delivery demand by its dealers, failed to support dealers with marketing collateral, and failed to curb discounting by Wal-Mart. Meanwhile rival Michelin held its price, even as Goodyear "failed to justify the increases [or match] Michelin's reputation among consumers for safety."[12] A perfect illustration of how *not* to coordinate price moves with other elements.

[12] "Deflated. How Goodyear Blew its Chance to Capitalize on a Rival's Woes," *The Wall Street Journal*, February 19, 2003.

Chapter Seventeen
Turning Online Auctions to Your Advantage

Since eBay first opened its doors in 1995, nothing is sacrosanct—from the commonplace, items such as books and toys, to the extreme, airplanes and cow hides (leather irregulars that go for $50 a hide in every color but purple). Even countries. Iraq and its oil fields landed on eBay's capacious block, but turned out to be a prank.[1]

In 1995, online auctions were also capturing the imagination of the business world. Procurement officers and their minions recognized the potential for saving money and began using Internet "reverse" auctions to procure a variety of products from competing suppliers.[2] By the end of 2001, the global value of goods and services managed through e-sourcing solutions (which include online

---

[1] Scarlett Pruitt, "Iraq Goes Up for Auction on eBay," *PCWorld*, January 31, 2003

[2] In a reverse auction, a sole buyer procures goods and services from multiple competing sellers. Reverse auctions are distinct from exchanges, which bring together multiple buyers and sellers. The discussion in this chapter is limited to the former. Internet commerce in the business-to-consumer (B2C) context is another major lowest price situation.

auctions) was about $135 billion; by 2005, the number is expected to reach $738 billion.[3]

There are good reasons for businesses' mounting interest in online auctions. For one thing, they are more efficient and less expensive than traditional procurement approaches. A typical bidding process is paper and time intensive. The buyer prints and distributes requests for information (RFIs), quotations (RFQs), and proposals (RFPs) to the eager candidates, who do their best to fill in the blanks. Weeks pass, three or more firms shrinks to two, and a supplier is finally selected.

In an online auction, the entire process is automated. RFIs, RFQs, and RFPs are circulated online, as are sellers' responses. There is no need for countless face-to-face negotiations or travel, and geography is less of an issue. Indeed, a typical auction lasts only a few hours, and, according to A.T. Kearney estimates, can reduce the entire purchasing cycle by 25 to 35 percent.[4]

For buyers, online auctions are a way to get bargain-basement prices. The price of a product or service can tumble anywhere from 5 to 12 percent on average, and in some cases can drop by 20 percent.[5] In fact, according to A.T. Kearney estimates, those who participate in auctions run by e-Breviate or FreeMarkets, Inc. will see a 16-percent average drop in price.[6] In an online auction, buyers have the upper hand: They sit back and wait for a good price.

---

[3] Aberdeen Group, Making e-Sourcing Strategic: From Tactical Technology to Core Business Strategy, September 2002. e-Sourcing refers to all Web-based procurement functions, including online reverse auctions, electronic requests for information, quotations, and proposals.

[4] A.T. Kearney Procurement Solutions, op. cit. and Larry R. Smeltzer and Amelia Carr, "Reverse Auctions in Industrial Marketing and Buying," Business Horizons, March–April, 2002.

[5] Smeltzer and Carr, op. cit.

[6] A.T. Kearney Procurement Solutions Discussion Document, 2002. Also, Sam Kinney, "An Overview of B2B and Purchasing Technology," submitted to Federal Trade Commission Public Workshop on Competition Policy in the World of B2B Electronic Marketplaces, June 2000.

For sellers, online auctions might seem less appealing. In fact, some suppliers consider them heresy. "It's a perversion of the buying process," complains one supplier in the home furnishings industry in an interview with *Home Furnishing Network*. "In most cases, it is designed to squeeze more money from the manufacturer in a process that lacks any institutional control." Another supplier in the industry laments, "What did we win? We won the pleasure of selling the product."[7]

Suppliers' biggest complaint about online reverse auctions is that they are mostly price driven. Buyers choose suppliers solely on price with little regard for product quality, customer service, delivery time, or any of the other benefits that define a solid, long-term buyer-seller relationship. Some suppliers complain that online reverse auctions are "fixed," with the winners predetermined. Or they say auctions are a negotiating ploy, a way for buyers to wrangle a lower price out of a preferred (that is, incumbent) supplier. The winning supplier loses profit margin, while all other competitors become unwitting participants in a charade.

DEFINING THE STRIKE ZONE

Despite their complaints, not all sellers lose in an online auction. Some win, but usually only those who understand the rules of the game. In baseball, it would be equivalent to a pitcher tossing one just on the edge of the strike zone—getting the buyer to swing, but not hard enough to hit a home run.

The first rule is to use price transparency to your advantage. Unlike a sealed-bid auction, in an online auction, suppliers know what the best price is at any given moment, and they know where their price is relative to the competition. Such insight can be valuable. By observing competitors' bids in real time, suppliers get an idea of how competitors perceive their bids.[8] For those trying to penetrate a new market, an

---

[7] See "Auctions: Hitting Below the Belt," *Home Furnishing Network*, March 11, 2002.

[8] e-Breviate, "Auctions Bidder Guide," April 2002

online auction is an opportunity to gauge true market prices, thereby avoiding the dramatic underbidding or discounting, which often happens in a sealed-bid process. The acquisition cost for new customers is therefore lower than in traditional procurement.[9]

For new suppliers, online auctions provide a much-needed level playing field. Favoritism is out as all online bidders get the same information, and the same specifications, at the same time. No one does business under the table—meaning the incumbent supplier cannot step up after the auction and match the price of the winning bid. In fact, to forestall such after-the-auction shenanigans, some auctioneers such as FreeMarkets insist that buyers sign agreements forbidding any negotiations once the closing bell of the auction has rung.[10]

Also, in online auctions there is no room for questionable negotiating tactics, for example, where a buyer pretends he has a lower price than another supplier simply to get you to come down on your price.[11]

Finally, any supplier that wins an online auction is probably going to get a larger order. Because buyers want to entice as many suppliers as possible to their auction, they have to make it worthwhile by putting out a high dollar value of business.

THAT'S PRICELESS

Because no one wins in a price war, suppliers should do everything in their power to avoid one. How do you defend against auctions that make price the center of the process? That's easy. Expand the focus.

Today many online auction services use so-called multiparameter bidding to capture both the price and nonprice elements of a bid. For example, e-Breviate allows buyers to apply weights to nonprice parameters during the auction and then adjust the weight to test different sce-

---

[9] e-Breviate, "Thriving in the e-Procurement Market Place," Discussion Document, August 10, 2001

[10] Terry Kosdrosky, "Trade Group Boss: Online Auctions Used to Force Supplier Price Cuts," *Crain's Detroit Business*, April 22, 2002.

[11] Kinney, op. cit.

narios.[12] One buyer of parts might rank the value of a one-year warranty higher than the value of payment terms, while another might consider payment terms more important and give it a higher ranking. By calculating the value of different parameters according to their unique needs, buyers can compare products by the total cost of ownership rather than price alone.

With multiparameter bidding, suppliers can highlight their strengths relative to other bidders. If the process does not explicitly ask for nonprice parameters, call the buyer to find out where to insert your "priceless" information. Typically, including information about nonprice elements into a bid requires quantifying their value. For example, product quality might be expressed as the number of faults allowed per thousand pieces produced, or it might be a quality guarantee for a number of years. The following are a few examples of nonprice parameters that will help distinguish you from your competitors:

- Product quality
- Innovation record and plans
- Transportation costs
- Warehousing days
- Discounts and rebates
- Terms and conditions
- Maintenance fees
- Limited liability awards
- Lead time
- Training fees
- Summary billing frequency and cost
- Spare parts availability and cost
- Tooling and retooling costs

If you are an incumbent supplier, you will want to highlight the high cost of switching to a new supplier. For example, if you have enjoyed a long and deep relationship with the buyer, don't hesitate to inform the buyer about the risks associated with trying out a new supplier whose

[12] e-Breviate Discussion Document, January 2003.

quality, service, and reliability are untested. Moreover, to the extent that you have invested in meeting particular product specifications or have developed specific production processes or delivery capabilities, remind the buyer that a new supplier will be forced to make these investments as well just to match your value, never mind to achieve a superior level of quality.

New suppliers, on the other hand, will want to emphasize their competitiveness on all dimensions, not only price. If you suspect that the buyer thinks you are weaker than the incumbent supplier in some areas, offer to share or even fully bear the switching costs. One tactic is to guarantee that the total cost of ownership of your product will be no more than that of the incumbent. More generally, as a nonincumbent you should try to creatively identify "carrots" that are valuable to the buyer but do not cost very much to provide.

The disguised example in Figure 17.1 depicts an auction for power cords run by e-Breviate. Bids include not only price but a number of nonprice parameters as well, including lead time, payment terms, and warehousing days. In addition, the buyer's switching costs are addressed. What's interesting in this example is that the lowest price bidder didn't provide the lowest total cost of ownership to the buyer. For this reason it failed to win the auction.

DEFENDING AGAINST AUCTIONS

If online reverse auctions are becoming the norm in your business, the guidelines outlined in this chapter might help protect your prices. But they will not guarantee that you win the auction every time, nor that your prices will not be bid downward. The best long-term strategy for online auctions is to avoid them altogether, particularly if you are the incumbent supplier.

There are several ways to defend against reverse auctions:

Increase Complexity

The best defense against auctions is a good offense—increase the complexity of your offerings by adding innovative features. For example,

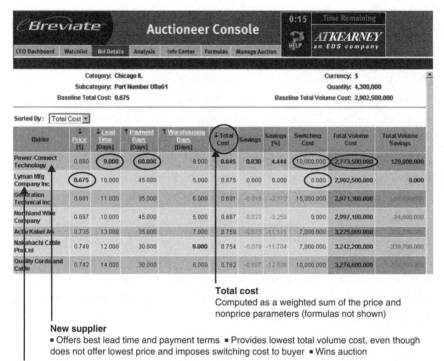

Total cost
Computed as a weighted sum of the price and
nonprice parameters (formulas not shown)

New supplier
▪ Offers best lead time and payment terms ▪ Provides lowest total volume cost, even though
does not offer lowest price and imposes switching cost to buyer ▪ Wins auction

Incumbent
▪ Offers lowest price and imposes no switching cost ▪ But less competitive on lead time, payment
days, and warehousing days ▪ Loses auction

Source: A.T. Kearney

Figure 17.1. The lowest price bidder does not necessarily win the auction.

Budd Co., an automotive supplier, came up with a proprietary technology for a self-dimming rear-view mirror.[13] This is the kind of advanced product that is a natural shield against mandatory price cuts at least until the competition catches up.

Online reverse auctions are best suited for buying or selling goods and services that are fairly straightforward: cables, locks, power cords, paper clips, and pens are all good candidates. If it is difficult to spell out a product's requirements or specifications, or nail down its intrinsic

[13] Doug Bartholomew, "The Big Squeeze," *Industry Week*, April 1, 2002

value, it should not be auctioned. Suppliers will not only find it difficult to put together robust bids for complex products or services; buyers will have a hard time comparing bids. One supplier's interpretation
of the requirements might differ from another's. And the more complicated the offering, the less assurance buyers will have that the winning
supplier can actually deliver the product or service. Bundling products
and services with complementary goods, spare parts, or repair and
maintenance services can also make it more difficult to quantify the
various nonprice features, or to compare the various product and service bundles, making it less likely that you will find yourself in a
reverse auction.

Pricing itself is often a good tool for increasing complexity, not to
mention confusion. Ask any carrier in the wireless industry about its
pricing structures and you will hear about a plethora of complicated
calling plans—from monthly fixed fees, per-minute charges, roaming
fees, long-distance rates, and different daytime, evening, and weekend
plans. Because calling patterns are difficult to forecast, and because
most buyers cannot predict their future requirements, mobile phone
calling plans are rarely found on an auction block.

Build a Brand

Branding can also be an effective weapon against reverse auctions
because brand value is difficult to quantify. Comparing different
branded products is far more difficult than comparing generic products.
In addition, the high cost of selling and marketing branded products limits the price concessions that suppliers can grant and in turn the price
reductions that buyers can achieve. The supermarket industry uses
reverse auctions to buy private label products but not to buy branded
goods. Department stores use reverse auctions to buy private label
apparel and soft goods but not branded merchandise.[14]

---

[14] Kathleen DesMarteau, "Major Retailers Usher in Era of Exchanges, Reverse
Auctions," *Bobbin*, September 1, 2002. An executive of the Hudson's Bay Company,
Canada's largest department store retailer, explains it this way: "Apparel and soft
goods procured through exchanges and online auctions could be branded, but we see
more upside for our private brands."

Become Indispensable

Suppliers that increase their role in the supply chain are seldom asked to participate in online reverse auctions. Investing capital and resources, retooling, and performing joint-process improvements with buyers can significantly reduce your risk of ending up in an online auction anytime soon. Do what the tier-one suppliers in the automotive industry do. Rather than providing stand-alone parts or components, these suppliers provide entire vehicle subassemblies and systems. Magna, a top automotive supplier, builds a cadre of unique, complex, and highly engineered modules ranging from subassemblies to complete vehicles.[15]

Have No Peers

Buyers use online auctions to secure lower prices. But lower prices are only possible if a sufficient number of suppliers (at least five[16]) participate in an auction. One counterauction strategy is to ensure that you have few true competitors. This will be the case if you own key patents, have access to key inputs, or have developed specialized production processes. If you do not have these advantages, consider making selective mergers, acquisitions, or alliances with close competitors. A consolidated supply market is unattractive to buyers using reverse auctions.

WHO'S ON FIRST?

We see far too many instances of risky bidding—suppliers who get caught up in the auction process and bid wildly because they must

---

[15] Magna annual report and various analyst reports. The Magna approach is consistent with procurement strategies in other industries. Consider a quote from the procurement manager of Owens Corning, a major manufacturer of building materials and glass composite fibers: "Supplier relationships are a vital part of the procurement process. For strategic materials you need a solid relationship with your supply base, so those are the things we leave off the table when it comes to auctions. The items we put into reverse auctions are not strategic to us." See "Owens Corning Builds Major Savings from Reverse Auctions," Supplier Selection and Management Report, March 1, 2002.

[16] Smeltzer and Carr, op. cit.

"win" at any cost. Later, these same bidders might be found meekly reneging on their unprofitable commitments. One participant in a reverse auction explained it this way, "[auctions are] almost like gambling. You get caught up in the moment and you don't want to lose it. You have to know your true cost, realize the bottom line, and just don't go below that number. If you can't make money, what's the purpose?"[17]

If you cannot avoid an auction, the following guidelines might prove helpful for participating in one:

- Participate only in auctions in which you have product or service strength.
- Make sure your corporate strategy and overall business development objectives are aligned with the auction (for example, is this must-have or nice-to-have business?).
- Form a cross-functional team to develop your response to the request for information, quote, or proposal and to participate in the auction.
- Plan ahead: Gather current and future costs for providing the product or service being procured over the duration of the contract (that is, bid profitability). Also, predict competitors' most likely bids and use information revealed by the other bids to identify other bidders.
- Define negotiation and bid strategies for all product or service categories: Determine the most desirable objective, the least acceptable agreement or drop-dead price (know when to walk away), and the best alternative.
- Define auction tactics: Determine initial and subsequent bids, the timing of each bid, and the rules that will guide your responses.

---

[17] See "Auctions: Hitting Below the Belt," op. cit. Another supplier concurred: "When you're sitting in front of that screen and you ask 'Can I slash another $10,000 or so off my price?' It's a gambling mentality." See William J. Angelo, "Reverse Auctions Raise New Specter of Bid Shopping on Industry Products. Some Contractors Worry About Services Becoming Commodities," *Engineering News Record*, November 4, 2002. See also Smeltzer and Carr, op. cit.

- Understand the auction process, including product and service specifications, auction rules, information available during the auction and the online bidding process. Participate in practice auctions and training sessions to become familiar with the process.
- Assign multiple bidders to different product and service categories for complex auctions.
- Obtain preapproval for price concessions and ensure that senior executives are available to approve "on the spot" concessions during the auction.
- Conduct a postauction debriefing session to capture lessons learned and to discuss what went well and what could have been better. Capture insights on where your industry is moving and realign pricing and marketing strategies with industry trends.

SUMMARY

In this chapter, we examined why online reverse auctions are a prime example of a "lowest price" situation, and what strategies sellers can adopt to defend against slashing prices and promote sustainable price premiums. Throughout the book, we discuss how to further protect prices through a strategy of product and service differentiation. Even in the world of online auctions, it is difficult to make price comparisons when a product or service is tailored to meet the unique needs of customers.

HOW THE OCEAN TRANSPORT INDUSTRY CAPTURED THE EFFICIENCIES OF AN ONLINE PROCUREMENT PROCESS[18]

When GoCargo, a B2B exchange for the ocean container shipping industry, launched its NaviPact auction tool in 2000, it had high hopes for automating the contract-award process. But most container carriers rejected the reverse auction approach, refusing to

---

[18] This case is based on information from three sources: (1) "The Container Case," *The Economist*, October 19, 2000; (2) Web site of "Ebituaries: Home of Dead Dot-Coms" (*www.ebituaries.whirlycott.com*); (3) Helen Atkinson, "Coming Back Slowly," *Journal of Commerce*, March 4, 2002

participate. They were emboldened by their customers—both domestic and international shippers—that preferred to pay premiums for end-to-end solutions. Their thinking was that container shipping was far too complicated for an online auction. Even though containers might look like commodities—that is, standard-sized sealed units—the sea is usually only part of the journey. Containers might also travel on trucks and trains, and pass through customs twice. And there are significant differences between container carriers' reliability records and the size of shipments they can handle.

Although GoCargo reworked its strategy, building a multiparameter bidding system to account for nonprice factors such as rated quality of service, it was too late. By May 2001, GoCargo had ceased to exist.

Today, GoCargo is dead but the idea lives on. A new breed of online reverse auction providers are pursuing the container shipping market. But rather than going for steep price discounts, these companies are focusing on reducing the paperwork and cycle time of the procurement process. So far the new online tools are being used successfully for domestic shipping, evident in reduced administrative costs, but not for international shipping. As one shipper puts it: "We don't want to treat international transport as a commodity. I think it's important that you have a relationship with your forwarder and they in turn with transport suppliers. If something goes wrong, you can recover relatively easily in the United States but when you're dealing with the other side of the world you want people you can rely on."

The lesson? Differentiate, emphasize the complexity of your offering, and build deep, strategic relationships with your customers.

The Aftermarket: Don't Let It be an Afterthought

"**D**on't let the aftermarket be an afterthought" is a familiar phrase. We all nod our heads in agreement, showing that of course we recognize the profit potential of the aftermarket, both long and short-term. Who among us can argue with the cumulative effect that annual price increases for parts and services have on cash flow? Despite this knowledge, and long-held intentions to pay more attention to their aftermarket businesses, few executives today have taken the time to systematically assess the fundamental questions related to their aftermarket business:

1. How high is the price ceiling? What is the maximum margin available?

2. How can we increase the proprietary positioning of the accessory, part, or service?

3. What are the price elasticities and price-demand responses of parts and services? How will aftermarket pricing affect marketing campaigns for existing or new products?

4. How visible are prices? Are there competitor reference prices on the majority of our parts?

5. What services can be bundled with the aftermarket? What is the role of financial and service engineering? For example, can we create an annuity product, such that the customer pays for usage or availability? Rather than having the customer perform difficult, risky maintenance tasks, can we provide these services?

These questions just scratch the surface of the range of possibilities and ideas to pursue in the aftermarket business. For purposes of this discussion, we define the aftermarket as spare parts, maintenance services, accessories, kits, upgrades, or extensions of products. Yet the pricing concepts for the aftermarket can be applied to a wide range of consumer items as well, such as snacks and beverages found in gas station food marts, or cables and printer cartridges found in electronics stores.

PROPRIETARY POSITIONING

A useful starting point for discussion is a product's life cycle and the proprietary nature of the associated stream of parts and services. Normally, the longer the life cycle and the more proprietary the service part, the more value in the aftermarket. Perhaps one of the most dramatic examples of a long-life-cycle product is the jet turbine engine business, where the annuity can and often must last 25 to 30 years, to offset the typically huge development costs.

Long life coupled with a proprietary position makes the aftermarket opportunity even more interesting. There are several ways to reduce competition in aftermarket products and services: by regulatory means, such as the FAA required imprimatur called PMA in jet turbines; by product design, or tooling investments, such as style parts in automotive; or by supply chain incentives and penalties. Each of these helps to raise the price ceiling.

THE MORE PROPRIETARY THE SERVICE PART, THE MORE VALUE IN THE AFTERMARKET

There are many ways to increase the proprietary nature of the spare part or service. Typical strategies include:

- Prevent local suppliers from selling in the open market
- Control parts flows so they go to authorized service centers only
- Label unauthorized dealers as "nongenuine" and therefore of lesser quality
- Invest in packaging and providing marketing materials to authorized service centers, thereby boosting brand equity
- Retain used materials or trade-ins to limit repair and refurbishment opportunities
- Flatten distribution by selling direct to dealers
- Retain final part processes in-house
- Create information barriers by retaining special engineering or quality instructions
- Make warranty and insurance programs contingent on genuine parts
- Offset more competitive parts to low-cost regions, cross-subsidizing them via highly protective or safety-related parts

The next question is how high can you initially set prices? The answer should take into account the total cost of ownership from the customer's point of view—this relates to the customer's willingness to buy a new product from you again. In a complex product sale with many operating and maintenance costs, customers can calculate the total cost of ownership net any residual value. An OEM can make similar calculations to duplicate the customer's reasoning. If the OEM believes it still has an advantage, it can choose to raise its aftermarket prices, resulting in near cost-of-ownership equivalency with the next best OEM competitor. However, if the OEM is disadvantaged, it might be better off mimicking competitors' prices, in the meantime coming out with improvement kits or new designs to restore parity.

Other important pricing decisions in the aftermarket are the following: whether to apply price increases for spare parts across the board or selectively, how to value-price performance kits and full solutions, and how to manage aftermarket distribution channels. We'll discuss each of these topics in turn.

SPARE PARTS OPPORTUNITIES

To understand the pricing opportunity in spare parts, you must first segment parts and part families according to their proprietary position, repair alternatives, and part velocity (that is, how fast they move off the shelves). Although such segmentation schemes vary by industry, the basic logic is depicted in Figure 18.1.

In this figure, the part segment labeled "3A" has all the characteristics of an attractive pricing situation—the price isn't readily visible or easily referenceable with those of competitors. New entrants are unlikely to come in, given its maturity, and there are few alternatives from the customer's point of view. Also, it can be bundled in a repair kit to simplify handling and logistics. On the other hand, Part "1C" has a highly competitive outlook with clearly visible pricing, several repair alternatives, and sufficient volumes to amortize nonrecurring costs of new entrants. The pricing opportunities in this latter case are most likely limited to a brand premium.

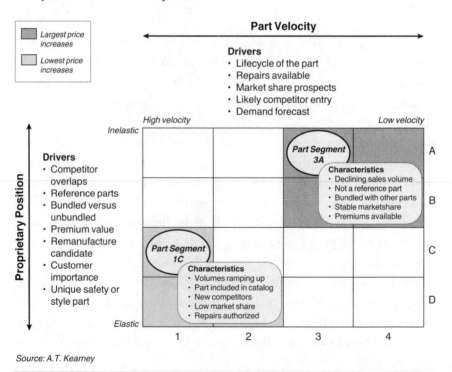

Source: A.T. Kearney

Figure 18.1. Developing the pricing matrix for a product line.

We can summarize by saying that the basic principle behind such a pricing matrix is that parts within the same category—that is, having similar velocities and proprietary positions—should have similar premiums or discounts. In other words, what matters is a part's competitive intensity, not its manufacturing costs. The less rivalry and visibility, the higher the price level. This would seem clear. Yet many companies fail to put this into practice, partly because they are reluctant to gather and synthesize detailed information on a large number of parts.

One of the myths associated with the aftermarket is that all parts need to be competitively priced, even though distributors typically track only the fast moving parts. In the automotive world, customer interviews confirm that "visible" parts pricing affects at most 10 percent of all parts.

Another myth is that parts can't be value-priced—definitely not true, because financial services and differences in extended cost of ownership can clearly be a significant source of value in the aftermarket.

The final myth—or perhaps we should call it an excuse—relates to the sheer number of parts to be analyzed, usually with only a limited staff. But what appears to be an overwhelming obstacle is hardly that: segmenting parts by value, part family, or business line, as well as by attribute, can help prioritize the most compelling parts to work on. Once this is done, the full lineup of typical parts can be assessed at a somewhat more leisurely pace. The most important utility of the price matrix is its use in annual or periodic price increases. Most companies tailor their price changes by product category, depending on their perception of competitor price points, market share objectives, and position relative to cost of ownership. However, within each individual product category, companies generally follow a "one size fits all" approach. This is a mistake, and it comes with a substantial opportunity cost in terms of lost profits. Inelastic, low-velocity parts can sustain relatively high price increases with little loss of volume, while at the other end of the spectrum, parts with low market penetration, highly visible prices, and strong competition might actually mandate a discount.

Software is now becoming available to help with the intensity of data and number of parts to price. Price lists can now be generated on a monthly, weekly, or even daily basis, allowing for the issuance of dynamic parts catalogs. As competitor and industry data becomes available, such data can be rapidly applied to a price matrix and the resulting price effects readily assessed. The savings in time can allow the pricing organization to conduct a wide range of experiments to confirm that profits are being optimized. Additionally, more time can be devoted to developing new part strategies, such as kitting, to increase the proprietary nature of the part and the opportunity to value-price it.

THE VALUE OF KITTING

Kitting is the bundling of parts, with the aim of simplifying customer logistics or improving a product's performance or reliability. From this definition we can see that kits have value to the customer only if they improve the total cost of ownership—that is, they must either save time or money, or else improve product performance.

Consider the following example in jet turbine engines: One turbine engine manufacturer's design was superior in fuel-burn performance. Unfortunately, that advantage was more than offset by more expensive maintenance and lower reliability. Consequently, this OEM was slightly disadvantaged in overall cost of ownership. This was bad enough, requiring up-front discounts in new turbine engine sales. But it also put a ceiling on spare parts increases for turbine engines already in service, because the OEM didn't want to increase the cost of ownership differential. To counter this, the OEM designed an upgrade kit that significantly improved reliability and durability. The question then became— how to price it?

The pricing organization's first instinct was to use the superceded parts list price as the starting point. Others advocated a margin requirement of 50 percent to recover the engineering investment. Still others wanted to achieve price parity with the competitor. Essentially, these convenient solutions were all forms of cost-plus pricing.

However, by quantifying the improvement in total cost of ownership (less maintenance cost, higher reliability, increased efficiency), the OEM could split the increased value with the customer. Knowing that the customer would be reluctant to buy anything that didn't have a one-year payback, a new price level could be set that shared the value. This would encourage high adoption rates while ensuring competitive parity on cost of ownership. A sensitivity analysis was also performed to judge the potential impact on price if a competitor followed suit with a similar improvement. As it turned out, value-pricing in this fashion resulted in a price nearly double that of the initial cost-based recommendations.

FULL CUSTOMER SOLUTIONS

If performance kitting has intrinsic value, imagine what *full customer solutions* can achieve. A full customer solution in the aftermarket is typically a guarantee to the customer that the product will be available, reliable, and upgradeable. One such solution, again from the jet turbine industry, became known as "power by the hour." It works like this: For every engine flight hour, an airline pays a fee to the engine OEM. The OEM for its part performs the necessary maintenance at shop visits and restores the engine periodically to its initial performance condition. If necessary, the OEM can supply a spare engine to ensure availability. The OEM manages the full costs—material and labor—as well as the risks.

From an airline point of view, such a solution makes perfect sense. An airline has a high cost of capital and naturally prefers to offload its expensive maintenance and part inventory assets. Advantaged airlines such as Southwest have followed exactly this model. Ultimately, "power by the hour" might prove to be the first of a series of financial and risk-managed solutions that eventually lead to an OEM managing an entire fleet—engines and airplanes.

In designing full solutions, it's useful to look at the entire ecosystem of players. Consider accessories for large trucks: A complete solution might wrap services, information, and channels into a fully integrated format, available at a convenient location and with financing. Taking the friction out of the supply chain might prove attractive to all parties involved.

GETTING THE PART TO MARKET EFFECTIVELY

The notion of ecosystems highlights the importance of distributor and retail channels in the aftermarket. In many industries, wholesale distributors are relied upon to get parts to the various retail outlets—dealers, authorized service centers, jobbers, and others. Considered as customers of the OEM or parts manufacturer, distributors vary in size, capability, exclusivity, and market focus. In large urban areas, it's not unheard of that the required service level for an auto parts distributor needs to be measured in minutes.

In spite of these obvious differences, many OEMs make the mistake of treating distributors as if they were all the same size and had identical needs, offering all of them the same promotional and discount programs. From the OEM's perspective, the actual distributor margin is based off the net/net price. But from a distributor's perspective, it's not so clear—is it the net distributor price? Invoice price? The initial distributor price? OEMs typically want a homogeneous price ladder—the same programs and discounts for all distributors. But why should a distributor that caters to dealers have the same value of co-op advertising as a distributor that primarily serves independents?

A return reserve might be much more difficult to administer than, say, a volume discount program. However, for a small distributor, volume discounts might not be valued anywhere near the ease to handle returns. And on the other hand, a larger distributor might not even recognize the timing and magnitude of annual volume bonuses. The point we're making is that there are distinct distributor segments, each requiring a specific value proposition that delivers the benefits they value most, and at an attractive cost to serve.

Effectively tailoring the price stack should accomplish two things: First, increase distributor satisfaction, and second, allow your company to retain more of the value it has earned from improved pricing capabilities.

In summary, the aftermarket can be a significant source of improved profits. Once the basic capabilities for pricing spare parts are in place, new initiatives in kitting, solution selling, and distributor management can provide additional profit opportunities. The organizational effort required is significant—but so is the payoff.

| Chapter
Nineteen | # Quick Hits |

Pricing requires effort, and some of the most rewarding price initiatives take some lead time and investment. However, there are some price initiatives that can, under the right circumstances, produce a material benefit with little lead time and minimal effort. These are the "quick hits." Each serves a different purpose. Some improve both the top and bottom lines, some only the top line, others only the bottom line, and some improve cash flow. Pick those that apply to your company's needs and ignore those that don't.

We urge you to use these quick hits as proof to the organization that pricing skills do produce real rewards. Forge an agreement that the monies generated by these quick-hit efforts can go to fund more price capabilities and major price projects listed elsewhere in this book. It's an approach that can convert skeptics.

Quick Hit #1. *Increase the revenues from stable accounts by offering all-you-can-eat pricing.* The idea here is to take an account that has been relatively stable, growing, or shrinking slightly from year to year, and offer that account all the product they want for a flat fee that is somewhat higher than their current spending. For instance, one legal

publisher had a law firm customer that spent $97,000 per year on the
publisher's books. The publisher offered the lawyers all the copies they
wanted for $110,000 per year. The firm found the proposition com-
pelling. As a result, revenues grew 11 percent while actual product
shipments grew very little.

Quick Hit #2. *Move from billing in arrears to billing in advance.*
Some industries commonly bill for services and goods before they're
performed or produced—examples are newspaper subscriptions,
airline tickets, and monthly telephone service. If your company
bills in arrears (that is, after you've performed the service), consider
a shift that puts your company ahead one month for the year. Objections might include the worry that the precise amount of charges
isn't known in advance—however, you can either bill an estimated
amount, or else separate the fixed and variable charges in different
bill cycles (which by the way is what your local phone company
does). Another objection is that it might be difficult to switch over
existing customers, and this might be true. But you can still begin
with new customers.

Quick Hit #3. *Launch a product bundle.* Often a bundle is an excellent way to grow your market share: It allows you to offer more value
without much danger of cannibalizing other revenues. And as described
in Chapter 10, bundles can be so powerful they permanently change
the competitive landscape. An ad hoc bundle is not likely to do quite
this much, but it will still lift revenues and start to build market intelligence regarding customer bundle needs.

The "quick hit" part of this idea is that we find that many bundles
can be successfully launched to the market *before* all the normal back-
office changes are made. The IT department will typically object that
supporting the bundle requires many millions of dollars of investment
for billing and customer service, among other things. But this isn't true,
as there are many workarounds to such infrastructures. As Figure 19.1
illustrates, a hierarchy of ways exists to address the billing of bundles
and provide customer service support. In most cases customers are so

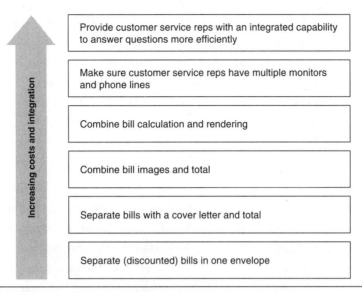

Figure 19.1. Bundling "workarounds."

happy to get the bundle they want, they don't care about the lack of elegance to the solutions.[1]

Quick Hit #4. *Add on extra charges for valuable services.* Such services might include rush orders, shipping out of state, special billing arrangements, custom products, training fees, and setup fees. In most cases customers won't react to such charges, and they provide a quick revenue lift.

Quick Hit #5. *Convert revenue offsets to expenses.* If your objective is to improve top-line growth, but your net income is meeting plan, there are nonetheless ways of lifting reported revenues. One way is to suspend early-payment discounts and instead offer free shipment or other services in lieu of the early-payment discount. Another way is if your company separates out sales taxes from revenues: In some circumstances you might be able to count taxes in revenue figures, and then pay sales taxes as an expense.

[1] As one Silicon Valley, ex-Apple product development guru said, "Don't Worry, Be Crappy!"

Quick-Hit #6. *Pull forward a product release.* R&D and other product development organizations, by their very nature, like to release new products and services in an orderly fashion, preferably after extensive testing. Consider offering a discounted "prerelease" version of your product or service. Make it clear that because this is a prerelease, there might be some flaws, but that the customer is nonetheless getting a good deal. (This is a notorious practice among software developers, but for reasons that have to do with time-to-market rather than pricing.)

Quick-Hit #7. *Change price structure to reflect value.* While changing some price structures can be difficult, often there are obvious ways to capture value that can be executed quickly. For example, Russell Cohoon, the island manager for Dog Island, Florida, was inspired to change the charging structure for the ferry that transports cars from the mainland. Switching from a flat per-vehicle charge to a fee by weight, he found this instantly brought in higher revenues from contractors and others bringing over trucks and building supplies. Overall, the change increased revenues by 35 percent with minimal administrative effort.

Quick-Hit #8. *Suspend sales discounts for a short period of time.* We find that in many markets a brief suspension of discounts or promotions can work to increase price levels, without hurting sales.[2] We suspect the explanation is that the sales force seeks out its less price-sensitive prospects during the no-discount period and sells to them at the higher effective price. After the discounts come back on, the sales force goes back to normal customers. Theoretically, with a good discounting model such as that described in Chapter 15, you should be able to capture this value at other times—but if such a model is lacking, this program will make some small progress in that direction.

Quick-Hit #9. *Temporarily unbundle your most valuable product or service.* Many companies—quite correctly—bundle their lead product in with other products and refuse to sell it independently. This is a

---

[2] An analogy can be found in a Volkswagen owner's manual (one of the authors was for many years an avid VW driver), dating from a period of high gasoline prices. The manual notes that when driving at a constant speed, slightly reducing gasoline-pedal pressure will reduce gasoline consumption, yet without slowing down the car.

highly rational price strategy because good bundling can increase total revenues over time. However, the strategy does have an offsetting cost, in the form of customers who choose not to buy the bundle but *would* buy the lead product if it were offered alone. If you manage a temporary offer right, you can sell more of the lead product than you lose in bundles, because those prospects that have previously refrained from buying now rush forward to buy before the interval expires.

Quick-Hit #10. *Reduce barriers to sale, at least temporarily.* The General Motors offer of free financing that jump-started that company's sales during 2001 to 2002 is a good example of removing a price barrier. Although such a move might not be sustainable in the long run, it can be extremely effective in the short term. Other situations lending themselves to this idea might include the conversion of sales to leases, or vice versa, selling something that formerly was only leased.

Another barrier to sale might be if customers hold large existing inventories of a competitor's goods. A good tactic here might be to offer to buy those inventories, thereby opening up space for your product.

Quick-Hit #11. *Charge for unintentional abuse by your customer base.* After reviewing your operational costs, you probably can identify several ways in which undesirable or unusual customer behavior is increasing your operational costs. Typically, these behaviors flourish in connection either with fixed-price usage, or with features or services for which there are no explicit charges at all. Examples are excessive use of an online service by fixed-price customers, too many requests for rush production, oversized packages, heavy claims by insurance policy-owners, and so on. Your counterbalancing price increase might be quite modest—or even offset by a linked price reduction—but the resulting operational cost savings can be significant.

Quick Hit #12. *Look for a "tuck-in" addition to the product offer.* If you can find a product or service to resell in conjunction with your existing products and services, it can create a significant revenue boost—both from recouping the cost of the item and marking up the resold item. Examples include IBM reselling a high-end multiplexer in connection with its data communications devices, a tax service acquiring and selling a related tax newsletter, and a telecom reselling business interruption insurance to call centers in case the telecom's network fails.

Quick Hit #13. *Take advantage of a growth in demand for your product or service—and be creative about it.* Pay attention to unusual or sudden increases in demand for a product or service. This can highlight what is effectively a new market, or else better reflect shifting changes in value. For example, the rationale for medical MRIs has changed from "better diagnoses" to a legal necessity to avoid malpractice claims—as a result, the test is more frequently ordered. When risks of terrorist biological attacks became known, gas mask manufacturers raised their prices. Similarly, Coca-Cola is looking at ways of changing the prices on its vending machines so that it charges more on hot days and less on cold days. A neater instance of price mirroring need can hardly be imagined.

Quick Hit #14. *Raise prices ahead of the normal cycle.* Although this tactic is quite obvious, it's worth considering. As described in Chapter 14, you need to communicate a convincing reason for any unexpected price increase, so that customers will accept it as necessary and not balk or worse rebel. However, with a little creativity, there are nearly always excuses—new features, changes in demand, additional costs, operational necessity, are all good excuses. Whether they will be convincing depends on the market and the magnitude of the increase, as well as how often you attempt this tactic.

Quick Hit #15. *Raise prices to your trailing-edge customers.* Very often there are subscribers or leasees of products and services who haven't paid attention to their bills for a long time. For example, some users of high-capacity data lines are still paying tariffs from a decade ago, even though market prices have dropped in the interim by more than 50 percent. Likewise, some leasees of computers and copiers from the late 1970s truly *haven't* looked at their bills in years. You can leverage the inattention of such users by raising prices on trailing-edge products.

Quick Hit #16. *Raise prices on mandatory parts.* Raising prices on required parts exploits the high switching costs of customers that have already bought into your product or service through a capital purchase or extensive training. The price focus of most organizations is all too often on the initial sale, not the follow-on purchases.

Summary

Quick hits are useful if you need to meet budget goals, and can also be useful as a way to try new pricing tactics, or even (provided you have buy-in from the organization) as a means to fund other price initiatives. Yet to be truthful, their very nature makes it unlikely they will play the role of transformational initiatives. In addition, there is usually an offset of some sort, whether it is increased administration, greater downside risks, reduced customer satisfaction, or simply that the benefits are merely temporary. This is another way of saying there is no free lunch—only specials of the day.

And note that in some cases a quick hit might move your price position in the wrong direction. A company whose price levels are above the optimum might still see short-term improvements from an out-of-cycle price rise—but in the long term there might be negative NPV to pay if a sufficient number of customers become sufficiently irked that they'll defect to the first competitive offer.

Quick hits do have their place, otherwise this chapter wouldn't exist. But for price measures that represent sustainable, systematic, lower-risk initiatives with bigger long-term gains, read the rest of this book.

Part Four

Building Revenue Capabilities

A Supporting Organization and Process

This final section of the book provides a blueprint for how to build up your institutional pricing and branding capabilities. By institutional capabilities we mean the ways to ensure that your company excels in pricing and branding as a natural outcome of its organizational structure, standards, culture, process, systems, and strategies.

By now, you have no doubt concluded that there is a hefty payout to integrating your price, brand, cost, and product development. But do your current organization charts and processes support this integration?

Typically, organizations have flattened the pyramid, reducing the vertical layers between top management and first-level managers to achieve cost reductions and faster execution. But also typically, little is done to *horizontally* integrate exactly those functions we have been discussing. You can argue that the gaps can be bridged through a knowledge-sharing system, whether software-based or other. But while such systems can be powerful, they aren't up to the task of single-handedly bringing managers together to change strategies or reallocate marketing efforts.[1] Much more is needed for completing the integration needed for

[1] "Putting Knowledge to Work," *Internet Telephony*, December 1996.

success. Hence, this chapter. If your current reporting structure, information flows, and decision flows aren't getting your company where it needs to go, then the remedies suggested here should be of great interest to you.

First, some groundwork. We have found that to truly integrate different functions, a company must blend three things: performance measures—that is, how each department measures its productivity and success; compensation plans for managers in each function; and decision processes for product branding budgets, overall price plans, and new product development. Let's look at each of these.

Performance measures today tend to be quite disparate. Take branding. Typically, success in branding is measured through awareness—how favorably customers view the company and sometimes the lead streams that support the sales force or shop-front. All worthy measures, but they are sufficient only if branding intends to operate in a vacuum. If not, we suggest that brand must also be measured by how it is contributing to corporate profits, that is, by its effect on price.

Specifically, you must be able to compare pricing power for your company versus the same for competitors.[2] This shouldn't be a burden, as normal competitive monitoring should include keeping tabs on competitors' prices. For example, in a particular reference book market, two rival publishers regularly tracked the "ratio," meaning the difference in subscription prices (net of discounts) between their respective publications. When one publisher saw his side of the ratio deteriorating during the late 1990s, he spent money to ensure that his publication updates were prominently reviewed by influential third parties. This helped him regain brand advantage.

Compensation plans must be merged—this is essential. Without merged incentives, the impact of other measures tends to be muffled. Should you suspect that merging compensation plans isn't bringing

---

[2] By all means, continue the existing measures for brand success, such as awareness and customer ratings of quality. However, if it doesn't relate to price, it might not be contributing to your bottom line. As Duke Ellington said: "It don't mean a thing if it ain't got that swing."

about enough cooperation, you might need to consider additional tactics, such as the following sly maneuver developed by Bell Labs.

Historically at Bell Labs, there were many times when disparate research and software development efforts needed to work together for the common good—yet independent-minded researchers and technical staff could be quite creative in resisting such efforts. Often, this took the form of one department warring against another. To bring about peace, Bell came up with the novel scheme of having the *head* of each department write the annual appraisal for the *second-most* senior manager in the other department. Apparently, this was enough to restore cooperation—no one wanted to see a manager in their group get a poor review.

Decision processes must include checkoffs and consultation among price, brand, and product development areas. Product-specific branding budgets require comment and perhaps approval from pricing. Overall price plans need brand management's perspective. And new product development must build approvals into its process to coordinate with pricing.

The above points are crucial, and yet typically they cannot be accomplished without first improving the pricing process. This is not just a matter of shuffling pricing managers. To truly integrate pricing, branding, cost, and product development, we must first make sure the pricing function is sturdy enough to stand on—much like restoring an atrophied limb through vigorous physical therapy, so that the patient can walk again. The remainder of this chapter is directed toward this fundamental goal of restoring pricing health. We will look at improving pricing in four specific areas:

- Pricing and product or service portfolio allocation
- Ongoing general line management
- New service and product pricing
- Unique competitive or major bidding situation

Each of these events requires different skills, senior level involvement, and resources. The organizational and process principles also differ.

PRICE AND PORTFOLIO ALLOCATION—
RELAUNCHING THE PORTFOLIO

The first issue concerns how to best define the various pricing organizations within the business. Like every P&L manager, price managers face issues of how to address customer needs, react to competitors, and maintain margins. Thus, the higher organizational principles for organizing the company apply to the pricing organization also.[3] Ideally, each separate P&L and pricing organization should be concerned with:

- Distinct customers (considered as buying organizations)
- Distinct competitors
- Distinct economics—that is, profit margins
- Distinct infrastructures or resources

In practice, companies must compromise these principles because it is not feasible to establish dozens of pricing organizations—costs would be prohibitive and coordination next to impossible. Still, these principles can be used as a guideline for defining business units and pricing mandates, as many medium and large companies have done with success.

The reasons for separation based on these criteria lie in the limits to management focus. To the extent that a single pricing organization faces many different customers, it will tend to blend the distinct requirements of these customers. With too many competitors, the organization won't be able to keep track of all of its strategies and initiatives. If some services or products enjoy large profit margins, while others face narrow profit margins, pricers won't be able to invest the time needed to adequately develop or exploit each. And finally, if pricing organizations share a common infrastructure or resource, then this resource—be it an IT platform, sales force, or advertising program—will subtly align itself to favor the most politically astute of its client groups.

---

[3] The broader organizational principles have been refined in various articles and speeches by Barry Jaruzelski and Reggie Van Lee.

Careful thought is required to decide if different divisions of product lines truly have a common customer. For example, if two different groups are both buyers at a client company, there might be little commonality between their requirements, despite the common parent. A purchasing department will want discounts and alternatives, while an operating division will consider price secondary and focus instead on such things as delivery schedules. This divergence of goals is a perfect opportunity to price differentially. Naturally there is some danger that the two groups might compare prices, especially with the increasingly sophisticated software now becoming available at an enterprise level. Yet more often than not, larger companies will buy the same good from the same vendor at different prices. Even when price differences come to light, they are rarely reconciled permanently.

Economic differences are an obvious distinction, but one that many managers apparently don't consider valid as a basis for organizational division. Actually, we believe this is *the most important principle*. This is why some of the more dramatic successes have come from instances in which companies have split out organizations to deal with new and different economics. For example, during the 1980s, when IBM came from behind to seize the PC market from Apple, it established a totally separate business unit for PCs—in large part because PCs offered very thin profit margins compared to mainframes. On the other hand, when Bell Canada's Yellow Page unit acquired an online information provider and local advertiser, it failed to separate out the near-zero margin acquisition from the print business with its 70-percent-plus margins. As a result, the acquisition became progressively crippled by resource allocations and inappropriate strategy choices, losing its market lead as a result.

In principle, financial evaluation of alternatives should be able to equalize long-run growth investment with short-term return opportunities—yet one reason that different economics prevent unified management is that managers and analysts never correctly estimate the relative potential of low-margin emerging businesses, or the decline of primary businesses in the long run. Such forecasts are too troublesome politically and require too much justification when they show a big drop in the numbers. Also, analysts typically use a single discount rate for both opportunities, although in fact the risks aren't at all similar.[4]

The impact of economics on pricing is fundamental. In a narrow-margin business the technique for superior pricing is to work the patterns in demand—for example, there might not be significant profit margins in baseload demand, but rush orders, special orders, or innovative products command high profit margins for a short time. Also, low-margin businesses emphasize related services and products: for example, financing, warranties, and add-on products. The result is that narrow-margin businesses tend to be highly tactical, with rapid price changes and complex structures.

Higher-margin businesses, meanwhile, operate under a simpler model. Regardless of whether it originates in patents, superior technology, or some other attribute, a generous profit margin sets the standard for pricing. The company is thus less interested in tactical pricing because the gains from this approach pale in comparison to those from the main product. Similarly, few add-on products can justify much diversion from the main product. For example, for many years Microsoft products such as Microsoft Word offered much narrower margins than DOS and Windows. It was only good long-term judgment by senior management at Microsoft that kept these add-on products alive. Today Microsoft Office is highly profitable, but that would have been a difficult financial argument 15 years ago.[5]

ONGOING LINE MANAGEMENT

How to run the pricing process once you have made the basic organizational division? For this, you need a list of the types of pricing activ-

---

[4] As a former CFO, one of the authors (Rob Docters), found that operational management rebelled when CAPM-based discount rates were used that were either lower or much higher than the corporate weighted average cost of capital. Consequently, not even the financial organization had the influence to balance long-term versus short-term.

[5] In the case of MS Word, it's clear that this program is a complement to the operating system. However, in many cases, narrow-margin pricing tactics (for example, extra charges for rush orders) are seen as detracting from the main product's appeal.

ities your company is engaged in. Some typical activities are shown in Figure 20.1.

The top five or six items in this list are characterized by their relative frequency, and by the fact that they represent incremental adjustments, requiring familiarity with the market more than deep pricing expertise. On the other hand, the bottom three or four items are sufficiently unusual that they fall outside the routine. We shall address these shortly.

To handle the routine pricing processes, you need a well-defined process. This will vary from company to company, but should embody the following principles:

- All price decisions are easily and formally made known to the pricing organization and to senior management as desired.
- Managers with operational responsibility for the market affected by a price decision—for example, account managers or product line managers—must be given formal opportunity to approve or veto the decision.
- The owner of a price decision must be explicitly recognized because this is the person who will be hurt if the process breaks down. This highlights who can legitimately complain if the process is bypassed or stalls.

Routine price moves	Unusual price moves
Change to list price	Major competitor initiatives
Bundles	Major bids
Discounts	New service and products
Credits and returns	
Price-related sales compensation issues	
Changes to product and services (a new technology)	

Figure 20.1. Typical price activities.

- Only one pricing process is allowed for any given category of price decision.
- Sufficient notice is given for each pricing decision, so that relevant parties can involve themselves without compromising market time lines.
- The process must be cost-effective.
- There is provision to handle disputes, but price decisions are revisited no more than once (if at all).
- Price specialists are given the chance to inject their experience and expertise early in the process, as appropriate.
- The price decision can't be subverted or countermanded without notice or sanctions as appropriate.
- A feedback process exists to gather information on when and how pricing decisions are implemented.
- If possible, a feedback process exists to document the effectiveness of a decision—for example, monthly sales volume reports and measures.

Although this list might seem long, it does not necessarily imply that pricing must be a resource-intensive or complicated process, or involve many players, or be paper-intensive—just well-designed. In some businesses a weekly staff meeting will suffice. In others a paper or electronic bulletin board might be all that is needed.

An example of an effective pricing process is shown in Figure 20.2. Note how all the sources of pricing decisions are funneled to a central consolidation point and separated into two levels of decision making. The process supports both a forum for different views and a feedback mechanism via an intranet bulletin board.

Of particular interest to some organizations is the idea of a "single voice to fulfillment" or some similar organization that actually executes the price change. If your company is accustomed to handling pricing decisions informally, initially you should probably create such a choke point. It effectively thwarts anyone who tries to end-run or otherwise subvert the process.

Alongside the process flows, and supporting these flows, you should have an explicit chart of approval levels. See Figure 20.3 for an

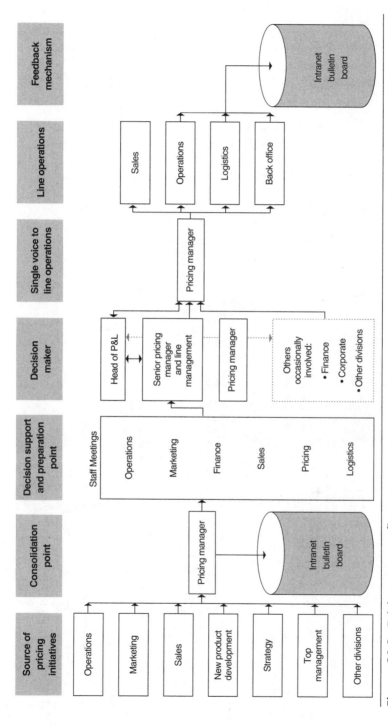

Figure 20.2. Pricing process flow.

	Change in list price	New products and product changes	Bundling of products (more than one sale)	Promotional pricing	Special pricing (one-line, one-account, discount or change in terms)	Credits and returns	Sales compensation issues
Manager of pricing	None	May establish prices for single-state products with expected revenues under $10,000 per year Must notify line management	Lower of: 10% off combined list prices[†] or $20,000 in total discounts expected to be awarded (i.e., total bundle sales times 5%) per year Must notify line management	None	Lower of: 30% or $1,000 on-line, or 50% or $2,000 off-line[†] Must notify line management in writing	Up to $10,000 in credits or returns per "event"	Unlimited (work with sales)
Senior line management	May decrease prices: 30% on-line or 50% off-line May increase prices without limits Must notify P&L head if price decreases are more than 10% on-line or 20% off-line or if expected impact is more than $100,000 per year	Establishes all prices Must notify P&L head if expected total revenues are more than $100,000 in lifetime revenues Strategy and pricing sign-off for new products	May offer bundle discounts up to 60% of combined list prices Must obtain strategy and pricing approval for bundles with expected total revenues of more than $100,000 of lifetime revenues Must notify P&L head if bundle discounts are more than 30%	May offer promotional of up to 20% on-line[†], 40% off-line[†] for up to 3 months Must notify P&L head if product has been promotion-priced for more than 5 of the past 12 months May offer promotions up to 15% more if sales force is precluded from discounting	May authorize discounts for up to 70% or up to $100,000 per year[†] Must notify P&L head and line management in writing if discounts are more than 40%	More than $10,000 in credits or returns per "event" Must notify head of P&L and operations of all credits or returns over $20,000	May request notification
P&L head	Significant involvement	Significant involvement	Occasional involvement (for example, on cross-business-unit pricing)	Should be highly involved in the event of major competitor initiatives—in coordinating regions, and ensuring promotional pricing does not become de-facto list price	Little or no involvement except to ensure that non-scorecard discounting remains limited	Little or no Involvement Will set general direction	Little or no involvement May establish direction

† Discounts calculated as a temporary decrease in the list price

Figure 20.3. Approval limits.

example. We have found that one approval limit does not fit all circumstances, primarily because dollar amounts aren't enough to fully capture the potential harm to the organization. For example, a $1000 refund is typically a one-time event, which must be executed rapidly to assuage an angry customer. On the other hand, a $1000 discount on new service can have widespread impact if word gets out. This suggests different approval amounts, as well as different ways to measure those amounts.

A related subject is the level of resources required by pricing organizations as they go about their routine activities. In practice, this question revolves around a balance between market understanding and internal pricing expertise.

Pricing specialists have the advantage of understanding pricing principles and executing pricing strategies. Given time, they can apply those principles to the various markets served by your firm. However, if your company has a lot of disjointed products and many segments, bringing price experts up to speed will take too long. This suggests that business unit staff members should perform much of the pricing analysis. Conversely, if you serve a fairly homogenous, unitary market, a centralized pricing function is appropriate.

For example, centralized markets such as automobiles, steel, airlines, large systems development, enthusiast magazines, television, insurance, commercial loans, and education, are all candidates for centralized pricing organizations. On the other hand, fragmented markets such as construction, specialty electronics, local newspapers, local transportation and communications, and commodity plastics are in quite a different boat. They face different competitors, diverse product requirements (low standardization of product and services), low-order quantities, and deal-by-deal (that is, feast or famine) economics. In such circumstances, it's line managers who know the specific circumstances, customer, and scheduling. Thus it's line managers who are in the best position to price successfully, not a centralized organization.

NEW PRODUCTS AND SERVICES AND MAJOR BIDS

New products, new services, and major bids all require pricing processes outside the routine. One reason is the much greater uncertainty as to outcome—both in winning sales and in achieving profitability. Unfortunately, two common responses to this increased uncertainty and complexity are to either ignore pricing until the end of the process or else create an elaborate institutional way of working out the details. The first choice is ill-advised if price matters (and it usually does), and the second choice might be both overly expensive and too slow to meet the window of opportunity.

A better way of approaching these situations is to develop an *expert hypothesis* early in the product development or bid process. This provides a price concept to go along with the product or service concept and generally improves results.

An example of using such a hypothesis to improve pricing comes from a manufacturer of special-purpose computers. This company had 500 engineers in its R&D group, which periodically responded to customer requests for new application software. In this market, the price for such software was crucial. Historically, developing a quote involved almost all 500 engineers, as they assessed in detail how to build the desired application. This meant that each quote cost the company more than $1 million worth of engineering time and talent and took more than two months to produce. More often than not, upon hearing the cost, the potential customer would lose interest, or else change its specifications to lower the cost.

The company engaged consultants to improve this situation (as it happened, these consultants included some of the authors). They found that an expert hypothesis would do a far better job of producing quotes: Instead of a detailed analysis by some 500 engineers, a small group of four senior engineers who knew all the functional areas involved could spend one intensive week working up a nonbinding proposal and quote. If the quote needed modification, it could easily be reworked, typically for less than $10,000. This approach was not only quicker and more cost-effective, it promised the additional benefit of landing more assignments.

Regardless of industry, a focused team effort is almost always the best way to price major, nonstandard bids for existing products or services. The bid team's first step is to plan the bid process, which might differ each time. Next it must define the scope and context of the effort. Simultaneous to scoping comes the gathering of data to supplement the RFP. Next, the team decides the best structure for the bid, as well as which basis to use for pricing (that is, what pricing engine). (See Chapter 8.) The choice of price engine will reflect both the degree of uncertainty and the need for precision. Finally, the team writes the proposal or places the bid.

As described in Chapter 8, if the scope of the proposal is quite broad, and both uncertainty and the value of the bid are high, more elaborate pricing mechanisms might be warranted. For example, to prepare its bid for a next-generation commercial airliner, one leading airframe manufacturer conducted a war game in which dozens of senior managers, including retired executives from airlines, were brought in to judge the outcome. To its surprise, the airframe manufacturer discovered that a major factor in the bidding would call for the manufacture of some key components, such as auxiliary power units. This led to a change in strategy. War games are an expensive process, but in this case, the expense was well worth it for it averted a nasty surprise some months later. On other occasions, simple economic value analysis is enough to produce the right quote.

PRICE ORGANIZATION REPORTING

Regardless of whether pricing is centralized or a shared resource, we recommend that the chief pricing officer report to the top—to either the P&L head or the CEO.

Key market decisions are made at senior levels, and at least for now, pricing needs to be represented at that level to inject pricing discipline into key decisions. Without a pricer at the table, pricing issues often go unrealized, even by otherwise smart top managers, and then require costly after-the-fact corrections. Good intentions to involve pricing specialists afterwards aren't enough, especially if situations require immediate action. A decision to make a big change in policy, an effort to switch focus of customer segments, a change in a product or distribution channel—these decisions often are not connected to price until it's too late.

A related question is which pricing decisions belong at the business unit level, and which at the corporate office. As Figure 20.4 suggests, there is no one answer to this question. Economics and competitive pressures will drive many of these choices. An illustration are the changes instituted at Home Depot by Bob Nardelli, the ex-CEO of GE Power Systems and successor to Home Depot founders Bernie Marcus and Arthur Blank.

When Bernie and Arthur ran the chain, Home Depot was expanding rapidly, and local store managers had significant discretion as to price and inventory. This made sense because Home Depot had an advantage over existing competitors, and the objective was to convert customers from other retail formats as quickly as possible. One of the reasons Bernie and Arthur turned over Home Depot to a seasoned manager such as Nardelli was because competitors such as Lowe's and

Business unit	Corporate office
Segmentation	Business unit definition
Single business unit competitive responses	Cross-business unit competitor responses and initiatives
Channel optimization (for example, price differences among channels)	Cross-business unit effects (for example, cannibalization)
Promotions	Product line life cycle management
Customer life cycle management	R&D priorities
Warranties, financing	Cost, billing, and IT platform leadership
Sales for compensation	Financial goals

Figure 20.4. Business unit versus corporate office responsibility.

other chains had become tougher competition. Lowe's enjoys the same centralized purchasing as Home Depot, and might have a superior distribution system. The logical result was that Home Depot had to streamline purchasing and tightly control prices and costs to defend against a comparable competitor.[6] Hence the shift from local pricing control to corporate control, to reflect the new competitive realities.

SUMMARY

Pricing studies show that buyers use context when judging a price. Ironically, we find that price setters are also sensitive to the context in which they price—and have trouble allocating their attention and effort between markets with different economics. The right way of organizing pricing groups is so they deal with price situations that are relatively homogenous. The best results will come when a group of pricers faces a common set of competitors, a homogenous group of customers, and common economics and infrastructure. The investment of matching price resources to these four factors is usually a positive one.

For day-to-day pricing decisions, a well-defined process is important. The best processes anticipate the range of pricing issues that need to be resolved and are robust enough to handle rapid turnaround and detect efforts to subvert price decisions. The better the up-front definition, the less costly any given price decision will be in terms of management effort and market efficacy.

For situations outside the norm, such as large contracts and bids, a focused team effort is often the most appropriate form of organization. If the bid is truly unusual in size, or the product or service truly innovative, there must be a parallel innovation in the pricing. The resulting price hypothesis will grow and develop alongside the bid or the new product.

Whether to centralize pricing at the corporate level or at the business unit level depends on the market situation—competitors, customers, and economics. Such decisions should be fluid over time to reflect changing situations. In all cases, however, senior pricing man-

[6] "Under Renovation," *The Wall Street Journal*, January 17, 2003.

agers must report to the top level of the appropriate organization—
either the business unit head or the CEO.

Effective integration of brand, price, and other functions isn't easy.
At many companies, culture, mission, process, and incentives conspire
to motivate these functions toward different and sometimes opposing
goals. Reversing this trend calls for both effort and ingenuity on the part
of top management—but it can be done.

The remaining chapters in this section of the book will elaborate on
channel management, processes, and technology—all key aspects of
profit maximization through price and brand.

Chapter Twenty-One | Sales Channels

Price structure and sales channel design flow from the same motivation—to increase revenues. Regardless of whether your company seeks to sell its services and products through one or multiple channels, or outsource its sales channels to third-party distribution, you need to ensure that the price structure and the distribution system work in harmony toward this ultimate goal.

In this chapter, we'll start with an overview of a primary channel selling directly to the customer, then move on to describe the guiding principles for managing price across multiple channels and within a retail and wholesale context.

ONE PRIMARY CHANNEL

The joy of simple channels is limited by the continuing reality that customers remain heterogeneous. Thus the objective of even a single channel is to premium-price the least price sensitive segments, while obtaining the best price possible from marginal segments.

Different sales channels have different abilities to support segmentation and price discrimination. We have found that a major cause of customer down-migration—that is, customers moving to lower-revenue price plans—is that *the company's own sales force suggests that the customer do this*. In consumer markets, where customer communications are more centralized and controlled, the incidence of down-migration among products and services is very small—usually, fewer than 20 percent of those who could down-migrate actually do so over the course of a one- to two-year period. Thus, one price requirement for direct channels is to limit the sales force's tendency to down-tier customers. This might involve including sales force compensation incentives that discourage such behavior, devising long-term customer contracts, or imposing penalties for switching.

The second important characteristic of sales channels is that they are poor at selling a mixture of independent goods and services—unless there is a clear structure that tells them when to sell what. This applies to telemarketing sales representatives who are not given clear selling rules, as well as to in-person salespeople. In the latter case, salespeople tend to emphasize the products or services (usually the products) with which they're most familiar.[1] To counteract this tendency, you need a product and price structure that sells your company's lead product or service first, and later sells the add-on products or services.

You begin with your lead product either because it offers the highest total profit margin to the company, or because it offers the best basis for selling valuable add-ons. The lead can be higher- or lower-priced than these add-ons, depending on the situation. If the lead product has the greater market power, then it should be priced higher. If the lead product lacks appeal by itself, but serves as a useful platform for follow-ons, then it can be priced attractively low.

Microsoft Windows is an interesting example of a lead product that has considerable market power, but also serves as a useful platform for follow-on. With Windows as its base, it's easier for Microsoft to sell such products as Microsoft Word and the Microsoft Office suite of applications. Without Windows, these products would enjoy far lower

---

[1] Al Hahn, "New Models for Selling Services," *The Professional Journal*, June 1998.

market share. Microsoft understands this fully and has built in price and product incentives for customers to buy the add-ons. These include continuing reminders to the sales force to explore customer requirements in the right order.

Does your company do as good a job as Microsoft in clearly identifying its lead and follow-on products? In practice, we find most companies do *not* explicitly or rigorously do so. Even fewer companies support this sales pattern in their pricing. For example, if you have a market-beating lead product such as Windows, you need to structure your pricing so that customers are led to buy warranties, service agreements, and related products, preferably along with the initial purchase.[2] If you don't have a chart showing which sales lead to other sales, you haven't optimized pricing from a channel perspective.

To identify the sales pattern, and the linked selling patterns among products, the marketing department must have tools to examine both the existing customer base and the sales process ("motion"), and to identify high-potential prospects in the market. This often means the ability to query databases for the most valuable customer prospects and tag those that fit a model.[3] Access to both the right data and the right model is an important aspect of a company's marketing capabilities.[4] American Express is a good role model for this: its managers enjoy one of the most powerful databases in the world, allowing them desktop analysis of the entire customer base.

These capabilities have a direct impact on price. If a company enjoys stronger segmentation capabilities and superior channels, it can more often target the best customers without using price level as a lure.

---

[2] If your company has monopolistic market power, tied goods can be a legal problem—however, most companies don't enjoy such power. Note that Microsoft, with a 90-percent market share, may be allowed to link its prices and products.

[3] S. Farrar, "Fancy Maths Give Banks Your Number," *Sunday Times*, April 18, 1999. This article describes how banks have hired mathematicians to use Bayes Theorem to identify the best prospects for credit cards and loans, based on observable patterns. These models can range from the intuitive to highly complex math.

[4] For a more general discussion of marketing capabilities, see R. Docters, R. Katz, and Carolina Junquira, "Strangers in Their Own Land," *Telephony*, July 31, 1995.

On the other hand, without these capabilities, companies must always use price as a tool in customer self-selection.

Channel not only influences price strategy, but also it enables or limits your company in the execution of that strategy. Price level changes are required by the market from time to time, for example in response to a competitor's price. These changes can be successful or not, depending on the capabilities of your sales channels to adapt. Ideally, changes should be rapid and low cost. The processes involved span marketing, sales, operations, and billing:

- Marketing must have the information sources and frameworks to understand when change is necessary and how to develop new price levels.
- Sales must strive to understand the new prices and handle customers who are caught in the transition.
- Operations must make sure that price literature—for example, price tags—is updated.
- Billing must be able to base invoices on new charge rates. Ideally, billing's turnaround time shouldn't be the limiting factor for price changes, but often this turnaround is measured in weeks.

The other kind of change is to price structure. Changes here are less frequent, usually require significant administrative effort, and are on an order of magnitude more laborious. This is because structure change requires sales force education as well as simple information dissemination. The underlying pricing programs used for quotes, billing, and other purposes (for example, taxes and royalties) might have to be rewritten, as opposed to making mere table updates. Operations might have to do more than change price tags—customer behavior should change sufficiently that operational requirements must also change.

Launches of new services or product bundles provide an example of how different companies implement new structures. One example involves two service providers that use telemarketing to launch service bundles. One company has a modern IT infrastructure that allows it to place instructions for how to handle new bundles on the telemarketing

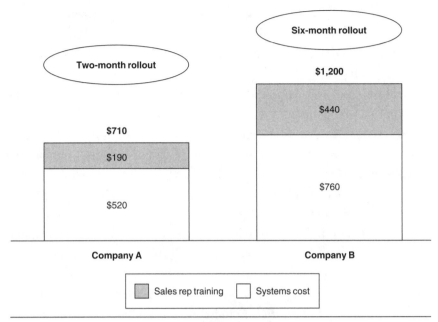

Figure 21.1. Channel costs of rolling out new price structure.

representative's computer monitors. The other has an older system, which does not allow instructions, and so must train its telemarketing salespeople and provide them with paper manuals. Figure 21.1 shows the relative costs of the two approaches:

Thus one company had the ability to rapidly launch many new bundles by adding instructions to computer screens, while the other had to pull its people from their jobs to train them. Clearly, the more automated company was able to launch more bundles more quickly and refine its price structure more cost-effectively over time.[5]

MULTIPLE CHANNELS (HYBRID MARKETING SYSTEMS)

In a simple world without constraints on channel capacity, with reliable insight into the future, and with a solid understanding of profit margins,

[5] The actual level of service differed between the two companies also. Company A could handle variation better (relying on its sales reps' skills), while Company B's sales reps could be more precise (for example, on geographic coverage).

most companies would choose to maximize profits by selecting the highest-margin sales channel and moving all of their products through that channel. Often, this is exactly what companies do, and it works perfectly well.

Unfortunately, in many industries, there are limits to the sales volume that can be economically generated through a particular channel, and so companies consider expanding into new channels. This in turn leads to two issues: how to price the new channels for profit maximization and how to avoid channel conflict.

Some managers believe that all their channels should be priced alike. Although that might offer simplicity and mute criticism among channels, it might also effectively cripple some channels. Customers do not see all channels as of equal value. Because the sales process is part of the value of the offer, a premium might be appropriate for one channel, a discount for another. For example, boating equipment sold through catalogs is often discounted compared to equipment sold in a retail establishment.[6] This is because telephone and online sales don't offer the same opportunity to touch and assess the good, and the online sales environment in particular offers almost no opportunity for advice from a salesperson.

Companies will usually seek out the most profitable incremental channels, but sometimes existing channels form a constraint. For example, for many years Coach sold its leather handbags through upscale department stores. After a while, it added a mail-order channel, but catalog merchandise also sold at list price to avoid upsetting its important department store channels. Next came brand-name Coach stores. These stores offered Coach the opportunity to vary its prices: Initially Coach stores were geographically separated from department stores,

---

[6] For instance, the Web site for West Marine offers prices not available in retail stores. A variation on that strategy is the Saks Fifth Avenue Web site, which offers excellent prices on clothing not easily found in the actual store. Web sites for airlines sometimes offer lower prices than are available via telephone. In addition, often telephone purchases escape state sales tax, which can be a significant saving for expensive items that are easily transportable.

and sometimes positioned as "seconds" merchandise outlets (although it was tough to find any flaws in the merchandise). These stores became a powerful platform for growth, despite the high costs of establishing and maintaining the outlets. Hence these stores were opened rapidly during the 1990s, with Coach revenues growing just as rapidly, even as per-unit margins fell.

The equation for such channel growth asks if a new channel cannibalizes existing channels at a faster rate than it offers new margins:

Total Margins = (Existing Channel Revenue × Existing Channel Margins) + (New Channel Revenues × New Channel Margins) − (Decrease in Existing Channel Revenues × Existing Channel Margins)

The tricky part of this decision is, of course, estimating the prices. In addition to the usual difficulties in estimating prices for new channels, there is the issue of cannibalization. For example, the Coach stores cannibalized its higher-margin mail-order channel. On the other hand, having its own retail outlets improved its bargaining power relative to department stores, and so we suspect it increased Coach's realized wholesale prices. Finally, the ability to expand through new outlets probably curbed a natural temptation to lower retail prices to build volume.

If different products and services are sold through different channels, there are no particular channel issues regarding price. Similarly, if different aspects of the sales cycle (for example, lead generation, qualification, and closing) are executed by different channels, there is also little danger of conflict. Unfortunately, with many larger companies, there is usually a slew of different channels trying to sell the same product or service, and the process is rife with conflict. As observed in one study, often a hybrid sales system of this sort doesn't segregate as cleanly as hoped.[7] This presents a problem for pricing, as there will be channel conflict, and if customers see different prices through different channels, customers might self-select in a manner not reflecting the

---

[7] U. H. Moran and R. Moriarity, "Managing Hybrid Marketing Systems," *Harvard Business Review*, November–December 1990.

company's best interests. At a minimum, the result will be a heavy administrative burden and some customer dissatisfaction.

Where channels cannot be cleanly separated, pricing must play an active role in optimizing channel mix. Your company must judge to what extent your customers will say, "I recognize that telemarketing is cheaper, but for me, in-person sales have an added value for which I'll pay another ✕ percent." If this isn't the behavior you expect or that trials reveal, prices must be brought back into line.

Trial is one sure way of determining what level of price differentials deliver the volumes desired in your business plan. The key thing that some companies seem to forget, however, is that channels are there to maximize revenues and gross profits. Revenues are not there to justify channels. Ideally you would rather have one successful high-margin channel than many mediocre-margin channels.

RETAIL AND WHOLESALE

Manufacturers or service providers rely on third parties to sell their services or goods either because a retail channel offers superior economics, better reach, or superior competitive capability. The classic examples of superior third-party distribution are electronics distributors such as Graybar and Merisel. These companies enjoy sales volumes aggregating the demand for all the manufacturers they represent, and so can sustain strong retail relationships that would be difficult to sustain if there are many companies selling individual devices to the same customers. Thus sales cost savings are generated (and shared) along with improved reach.

The choice to sell through third parties—that is, to go wholesale—is fundamental because it reduces your control over the final price to customers. Also, it might mask or eliminate important feedback on price issues that should influence your product or marketing choices—for example, the optimum price point in the market.

Why does this control matter? It matters because your channel's economic incentives are rarely aligned precisely with yours. Typically, retail channels face narrower margins than do integrated sellers, and so cannot afford to perform the price and product-offer experiments that

Price and volume	Retail price increase	Base case	Retail price decrease
Total minutes sold	268 minutes	300 minutes	339 minutes
Retail price-per-minute	10¢	9¢	8¢
Total retail revenue	$26.08	$27.00	$27.12
Network cost to retailer (6¢ per minute)	$16.08	$18.00	$20.34
Fixed retailer costs	$5.00	$5.00	$5.00
Net retailer margin	$5.00	$4.00	$1.78
Wholesaler revenue	$16.08	$18.00	$20.34
Wholesaler fixed costs	$11.00	$11.00	$11.00
Wholesaler variable costs (1.7¢ per minute)	$4.46	$5.00	$5.56
Net wholesaler margin	$0.62	$2.00	$3.78

Figure 21.2. Retail versus wholesale: The economic condition.

are often key to developing markets. For example, things such as free technical training on computers and first-line troubleshooting services have proven successful in developing some markets. This kind of bundling is likely to come only from an integrated computer provider—not a reseller.

More fundamentally, retail distributors are both by inclination and economic incentive likely to price higher than is optimal for the wholesaler. For example, take the resale of telephone services.[8] Figure 21.2 accurately reflects how wholesale service providers (for example AT&T) have a higher proportion of fixed costs than do resellers. The boldface text in Figure 21.1 reveals how increasing prices improves retailer margins, but decreases wholesaler (network provider) margins.

[8] Resellers are companies that buy network capacity from telephone companies such as AT&T and Sprint and resell long-distance phone services at a discount. The example is modified from a presentation to the Telephone Reseller's Association annual meeting in Desert Springs, Arizona, 1996, by Rob Docters. This was one crowd that clearly was not inclined to spend a dime to develop new markets unless there was an instant return.

To address these divergent economic incentives, the wholesaler should try to structure its wholesale pricing and related services so that its retail distribution channels have the same incentives to increase volume. Such measures might include a sharp volume taper, volume bonuses, or minimum sales agreements.

There are also situations in which the economic incentives are reversed, meaning that retailers might seek to lower prices below those the manufacturer has in mind. Examples include situations where the good is a prestige item and the manufacturer worries about damage to the brand should customers see it sold at a discount. Another situation might be if the manufacturer wants its retail channels to offer extensive customer education and services and fears a downward spiral if discounting leads to reduced education and services. One way of limiting such discounting is for the manufacturer to offer direct incentives or resources (for example, in-store personnel or end-user technical assistance) to ensure that the premium service is delivered.

Agents are a special case when it comes to channel incentives; these include sales agents, realtors, travel agents, insurance agents, and others. By definition, an agent pays nothing for the good or service being sold and is compensated by either a percentage of the amount sold or a flat fee. Regardless of who these agents work for legally, they have a strong economic incentive to underprice. Because the asset or service in question costs them nothing, they prefer to optimize their revenues on the basis of time and effort. Figure 21.3 illustrates the sale of a house. It assumes that realistically it would take three weeks on the market to hold out for a 5-percent better price.[9]

In this illustration, by pricing the house low, the realtor reduced both her effort to show the house and the time to sell. This resulted in a big benefit for the realtor, both in terms of the volume of houses she might sell in a year, and in the expected revenue per showing. On the other hand, the seller came off almost $10,000 worse, despite getting

---

[9] There is a typical price pattern over time: the time it takes to sell something below its full value will be brief, the time to sell something above its normal value will be longer (or possibly forever, if it doesn't sell).

Selling parameter	Right price for asset	Lower price for asset
Optimum seller price	$100,000	$100,000
Actual sales price	$100,000	$95,000
Time to sell	4 weeks	3 days
Number of showings	7	2
Realtor's commission	$6,000	$5,700
Revenue per showing	$857	$2,850
Potential sales per month	1	3
Realtor monthly income	$6,000	**$17,100**
Net proceeds to seller	$94,000	$89,300
Interest lost due to sales interval (at 7% per year)	($557)	($52)
Net seller result	**$93,443**	$89,248

Figure 21.3. Channel economics for a real estate agent.

his money faster, and despite the fact that nominally the realtor was working for him.

This is why selling your house the first day it comes on the market is very bad news for you—it means it should have been priced higher. The way for the seller in our example to optimize the sale would have been to force the realtor to list it at a higher number. The realtor would have argued, but resistance to price optimization in sales channels is routine, and usually the owner of the asset prevails.[10]

Wholesaler Skills

More globally, price must reflect the most important of the distinct capabilities and requirements of retail and wholesale. Flexibility versus

[10] If the realtor were truly flexible, she could have structured a fee with a strong taper: The realtor gets nothing if the house sells for $90,000, close to 6 percent if it sells for $100,000, and a bonus for a sale over $100,000. This might have been to both parties' advantage.

deliberation is the distinguishing difference between retail and wholesale pricing. Retailers have relatively little difficulty calculating profitability compared with manufacturers, so they typically know profit by individual sale. A retailer's main challenge is to find profitable markets and cut the right deals for access to those markets. In contrast, wholesalers face complex cost calculations, so they need to isolate profitability by account, as well as adjust pricing and related marketing levers to ensure profitability. This kind of profitability analysis recently led a leading office equipment manufacturer to use pricing to become more selective in the products offered its three largest customers, while raising prices to some smaller customers that had no alternatives.

BRAND AND CHANNEL

Brand is another distinguishing factor between retailers and wholesalers. The wholesaler must be principally responsible for the brand, given its control over product design, quality, wholesale cost, and other brand-creating attributes. The retailer, by comparison, must judge which applications or customers offer the greatest opportunity to leverage the brand through higher prices.

The tension in this division of labor is that the retailer might be looking for ways to liquidate brand—that is, raise or lower prices in ways that destroy brand equity, but boost sales in the short run. For example, one online distributor of continuing education materials for a University Consortium consistently charges too much for its materials, leaving online customers annoyed with the universities—even though the latter have little control over the retail price.

Brand is an intrinsic part of any channel decision. The character of the channel experience will shape the brand significantly. This is why IBM cares about how its salespeople dress—to project a reliable, professional image. It is also why some companies jumped to build Internet channels—to project a forward-looking, tech-savvy image.

MCI's "Friends and Family" program demonstrates a brilliant meld of brand and channel. As mentioned earlier, this program offers long-distance telephone customers a discount if the people they call frequently also subscribe to MCI. This price incentive produced a rich array of sales leads. Further, it resulted in a strong brand association: Instead of telemarketing as MCI, the company was able to call a prospective customer and give a friend or family member as the source of the referral. For a weaker brand, what better partner could you find than someone's parent or close friend?

Brand becomes more important in cases where the channel doesn't afford customers an opportunity to examine or test the products, such as the Internet (see Chapter 3). In these cases, companies with strong brand should exploit it, while companies with weaker brands should find a partner with the right brand. For example, although Home Depot initially considered building its own Web presence, it eventually chose to partner with *Amazon.com*. Although that partnership has some problems, brand strength isn't one of them. Amazon brought Web credibility and a superb platform, while Home Depot brought logistics and a strong brand specific to tools.

Pricing Technology— Vapor or Value?

Chapter Twenty-Two

C huck Yeager inspired the phrase the "right stuff" to describe a set of capabilities. Pilots who had it simply did not make a habit of crashing their rides into the sides of mountains when things got a little dicey. Bottom line, the "right stuff" was needed to optimize the pilot's chance of survival while gaining an advantage over the enemy.

In the technology-enabled world, the "right price" is not so different, although it doesn't tend to be the subject of many action-packed movies. The right price, as generated by a software package, optimizes a company's chance of survival by helping to accomplish key goals such as increasing revenues or profits, while allowing advances on competitors.

Software providers that understand that pricing is one of the most powerful levers to channel dollars to the top line have been immersed in building the "thinking" algorithms and user interfaces that form the basis of a very powerful set of technical revenue and profit optimization tools. The analytical leap forward that this band of merry statisticians is creating is the ability to understand the implications of pricing movement on demand, based on factual data relationships. The *value* is in understanding the impact on revenue or profit of these same demand movements. There are several highly competitive software providers out there, and their sophisticated products are well worth a look when pursuing "the right price." Yet the commercially available software applications that promise to provide the final piece of the pricing puzzle might not be the right stuff for every competitor. At least not yet. Given the nascent stage of these packaged solutions, the burning question is, can they improve the bottom line? The answer is yes—in some cases.

To shed some light on that qualified answer, this chapter examines the contribution, or lack thereof, of technology in the pricing domain, specifically addressing how these packages work, what they require to create valuable output, and why these requirements by definition create solutions that are effective in only some industries. Additionally, we outline the change management elements that should accompany an implementation of one of these packages, addressing the deeply traditional, and in some cases, tightly protected set of processes or policies that generate pricing decisions in most companies.

The discussion of these software packages is fairly high level. While the statistical depth and breadth of these software solutions could motivate us to babble on at some length, we will, in the spirit of brevity, address only the major components of these packages.

THE PRICING OPTIMIZATION ENGINE: STATISTICALLY UNDERSTANDING THE CUSTOMER

The primary value of pricing optimization software tools is their ability to statistically understand customer behavior at a microsegmented level—a level that is currently not available to most pricing decision makers. In fact, these statistical engines drive a new approach to pricing: predictive rather than reactive, resulting in the best possible understanding of the impact of a price decision before the price goes on the product or service.

The predominant statistical components of these packaged solutions are price elasticity of demand and competitive analysis. Although these are not new statistical concepts, they are newly captured in market-specific models in these packages, providing the first true commercial off-the-shelf pricing optimization capabilities. The three primary types of pricing—list, promotion, and bid—although different in specifics, are optimized through the same basic application of price elasticity of demand. That said, it is important to understand that not all packages include modules for all three types of pricing.

Price Elasticity and Customer Segmentation

The more a company can segment its customers based on demand profiles, the more it will understand its customers' behaviors. Customers in an upscale community in Scottsdale, Arizona, might show no demand change to a price increase for a soft drink, whereas students in a neighboring university town might show a significant decrease in demand. This is crucial, and segmentation analysis is among the first key steps in deploying a pricing technology software solution.

Identifying differentiated customer and product segments can be analytically challenging. Hundreds or even millions of sales transactions might need to be analyzed to parse a customer base into groups that exhibit statistically relevant differentiated demand behaviors. While some providers utilize highly robust proprietary segmentation tools to identify clustered demand curves that they bring as a part of the implementation, others do not, utilizing instead secondary tools available separately on the market. When making the decision to adopt a pricing solution, it's important to understand just exactly how your provider will do the analytical segmentation legwork up front that will drive this important aspect of pricing optimization.

Substitution—or cannibalization—provides another view of price elasticity of demand-driven segmentation, including trade-off decision making as a component of the statistical analysis. The university student who is highly sensitive to price changes in soft drinks might indeed respond to a price increase in a particular citrus-flavored beverage by not buying it. But if the price of another brand of citrus drink is not changed, will he buy that instead? Or will he choose a cola drink at the same lower price?

The substitution analytics in software packages that focus primarily on retail packaged goods pricing are formulated to answer these questions. By grouping products with historical substitution relationships, revenue and profit can be optimized by understanding how customer groups trade-off one product for another given different pricing levels. Needless to say, for any seller of closely correlated products, this is crucial knowledge that can make or break a pricing decision.

Competitive Analysis

For some companies, the pricing behavior of key competitors is crucial to determining customer demand. All one needs to do is listen to auto dealers or large furniture retailers battle it out on the radio for the best price deal in town, this weekend only. As such, some pricing packages include the ability to either factor in historical competitor pricing information or apply a current-state competitive index based on the pricing manager's knowledge of the competitive landscape.

In the B2B space where bids are won or lost, how a key competitor has priced historically can be statistically analyzed to influence the software's decision on which price will drive the highest probability of a win, balanced with an acceptable profit margin. Historical data for both the user's company and competitors is analyzed in the initial setup of the software to configure the statistical model that predicts the market response.

In the list or promotion pricing space, competitive pricing behavior might be equally as important. However, there has been a tacit recognition by most providers that very few companies maintain the transaction-level pricing of their competitors. While some providers offer the ability to integrate external sources of competitive information, others apply a competitive influence index, based on their own analysis of their market. When the software is being used to produce a pricing scenario, the user can adjust the competitive index to statistically influence the outcome of the price. A high competitive index would result in a lower recommended price to achieve a desired revenue or profit outcome relative to a moderate or low competitive index.

The fluid nature of any marketplace can change the market dynamics over time, and this can render the pricing model invalid, reducing the value that the software can provide. Thus, it's important to understand that adopting a technology solution will require some maintenance over time. In some cases, this will mean a visit by the software vendor to adjust the statistical market model based on market changes.

THE PRICING OPTIMIZATION OUTCOME: REVENUE OR PROFIT

As we mentioned in the outset of this chapter, pricing solutions optimize one of two goals: profit or revenue. This is done through statistical modeling that constitutes the software engine described above, as well as through configuring business rules in setting up the software.

The Difference Between Revenue and Profit Optimization

In general, revenue is optimized in the aggregate by determining the highest possible total price multiplied by the predicted demand for that price. Profit is optimized in the aggregate by determining the highest possible total of unit margin multiplied by the product demand at the recommended price.

The key difference between optimizing profit versus revenue is the availability of accurate cost data. There are substantially different approaches to managing cost data within these tools, and this is one area where user knowledge and skill makes a difference, as none of the packages in the market is terribly robust at assisting the user in building a fully allocated cost model. Some solutions provide an input for the cost, but it is up to the user to determine what level of cost goes into the model. Other packages include, in addition to the product cost inputs, activity-based costing for situations in which price changes result in additional labor and administrative costs.

The less-than-complete approach to costing in these packages is not a good reason not to consider them. They are quite valuable in driving predictive price decisions, which more than offsets their limited costing capabilities.

VALUE REALIZATION: WHO BENEFITS FROM THESE TOOLS?

The emerging players in the pricing optimization space have done a commendable job of developing a much-needed set of solutions that address pricing complexities. That said, not all companies will benefit from these products, and it's important to look before you leap.

There are three things to know when researching pricing optimization software:

1. They are only for companies whose business can support differentiated pricing
2. The algorithms are not "one size fits all"
3. You must have a substantial amount of transaction data

Differentiated Pricing

Assessing your customer base will determine whether or not your business can support differentiated pricing. As we mentioned earlier, segmentation is a crucial driver of pricing optimization, the basic premise being that not all customers are created equal, and therefore a single price does not necessarily need to be set for all customers.

A broad customer base is needed for differentiated pricing. If you have only one customer, you can offer only one price for a given product at a point in time. Conversely, if you supply a product to a large number of buyers, your customer base is likely large enough to segment. Analysis will reveal if you have differentiated elasticities across your customers that will allow the pricing optimization tool to be effective. Differentiated elasticities might reveal themselves based on a variety of customer attributes. In the B2B space these could be customer size, location, or buyer type, whereas in the B2C space, it might be attributes such as demographics. The bottom line is that you might find that you can employ different pricing to different customers.

All software providers will perform a viability assessment, most of them paid for by you. However, this requires that you either entertain a variety of assessments from the different providers that you are considering, or go through the vendor selection process before the assessment, which is a bit of a logic loop.

Another option is to use either a third-party consultant that is well versed in pricing tools or internal resources to conduct an independent assessment not driven by any one provider's particular objectives. The people assigned to this project should be able to understand what data to assess, how to determine its viability, and how to determine the statistical relevance of data patterns for your specific business.

Algorithms are Not "One Size Fits All"

All pricing technology packages incorporate some common elements of price elasticity of demand, but not all contain the same substitution or competitive influence algorithms, or business rule configuration capabilities. The available packages have evolved with a very distinct vertical alignment. Software vendors targeting retail customers have paid deep attention to the absolutely crucial element of substitution, as their products have little applicability to companies supplying manufacturing components. Conversely, software vendors targeting auctioneers in the B2B marketplace offer their services and capabilities in win probability, which is not terribly important to a retailer concerned with seasonal promotional pricing of garments.

The bottom line is that if you are considering a pricing solution, you can, and should, immediately eliminate some of the providers from your consideration. By understanding the statistical approach built into the packages, you can determine quickly which packages will suit your industry and which will not.

Data Requirements

Do not underestimate the need for a substantial amount of viable data. Historical transaction data is the basis for the predictive statistical model, and feeding the right data to the software will likely be your biggest challenge and concern in implementation. With this in mind, there are three things to think about when considering whether or not you have the data available to support a pricing optimization tool:

Type of data. The type of data needed varies depending on the industry you are in, but in general, the absolute requirements are unit sales and price if you are optimizing revenue, and cost if you are optimizing profit. In the case of list or promotion pricing, the price is the net transaction price applied to the product. In the case of bid pricing, it is the final accepted bid price. Additional requirements might include data such as customer attributes, inventory pipeline, competitive pricing, and win or loss data.

Volume of data. Regardless of what you sell or where you sell it, you must sell enough of it to different customers to generate sufficient data to support a viable statistical outcome. A good rule of thumb is that 500 to 1000 transaction points over the course of a year will render a statistically valid outcome. The beauty of software packages is that they can crunch as much data as you can throw at them. That said, 23 years of data would not be optimal because it will introduce influences that are no longer valid. One year's worth of data is workable if you do not have annual seasonal trends, but two to three years of good clean data is far better.

Availability and viability of data. Of equal importance to the volume of data is where the data resides and the shape it is in. It is highly unlikely that you will have all of the necessary data to make full and immediate use of the software nicely cached in tidy warehouses, so you will need to assess what you have and how you will aggregate it for use by the package. For gaps in data, you will need to determine how you can begin to capture and aggregate it going forward.

Keep in mind that available data does not mean viable data. While the ERP era has helped us considerably to organize data, rogue data still lurks in almost all companies. In addition to rogue data, there might also be data that is simply not appropriate to include in the statistical modeling. As a result, you will need to determine whether you can effectively cleanse the data to be the best representative of your current business model. Most providers, however, have data cleansing tools that address this need. The challenge is in ensuring that the users of the tool can interpret effectively the outputs of the data cleansing tools. This requires two core capabilities: a keen understanding of data relationships and of the pricing landscape that has existed both in your company and in the market. It also helps if your IT organization has robust documentation on system issues that might have caused irreparable data errors that could not be corrected or deleted from the historical data.

GOING LIVE

A change management focus is necessary to address cultural change in order to gain the most benefit from a pricing optimization solution. The focus should include:

Incentives. The incentives for employees, particularly those with pricing decision authority, must be aligned to ensure that behaviors support the pricing objectives. In other words, employees must be motivated to utilize the output of the tool, rather than making unilateral pricing decisions. As shown in the Ford case study in this chapter, Ford changed the goals for its sales force, shifting the focus from maximizing revenue and market share to maximizing profit. After this change was implemented, Ford used the pricing solution to determine the pricing and promotions of its products.

Process alignment. Corporate processes must be aligned to facilitate effective use of a pricing tool. Pricing tends to be very important in most companies, and as such input is typically derived from multiple sources; there is often a significant level of protectionist behavior around having the authority to make a pricing decision. Companies must balance their corporate culture with the reality that a software package will be able to utilize a level of quantitative sophistication that is not typically available to current pricing staff. This might require some level of mandate to accept the outcome of the tool rather than making more subjective decisions based on tribal knowledge.

Training. As with any system deployment, users must be trained. Any disruption that occurs in the sales process will be apparent in the company's top line, so it is important that adoption of a pricing tool accelerates pricing decisions, rather than slows the process by untrained users trying to figure it out as they go along. To ensure that the system functions before wider deployments, it's a good idea to begin with smaller pilot programs. If these are successful, they will help build credibility for the system and foster enthusiasm during the training sessions. Employees who participate in the test programs can also provide additional insight from their experience.

Adopting these three change initiatives will increase the likelihood of success for a pricing solution implementation. Failure to do so will drastically increase the risk associated with the implementation. With this in mind, we highly recommend that a robust change management strategy becomes an integral element of the overall implementation plan.

FORD MOTOR COMPANY: LIST AND PROMOTION PRICING

Until 1995, Ford Motor Company compensated its sales force by how many units it sold, regardless of profit margin. As a result, the sales force focused on selling inexpensive, low-margin vehicles. Although this strategy drove up volume, it did so at the expense of profit. To remedy this problem, Ford adopted a new pricing strategy.

First, Ford increased its market research to find features that "the customer was willing to pay for, but the industry was slow to deliver." Second, it made sales units accountable for profit and informed them of which vehicles made Ford the most money, reducing the focus on driving low-margin volume. Third, it adopted a pricing optimization solution to help it adjust list pricing to create an incentive for customers to purchase higher-margin vehicles.

In 1998, the first five regions that adopted this pricing strategy exceeded their profit targets by $1 billion. The 13 regions that had yet to implement the strategy missed their targets by a combined $250 million. By 1999, all 18 of Ford's regions adopted the strategy.

This change allowed Ford to cut prices on high-margin vehicles at an optimized level that drove an increase in volume without an erosion of aggregate profit. This resulted in a 600,000 unit increase of high-margin vehicle sales, such as Crown Victorias and Explorers, and a 420,000-unit decrease in low-margin vehicle sales such as Escorts and Aspires. Between 1995 and 1999, while Ford's vehicle sales increased just 6 percent, from 3.9 to 4.1 million units, revenue was up 25 percent and pretax profits were up 250 percent, from $3 billion to $7.5 billion. Ford estimates that two-thirds of this profit increase was attributable to its pricing and revenue management initiatives.

In 2000, Ford expanded the scope of its pricing technology efforts by addressing its $9 billion marketing and promotional budget. Every day, Ford analyzes sales data from its dealerships with its pricing computer models to predict which incentives will achieve the best results.

Ford now spends its marketing budgets promoting high-margin vehicles that aren't selling out on their own. For example, Ford offers a $1000 rebate on its popular Escape small SUV, but offers a $3000 rebate on its slower selling Explorer. In 2002, Ford spent an average of $3500 in incentives per car, $300 less than rival General Motors, which does not leverage pricing technology. This benefit improves Ford's bottom line by $5 billion per year in promotion savings alone. These dramatic benefits explain the increasing interest in pricing and revenue technology solutions.[1]

DHL BID PRICING

In 2001, DHL, the $6 billion shipping firm with a large international delivery operation, faced a pricing problem. After not changing its prices in five years, DHL was losing market share in its walk-up and call-up business because of competition from UPS and FedEx, which were undercutting its prices by 20 to 30 percent. DHL's traditional

[1] "The Power of Smart Pricing," *Business Week*, April 10, 2000; "Aided By New Software, The Automaker Is Using Revenue Management To Boost The Bottom Line," *CFO*, August 1, 2000; "Ford Tames the Rebate Monster," *Business Week*, May 5, 2003.

method of setting its pricing no longer allowed it to be competitive in the marketplace.

The scale of the pricing problem was huge. DHL needed to set prices for all of its shipping products across 43 international markets. Given its strong international brand, did DHL have to match its competitors' discounts to retain its customers? To answer this question, DHL had to find a way to price test its products and product bundles across its markets.

DHL engaged Zilliant, a Texas-based company that offers leading software tools to measure customer demand. The sophisticated analytics in Zilliant's offering allows large amounts of data to be analyzed to determine customer responses to price changes. Unlike other offerings, Zilliant's software does not predict the optimal price: Instead, it tests to find the right price and assess the impact on profit and revenue.

In September 2001, Zilliant installed its application for DHL in 14 days. The system sat behind DHL's own systems and randomly offered customers "experimental" prices to generate tens of thousands of data points of actual customer reactions to price changes. Based on this data, DHL changed its prices. In most cases it lowered prices, but because of DHL's strong international shipping brand, it did not have to match the price discounts offered by its competition.

One of DHL's key performance indicators for its walk-up and call-up business is the quote-to-book ratio, which measures the percentage of people who actually ship with DHL from those who get quotes. Before the technology, the ratio was about 17 percent. After the technology, the quote-to-book ratio stood at nearly 25 percent. As a result, DHL enjoyed increases in both revenue and profitability during an industry recession.[2]

THE FINAL WORD

Although we present only two case studies in this chapter to illustrate the real-world results that can be attained through the use of commercial off-the-shelf pricing technology, the value is real for many more

---

[2] "Which Price is Right?" *Fast Company*, March 2003: 92.

companies. Currently, none of the pricing software vendors is large, and as such they all tend to focus on a limited number of vertically aligned solutions.

We expect these players to survive for two primary reasons. First, with the ERP era mostly behind us, the focus on transaction-based management and its at-times-dubious rewards has dimmed. The potential for analytics-based software packages—which bolt on nicely to ERP backbones—is encouraging.

Second, pricing needs to change, and now it can. The tradition of executives acting on intuition must give way to analytically driven decision making. After delving into many of the software packages on the market, the statistical models are impressive, as are the teams that are crafting the solutions. There is little chance that a home-grown pricing team is going to out-think these companies, and this should be a welcomed relief to the legions of us who have spent years chewing on our pencil erasers trying to figure it out ourselves.

Although the future for technology-enabled pricing optimization is bright, the provider landscape will likely undergo some significant transformations. Given the symbiotic relationship between pricing and data, it is highly likely that one or more of the larger ERP providers will make a significant play in the pricing optimization space, with one or more of the current providers joining forces with a major software provider.

Building
a Price
and Brand
Powerhouse

E arly in this book we suggested that pricing and brand management are not only fundamental to win the profit game but a reflection of the sum of a firm's capabilities and product and service attributes that could lead to a competitive advantage. At the end of the book, we described the institutional capabilities necessary to become a superior pricer and thus take advantage of your competitive position. Between these sections, we hope we have added enough methods, tools, and techniques to help you become a smart pricer over the life cycle of your product or service.

In this final chapter, we discuss building the institutional capabilities to be a superior pricer and brand developer. Every decade sees companies building new capabilities. The typical pattern is that as the importance of previously ignored or obscure capabilities begins to be understood, these capabilities migrate to center stage. There, they offer competitive advantage for several years before fading by the end of the decade to become merely another standard requirement for doing business.

During the 1990s, for example, business leaders began to recognize the value of superior sourcing. As this view gained momentum, companies moved to upgrade procurement processes and the buyer-professionals who managed them. After all, in most industries 50 to 70 percent of costs can be attributed to direct and indirect material acquisition. Even so, initially most procurement leaders didn't report to "C"-level executives, and buyers were largely staffed from those who had fallen from grace in engineering, finance, and operations. Tools and methods were limited, and e-procurement, supply networks, and auction technologies were in their infancy.

Pricing is at the same crossroads as procurement was a decade ago. Pricing is often buried in the marketing and sales organization. Judgment and history are seen as the guideposts, not well-developed tools and methodologies. Senior executives view pricing as a quick and reversible decision—notwithstanding "unpredictable" channel backlash. New software technology for pricing is beginning to emerge, tailored to the needs of industry, but hasn't yet won wide acceptance.

The imperative is clear—the buyers have long since armed themselves. Now the sellers must follow suit or perish. Companies that fail to develop institutionalized pricing and branding capabilities will be crippled, unable to extract a large enough share of the value they have created. Meanwhile, competitors who have invested in pricing and brand capabilities *will* be able to extract more value, and with less customer irritation. These competitors will be the winners.

PRICING AS AN INSTITUTIONAL CAPABILITY

The hiring of a few pricing practitioners doesn't necessarily lead to superior pricing performance. Pricing capabilities need to be embedded in an organization: strategic direction established, value consistently delivered, supporting infrastructure developed. In fact, creating advantage through superior pricing requires excellence in five dimensions—six, if you count infrastructure. Let's go through the five dimensions one by one.

1. Creating Value Through the Strategic Use of Pricing

The ability to extract price premiums is a direct reflection of the competitive advantage of a product or service, a brand, and a business.

Pricing needs to be linked to strategic objectives—to gain share, optimize profits, penetrate as a new entrant, or secure incumbent advantages. Creating innovative price structures—such as "power by the hour" versus up-front purchasing of turbofan engines in commercial aerospace—might help change how a business competes in the marketplace. Pricing strategically means raising the willingness of customers to pay in accord with value received.

2. Setting Up a High Value-Added Pricing Organization

Who sets price in an organization? The answer is sometimes painful or unclear: lower-level managers, independent and intermittent decision making by sales or finance. Often price is set merely in reaction to competitors' moves. In a recent survey of clients, A.T. Kearney found that most lead pricing practitioners reported within the marketing and sales organization. A few reported to finance, especially those with aftermarkets, while even fewer reported to the CEO or COO. If pricing activities remain at a departmental level, isolated from senior management, pricing will always remain tactical. Upgraded pricing skills need to be networked throughout the organization and teamed on most important business developments. After all, price is the firm's language to the customer.

3. Getting the Best Results from Ongoing Pricing and Price Setting

The best firms use the introduction of new products or services and the repositioning of old ones as opportunities to fundamentally set new price levels and develop brand. This means new products must be developed with pricing and branding in mind, not as afterthoughts. To this end, the chief pricer and chief branding architect should sign off on all new product or service developments before they go into final development, as well as give the okay to final development before going into production. Only then will there be the lead-time to develop appropriate pricing and billing structures and refine the message to the market.

4. Obtaining Maximum Value from Pricing Processes

The organization must capture those lessons that have been learned. It must have the sophistication to not only discount the price to win, but understand the probability of winning at any price level. Other dictates: Know in advance the likely effectiveness of promotions. Lead the pricing process—whether in response to an RFP, a quote, an auction, or an annual price change. Share information extensively with internal constituents.

5. Establish Day-to-Day Channel Management and Communications and Synthesize Customer Feedback

Strive to maximize volume through the highest-margin channels. Also, obtain the market intelligence required to formulate the price structure necessary for various channels to operate harmoniously. One aspect that needs reinforcement is that customers, even long-time users, need to be reminded what the product or service is worth to them. They need a quantitative and qualitative reinforcement of the value received. Build internal measures to correspond with customer experiences.

6. Building a Robust Supporting Infrastructure

Without tracking and rewarding of effective pricing and branding, these tools will remain tactical considerations. Four aspects of supporting infrastructure are key here: performance management, human resources management, technology and software systems, and knowledge management. Metrics are necessary to show the economics of better pricing. A strong human resources capability is crucial to get skills in pricing to function in their new, transformed roles, to recruit to fill skills gaps, and to develop compensation approaches to reward and motivate pricing practitioners.

With the plethora of new technology and pricing software, an organization can fundamentally reinvigorate pricing processes and leverage science in designing promotions and new segmentation schemes. Knowledge—whether of competitors, customers, pricing histories, or tools—needs to be available to the pricing organization and to cross-functional teams. Knowledge management systems that can facilitate this are relatively cheap, easy to use, and indispensable.

PRICE SKILLS

Pricing as a function is at the borderline between the internal enterprise and the customer-channel marketplace. Its goal is to maximize the value generated by other functions within the enterprise. We can list five key macrolevel skills associated with pricing to counterbalance strategic buyers:

1. *Gain creative advantage.* Create innovative price structures, solutions, and customer value propositions that help the enterprise set attractive price levels and achieve its strategic goals.

2. *Optimize profit.* Manage ongoing prices to ensure profit optimization over a product or service's life cycle.

3. *Value-price.* Leverage all marketing, communications, and brand activities that can help raise the willingness of a customer to pay for the value received.

4. *Manage effective processes.* Manage the various pricing processes from auctions to RFPs and supporting information to include competitor pricing.

5. *Add science.* Bring new methodologies and technology to pricing processes.

Skill	Sophisticated	Basic	Needs work
Identify customer needs	Lead discussions with customers to fully understand their needs, problems, and problems, and determine potential solutions	Test customer needs with "what if" or "what would it take" statements	Wait for customer to volunteer unfullfilled needs
Design pricing experiments	Build a model of demand and price responses prior to experiment Refine experiment based on model results, and improve the model with feedback from experiments	Design experiment and track results compared to expectations and explain differences	Use past history as a guide to future promotions

Figure 23.1. Skill assessment.

Microskills associated with these more macrolevel skills are outlined in Figure 23.1. These represent a preliminary cut of the knowledge needed to price in a superior fashion.

BRAND CAPABILITIES

Everyone who's had a long-term romantic relationship knows the basic elements of branding capabilities. There are two parts:

- A successful day-to-day relationship
- Building the relationship, so as to build the bond

Developing a successful day-to-day relationship requires effective communication with both your partner and your customers. Some ways of communicating work; others do not. Moreover, such communications go beyond the spoken or printed word. As discussed in Chapter 7, strong messages are embedded in your price structure and changes in price. The organization must become keenly aware of these messages and learn to use them for maximum effect. Similarly strong messages, but this time in regard to quality and use, are embedded in your product or services. Besides learning to communicate well, companies need to learn to avoid brand mistakes in dealing with customers. Examples of such mistakes are described in Chapter 3.

Yet more is required. In the same way that communicating clearly and avoiding mistakes aren't enough by themselves to build an important relationship between two people, merely avoiding mistakes won't build brand equity so that it translates to the bottom line. You must add to the relationship, building new forms of connection and mutual benefit. In corporate branding, we can identify four dimensions along which to build brand equity. These are important because—when developed in conjunction and in harmony with pricing—they build profitability.

These brand dimensions are as follows, progressing in order from the most basic to the most refined and valuable:

Brand awareness. This means ensuring that your offer is foremost in the minds of the relevant target audience or segment. Awareness should have the beginnings of a message incorporated in it. Merely announcing your existence is a waste of resources—possibly even a costly mistake.

Perceived quality. You communicate your value proposition through market communications, your product or service, and activities related to your customer dealings (sales channel, customer service, billing, after-sales). If these messages are mixed—some good, some mediocre—then your company will have to work extra hard to get to the next stage, which is brand loyalty.

Brand loyalty. While there are benefits to the above elements of brand equity, the real benefit comes when customers are loyal to your brand—that is, willing to pay a premium. Brand loyalty increases retention, reduces channel and marketing costs, and paves the way for new products. If you're not able to command a material price premium, you don't yet have brand loyalty.

Brand associations. Your brand will be perceived in a particular context. Outside of that context, it might mean little. This is okay. You don't need to think of Microsoft when buying a candy bar. However, you *do* want your company to be included in the short list for an RFP within your market focus, for example. To get potential customers to think of you at the right times, and moreover to recall the reasons they should buy your company's product, you need to be involved in the nitty-gritty of customer perception and workflows. Examples of this are an icon for your information service on the relevant professional's work station, or a motorist remembering the name of an after-market supplier at the precise moment she discovers that her car's muffler has rusted through.

Improving in these four dimensions calls for the right institutional skills. For each dimension, the skill must be focused precisely on brand and profit—a skill not oriented to profit is worse than no skill at all. The right focuses for each skill are as follows:

1. *Building brand awareness:* The demand here is for consistency in the brand message more than creativity. The three key elements are these: *Identity*—reputation and history, human character traits, sensory signals and visual images, all the sensory leverage to include symbols, signage, advertising, packaging, and design.

Product—those attributes that core customer segments find distinctive and valuable, as well as augmentations to the product or service that add further distinctiveness. *Value proposition*—emotional and personal benefits of the brand experience; the tangible and functional benefits of using the brand.

2. *Building perceived brand quality:* The key for this skill is to reinforce the *promise* of the brand, not just awareness. Answers to three fundamental questions need continuous reinforcement: How distinctive is the brand from competitors? How relevant is the brand to core customers? How is the brand promise supported by the organization's functional capabilities and culture?

3. *Building brand loyalty:* This is about demonstrated performance and authenticity, *not* advertising. In other words, what matters is operational integration. All organizational functions need to live up to the promise of the brand consistently on a day-to-day basis. This includes design and innovation, procurement, manufacturing, selling and distributing, service support, pricing, and marketing. Allocation of resources should reflect priorities set by the brand. Gaining senior management support, guidance, and accountability is needed to succeed.

4. *Building brand association:* This skill addresses fundamental concerns of the business: How does the brand attract, convert, and retain core customers? What are the opportunities to become master of the category? What increase in effectiveness can be anticipated with a strong brand? Can one achieve emotional connection with the core target segments? Do we need to redefine or reprioritize customer segments? Capturing the value of the brand is aimed directly at building profitability—*not* at following a fashion or a trend.

SWINGING THE PENDULUM FROM THE BUYER TO THE SELLER

Let's keep this reiteration short but sweet: In order to shift the balance between sellers and strategic buyers, organizations must develop pricing and branding capabilities. This in turn requires that certain key skills are institutionalized to the extent that they become embedded in day-to-day processes. In some ways, price and brand can be considered not merely skills, but a very serious, very rewarding organizational game.

The power in smart pricing, brand management, superior operations, and solution marketing is not their separate elements but the ability to fully integrate them consistently throughout an organization. This means more than having joint meetings with advertising, marketing, and product and plant managers. It means that every function (even HR and Legal) and every partner in the supply chain needs to understand how customer and brand value are going to be created, delivered, and communicated to customers and what their role, responsibilities, and performance expectations are.

In summary, the leadership challenge is this: Do not allow pricing decisions and their impact on brand positioning to occur at the tail end of a process. In new product introductions, design reviews, and strategic planning—make the discussion of price front and center. When design engineers discuss pricing up front and advertising talks about customer segment profitability, than you are probably winning the profit game.

Index

Note: Boldface numbers indicate illustrations.

ABOUT THE AUTHORS

Robert G. Docters is president of Abbey Road Associates, New Canaan, Connecticut.

Michael R. Reopel is a senior officer in A. T. Kearney's strategy practice.

Dr. Jeanne–Mey Sun is a consultant with A. T. Kearney.

Stephen M. Tanny is a professor at the University of Toronto.

8/22